Bumps on a Lon Road - II

Bumps on a Long Road Volume II
© Cyril Belshaw 2011

ISBN: 978-0-9864725-6-5
Retail and printing: Lulu Books
Wholesale: Ingram Books

Webzines of Vancouver
2901 – 969 Richards Street
Vancouver British Columbia
Canada V6B 1A8

By the same author:

Island Administration in the South west Pacific

Changing Melanesia: Social economics of culture change (reprinted)

In Search of Wealth: A study of the emergence of commercial operations in the Melanesian society of South East Papua (AAA Memoir 80)

The Great Village: Economic and Social Welfare in a New Guinea urban community. (reprinted)

The Indians of British Columbia (with Harry Hawthorn and Stuart Jamieson)

Under the Ivi[1] Tree: Social and Economic Growth in Rural Fiji (reprinted)

Traditional Exchange and Modern Markets (republished India, translated Spanish Portuguese and Indonesian)

Towers Besieged: Dilemmas of the creative University

The Conditions of social Performance: An Exploratory Essay (reprinted)

The Sorcerer's Apprentice: An Anthropology of public policy.

The Complete Good Dining guide to Vancouver Restaurants.

Choosing our Destiny: Creating the Utopian World in the 21st Century.

From Youth Maturity to Global Government

Remuera: Memories of a New Zealand Boy Between the Wars

Bumps on a Long Road: Volume I

Fixing the World: An Anthropologist Considers our Future

---

[1] Pronounced "eevee"

BUMPS ON A LONG ROAD
Volume II

Essays from an Anthropologist's Memory

Cyril Belshaw

Webzines
Vancouver
2011

To Claudia Scheuermann
And
Kevin Davies

My essential friends

CONTENTS

Following Volume I

24. Africa Resurgent..................9

25. America Latina..............34

26. Around the World in Curiosity Mode..........................44

SHATTERED......................59

27. Disaster.........................59

28. Caged in France.............80

29. Caged Swiss style..........92

30. "Impeccable" Police ...108

31. How the Vaudois Conducted Trials......................128

32. Confusion Abounds.....157

TRAVEL AND FOOD – PART TWO..............................171

33. Gastronomy and the Digital Universe........................171

34. Iberia...........................182

35. Croatia.........................197

36. Egypt and Morocco......203

37. Quintana Roo...............211

38. A brother in New Mexico.......................................257

39. Hi jinks in Stockholm and Lively Leiden............................288

TWO SPECIAL MEN.......298

40. Raymond Firth: Mentor..298

41. Harry Hawthorn: Pioneer.......................................305

WHAT PRICE RETIREMENT?.........................315

42. Perish the Publication!.315

43. Ao-tea-roa....................327

44. Why Vancouver?.........337

Acknowledgements...........347

24. Africa Resurgent

My first experiences of Africa South f the Sahara was in the 'seventies and 'eighties, but I had additional exposure in 2006. The two sets of dates are in notable contrast.

The Canadian Research Centre for International Development sent me to participate in meetings concerned with the development of African publications, francophone in Dakar (with CODESRIA)[2] and anglophone in Nairobi. In both cases I was impressed with the ability and dedication of the participants. Unfortunately at that time they appeared to be a relatively isolated.

I enjoyed Dakar, probably because of the marked French influence. It has a notable Provençale style square which reminded me in a more sophisticated way of Noumea in New Caledonia, with relaxed cafes and a mix of colonial and modern architecture. Unfortunately I did not have time to explore beaches and markets or even take the train through the countryside to Mali as I would still like to do.

There was compensation when a senior official of CODESRIA invited two or three of the foreign participants to his home for a midday meal. This had been prepared by his tall gracious wife, a school teacher who was dressed beautifully in the photogenic Senegal

---

[2] Council for the Development of Social Science Research in Africa headquartered in Dakar.

women's style, an impressive blend of colourful African modes and modern fabrics.

She left to go to class before we men tucked into her preparations. We sat on a matted floor around a huge array of dishes, spooned onto our plates and then eaten with washed fingers. The fragrances and taste marriages were exceptional. Dakar is high on my list of desirable returns.

Nairobi is quite different. Over the decades I was able to make several visits to Kenya and had holidays in the Serengeti and elsewhere.

There I met A.B.C. Ocholla-Ayayo, an intensely able and in appearance miniature of Jomo Kenyatta.[3] A.B.C. (I never decoded his initials) had started life as a young man determined to be an engineer. His story of his youth, walking in the forest to school and confronting a lion on the way, always had my friends and I doubled up with laughter. His career, though, was anything but funny, evidencing major determination and high quality creative anthropological writing.

After school he first determined to go to Egypt to study. But he embarked on the wrong vessel and found himself working his way to India. There he was not well received, and found his way ultimately to work his passage to Cairo. I do not know how it happened, but Swedish aid authorities noticed him and he moved to Uppsala, still intent on engineering. In Sweden he discovered anthropology which entranced him and led him to his doctorate. He published numerous highly

---

[3] Kenyatta, the formerly imprisoned first President of Kenya, studied anthropology in Moscow and wrote a splendid ethnography, *Facing Mount Kenya*. There is speculation that he used his anthropological insights as he created the religion-base Mau-Mau radical secret society movement in opposition to the British.)

regarded papers, perhaps the most notable of which concerned the functioning of pastoralism, in which he successfully took issue with veterinarians and others who regarded the institution as archaic and unsustainable.

Despite Jomo Kenyatta's own background in anthropology, or perhaps because of it, Kenya like many other African countries in the days immediately after independence, refused to countenance anthropology as a university discipline, so it was some years before A.B.C. could return to Kenya and obtain a post in the University of Nairobi. And then his position was not in anthropology but in population studies, where he headed a research institute.

One of my visits to Kenya was in the mid-eighties not long before I retired as editor of *Current Anthropology*. One of my experiences was that African and other scholars from developing countries were at that time unable to get their papers published in major overseas journals and were discouraged from trying. So I decided to conduct a workshop for a limited number of social scientists from southern anglophone Africa. I put together a team consisting of John Ogbu, a Ghanaian who was pursuing a successful career as a professor at Berkeley, and Barbara Metzger, the wonderful copy editor of the journal, with A.B.C. as our local representative. The budget, provided mainly by Wenner-Gren, the U.N. University, and Canadian development agencies, was substantial and raised questions of security. Air ticket vouchers were distributed to scholars in most countries of south and east Africa.

The participants, who included historians, sociologists and social workers as well as anthropologists, were required to write a paper and bring it to the meeting. We held it in a small hotel on the outskirts of the city. A.B.C. hired a people mover and picked up the arriving participants at the airport.

They were entitled to a per diem and there were of course other cash expenses. Funds had been transferred to Barclay's Bank in the centre of the city. A.B.C. drove me there and waited outside. He was extremely nervous, disapproving of the insecurity of the process and wanted us to have a police escort. But I trusted my luck more than the police. Many thousands of pounds were handed over by the teller without fuss or raised eyebrows. A.B.C. drove us back to the hotel with backward looks, perhaps disappointed that he had no one to evade and could not say "I told you so". Relief washed over his wrinkled face and we both had a drink.

The participants were not used to our procedure. They expected to read their papers to test the content as at a conference. Instead we distributed the papers amongst Ogbu, Metzger and myself for evaluation from the point of view of structure and academic criteria. Each of the three of us gave presentations to the group about the procedures for submitting papers, the way the journals handled them editorially, and in my case the best ways in which to present their arguments. I stressed he necessity of defining a problem to be solved, locating that problem in the preceding literature so that its significance was apparent (not always easy at the time in Africa before the current expansion of libraries), establishing the logical steps needed to provide an answer to the problem, organising their data according to those steps, and then assessing the result. They were warned not to be upset as Barbara wielded her strict editorial pen, an exercise which often caused shudders amongst the most experienced writers, including myself, but to know that it was done with the best of intentions and applied to every author, no matter how well established.

The papers were returned to their authors and then re-written according to the comments of the team, I may say vastly improved. We did not address the validity of the content. That was a separate issue which would govern the acceptance or rejection of their submission. We said we had no expertise in that matter. In fact, given the short time for the writing of the papers, content on the whole needed improvement.

I also warned them about the overuse of portmanteau jargon. Words such as "colonial", "globalisation" figured too highly and obscured the message. The writers had to break them down analytically so that it was clear what they had in mind. I thought this might be controversial, given the loaded nature of such terms, but it was accepted straightforwardly with good results.

The incoming editor of *Current anthropology* published a report, and an elected committee assessed the results with approval, suggesting follow up meetings. I was starting retirement and found the business of raising funds a problem, especially when not having a university base. Although I toyed with the idea of doing something the same for South East Asia and other parts of Africa, I chickened out. All was not lost though, since several colleagues used the current Anthropology report to guide graduate students since the same principles apply to creating graduate theses. And by now this kind of advice is not needed to the same extent in Africa, such has been the growth of academia there.

Of course I did my best to find time to visit the Serengeti, and had one Kenyan holiday with a friend. We were lucky enough to have a guide-driver and land rover to ourselves and be there at the time of the great southward wildebeest migration. From the hotel pool we watched the evening fauna assembling to drink at the river in the valley, emerging one by one from the neighbouring forest. We cursed at the jabbering of an Italian roving party, a national trait that they couldn't help, but scaring the animals. We got out of the land rover and picnicked within ten metres of a pride of lions, lazily hugging their partners.

One evening at the hotel there was a hubbub. Along the boundary very close to the kitchens there was a substantial hedge of bushes. There was a leopard on top looking inquisitively at the domestic action and no doubt savouring the smells of roast meat. The staff came out beating tin cans and making the loudest noises they could summon up. The leopard with the glowing eyes departed silently.

At that time I had good eyesight with especially good peripheral vision. On one expedition I looked out of the top of the land rover and quickly whispered to the driver, "Stop stop". He did. There lying the grass savannah was a cheetah, almost invisible – the driver had missed it. He turned the land rover and the cheetah took flight. Like an arrow they say. Like a space rocket I would say. With incredible speed the animal reached a clump of trees, the land rover bumping off the road in a vain endeavour to catch up. As we approached the clump the cheetah came out flying. In no time at all it was down the slope and across a distant stream and out of sight in the distance. I wonder where it came to a halt.

On this trip we returned to Nairobi and took a plane to a small German run oasis resort at the edge of Lake Turkana. It turned out that the driver who picked us up from the plane was a Somali refugee by the name of Abdi. And then it turned out that he had studied anthropology under the guidance of an English colleague at his university. Of course immediate rapport. The management, with some surprise at having such a man on their staff, and maybe a little suspicion, recognised our rapport and gave him permission to use the vehicle to show us around. Which he did. He was a gentle man and we felt sad at his bleak outlook when we left.

He took us through desert countryside to a fishing community by the lakeside. The men fished for their own sustenance but sold some to the resort. One evening he took us to the nearby established village where men were doing their high jump dancing. Then men and women formed tight circles to sing and dance. We were pulled into the circle. Bodies close to bodies. Swaying movements. The women and my companion laughed at my awkward attempts, but she was having a ball.

Then there was Lamu, the mini-Zanzibar, with its rich Muslim culture and story. You take a little plane to get there. At the tiny airstrip there are dhows to transfer you to the island, and in our case to the Peponi hotel, separated from the main town by a rocky coast.

The town itself is largely a wonderful assembly of old mansions, one of which is open to visitors. They are the habitations of wealthy Red Sea trading families, accessed through narrow lanes, each with a beautifully ornate door. Close to the beach there are hotels, eating houses, and fruit juice bars and many back packers. In the harbour fishing and trading dhows nestle together.

One evening we were enthralled by the music, the dancing and the street vendors in the main square and took no notice of the time. We went over the slight rise inland. There women were dancing in groups, gaily, lightly, and beckoned my companion. She did not hesitate.

Then we needed to go home. We attempted to hail a dhow. No no. We do not sail at night. What to do?

We decided to walk along the beach. It could have been quite a mistake. Before long the beach was closed by high rocky formations. We had to strike inland a short distance where there seemed to be a path. It was quite rough going and we were not sure of our way. Then we were hailed from behind. A young man was following the trail. It turned out that he was on the hotel's staff. "This is the way", he said, and guided us a bit further inland until we gratefully reached our cabin.

On the other side of the hotel the great beach begins. Pure broad white sand for mile after mile with tussetted sandhills behind. We walked for an hour or two, passing only a couple of people on the way. Then we noticed the tide turning and creeping up over the sand. Time to go. Don't want to be cut off again. May the beach be ever protected from resort mania, may it remain open and pristine.

Back in Nairobi itself we hired a car for an afternoon. The affable driver took us through the suburbs and the acres of coffee growing small holders, and then he seemed to make a decision, no doubt after having checked us out. He took us to the huge, vast, massive shanty town and market area on the other side of the city. Several storied permanent housing blocks were being built, but it would take years to make a dent in the need of the squatters. We walked down into the market, the driver a little apprehensive, and found the vendors happy to show their wares and to talk. The driver had warned us not to take photographs without permission, which some of them refused to give.

The food in Kenya is a mixed bag, with old fashioned English, modern cafes, Kenyan eating houses, and some very good Indian food.

Despite the pressures, few people in the countryside go hungry[4]. There are agriculturalists, like the Kikuyu, whose farms handle cash crops such as tea and coffee, and local foods from cassava to bananas and vegetables. There are nomadic pastoralists and fishermen like the Turkana and Samburu, whose diet is almost entirely protein, and whose spirits are repressed if there is no fish (the world famous tilapia stocks the lakes) or good meat, like beef or camel or giraffe (instead of goat). In Loiyalangi the young people dance at night, but only if their bellies are full.

Many of the city restaurants reflect the African village traditions. Of these, the most famous cuisine is Swahili, that of the coastal people whose religion is mainly Muslim, and whose ancestry is African mixed with strong Arab inter-breeding.

Swahili cooking is well represented in Nairobi. I took my friend to a famous little place called Malindi Dishes, named after a coastal community. You can get there from the Hilton Hotel by walking across the plaza to Gaberone Street, past busy workshops, simple cafes and beer halls, peddling trays, along crowded narrow streets with workers and office clerks. You will probably have to ask your way, as I have had to do on every visit. Friendly Kenyans seem to feel hospitably privileged to direct you.

We arrived about one o'clock on a Friday. The place was shut, although a couple of the staff were within. A man and woman, dressed for the office, stood outside patiently. "We think they will open soon", they said. After a while they spoke through the window. "The

---

[4] Since then Kenya has been severely torn by drought and rivalrous massacres threatening the survival of thousands.

management is at prayer at the mosque. We must wait." We were joined by working people. It was nearly two when the management arrived, and a tall slim waiter took our order at a simple cafe table. A mixed clientele arrived as if by magic.

The rough menu lists standard cafe items like fish and chips or barbecued chicken (Nairobi is full of little fast food fish and chicken places). But there is was a small section that took our interest. We had one of the famed fruit juices -- passion fruit, there is no liquor, and well herbed meat samosas and a "shish kebab", here meaning a long sausage shape of spiced minced meat, cooked with a crust. I had *matoke*, soft cooked vegetable banana, one of the staples of Kenya. Some items on the menu were not available, but we were able to enjoy the recommended chicken shela and fish *takaungu*, both in the same mild coconut spiced sauce. The fish skin particularly was spiced dry, with complex exotic flavours and the fish itself of perfect calibre.

There is a famous store in the more fashionable part of Nairobi called African Heritage, assembling both tourist and artistic crafts from table stoneware and beads to clothing from all over Africa. Off a parallel street at the back the cafe hosts coffee and tea and informal food. Once it was noted for Ethiopian cooking, with buffet style stews, but that had disappeared. Indeed, there is better "rest of Africa" cooking in Vancouver than in Nairobi, where two Ethiopian restaurants serve their spiced stews (*wat*) and chutneys on proper Ethiopian *injera* soft breads, and fingers are the only utensils (available in Nairobi at the New Paradiso Hotel). If you keep looking you will find more Kenyan rustic foods. The Thorn Tree Cafe of the New Stanley Hotel on a busy downtown corner was a traditional colonial meeting and watering place, now beloved mainly by tourists and back-packers. It still sports a message board where you can try to make contact with fellow travellers. It had a pretty poor example of the traditional meat stew, tough beef chunks with just a touch, English style, of carrot, beans and green pepper. There was, when we sampled, no attempt at spicing or herbing, and the garnish of spinach shreds was almost as tough as the meat itself. The main interest was the *matoke*-like *irio*, a corn mush including bean and potato (often peas and other vegetables). You can also have it with the popular *ugali*, a stiffer maize "porridge".

Rice, cassava (tapioca, manioc), potatoes, are introduced foods that have become staples of African diet along with bananas (the harder green varieties are best for cooking). But the Portuguese seafarers introduced chili, especially in the form of hot piripiri sauce, centuries ago, and you will find dishes like prawns piripiri in fancy restaurants, perhaps with the wonderful giant prawns of the elegant Tamarind restaurant (alas, when we sampled, the chili was blandly toned down, English style). And the Indian settlers introduced chapatti, pilau, biriani rice, samosas and kebabs so that they are now popular staples in African cafes.

One place which should be a showcase of good African and/or Swahili food is at the Bomas of Kenya, a living archive of dance and village architecture, centred around a huge round stage unsupported by pillars. But here all the cafe could provide when I took the workshop there was tough unsubtle barbecued chicken or greasy fish and chips, or dull samosas or kebabs. A total disappointment.

At the other end of the luxury scale, a must on any visitor list is the Carnivore.[5] Here the supposed emphasis is on barbecued meats, grilled Brasilian style on spits over a round open fire. I say "supposed" because you would expect the finest of the fine, whereas the standard meats can be dry and tough, and the exotics, like giraffe or antelope even tougher. The real attraction is the ambience.

The Carnivore, and its associated Samba Bar, lies beyond the Wilson Airport some fifteen minutes from the city centre. (Your taxi will willingly arrange to pick you up after the meal). The large roofs cover terraces separated by low walls, extended onto open patios. The grill menu is *prix fixe*, the price including soup (during my last visit a dull potato-asparagus), salad you put together yourself, a good range of sauces and chutneys, and as much meat as you can stomach. Waiters steadily ply drinks and wine. Others (they seem innumerable) maintain a continuous procession of spits from the fire, cutting slices from the roasts, or pushing *à la* kebab chicken wings, livers, whatnot onto your hot stone plates. During my 1990 visit there was no poultry other than chicken, but be prepared for anything. We did have chicken liver, beef, lamb, pork, giraffe and antelope. In addition to the main offerings, there is an *à la carte* menu for vegetarians, plus farmed trout. In case you are wondering, the exotic game comes not from hunting, but from a food-game farm near the coast.

To explore Kenya food further, I recommend you get Kathy Eldon's *Eating Out in Kenya*, (if as I hope there are uptodate editions available) one of the most useful little guidebooks for any country, except for the

---

[5] Although visitors in 2008, on my recommendation, reported disappointment. Much depends on what kind of meats are in season.

famous French and English ones. Try and get an earlier addition as well as the current one, for they list eating places by type of food, an index omitted from the 1987 version: several of the hotels specialize in African or Swahili cooking.

Kenyan cafes make wonderful fruit juices - passion fruit, banana, tamarind, mixtures of orange and lime. On the narrow-streeted, dhow-fronted, donkey populated streets of Lamu, Islamic rules prevent the consumption of alcohol except at two specially licensed hotels. So fruit juices reign supreme. There are several little terrace-shaded watering holes, easy to come across -- the Juice Garden, the Papaya Juice Bar, the names say it. We gulped down huge beer tankards of exquisitely pure mango juice, rich and powerful, for ten shillings (fifty cents); and in the Equator Restaurant, more fancy, sipped pure tamarind juice through straws.

Most Kenyan restaurants derive from a traditional English colonial style, some modified by contemporary standards, some (in the resort hotels) German, and a great deal of Indian and Ismaili. You will also find poor Italian, creditable oriental, and some excellent light food cafes and buffets, like the Jax or the Tate Room of the New Stanley Hotel, or the swimming pool of the Norfolk Hotel (NOT the dreadfully old-hat English food in the Norfolk's Delamere Terrace and Restaurant)[6]. These feature first class curries, salads, dishes from a variety of cuisines.

Let's deal with the archaic English influence and get it over with. Sometimes, as at the Mara Serena Lodge, the hotels try very hard to produce, under

---

[6] In 2009 I heard tghat the hotel was being heavily redevoped so much will have changed. I hope the good has not gone out with the bad.

extremely difficult supply conditions, a wide variety for their guests. The Marai Serena produces an enormous breakfast buffet -- fruit, juices, porridge, cheeses, meats, sausages of several kinds, bacon, many kind of eggs, varied breads and toast. The lunch salad bar is equally huge and includes fish and meats with their sauces, soups, a choice of at least three protein dishes with curry, chops, chicken, stews for example, and a buffet of the most stodgy desserts, heavy heavy, as you could imagine plus fruit salads. At dinner, the same buffets made their appearance for salad and dessert, but the proteins were served *à la carte*. One could not but admire the ingenuity and imagination that went into getting the ideas together -- and despair at the near total lack of delicacy of taste or imagination.

Similarly at the unique Peponi Hotel at Shela on Lamu Island, where the German-language chef managed to serve English stodge as only the old-time English could think of it. Hardened grills, tiny uninteresting oysters, crab piripiri which was nothing but crabmeat unadorned and a bottle of commercial piripiri sauce, tough rouladen stuffed with whole carrots, heavy desserts, but good potatoes and chips.

From there to the Oasis Lodge at Loiyalangi on Lake Turkana, where the influence is homely German, nothing haute cuisine about it, but at least recognizably interesting despite the almost impossible difficulties of supply.

Here there was excellent fresh lake fish, mostly tilapia, caught on demand by El Moro tribesmen. In the company of Abdi we spent time in the simple grass El Moro villages, set by the barren lake shore some eight kilometres away, like blips on a moon face, and we accompanied him one day as he ordered fish and then late in the afternoon picked up what must have been a week's supply.

The sashimi one day was in fact a simple ceviche. The rouladen one day was as tough as old boots. Fresh vegetable salad one day only. Excellent potatoes and very reasonable sauces. Strangely, no attempt to grow their own papaya, bananas, etc., although there is good water supply (and it tastes good too). At breakfast, in addition to fruit, they served some of the best poached eggs I had in Kenya, full yolked, softly firm, spoiled by totally un-German coffee. One of the great mysteries of most hotels in Kenya was that, despite using those famous Kenyan coffee beans, what arrived in the cups was bitter and coarse; here, it didn't even have that character to complain about.

I was told that the best coffee beans are reserved for export, not sold locally, though you can buy them at the airport. We discovered when we tried that the coffee boutique in the departure lounge did not at that time accept credit cards and that its prices were at least half as high again for the same coffee and tea as was available in the official duty free shop, which also did accept credit cards.... (At this time credit cards were important because Kenyan money had to be left inside Kenya, and my dollars were used up in airport departure tax.

By far the best English style influence I experienced was at the two Tamarind restaurants. On the outskirts of Mombasa there is one with a patio view of the estuary, a little out of town, where I remember having excellent seafood. Indeed, although there are other items on the menu, the Tamarind went in for elaborate seafood, treated with more delicacy than the meats of its brother the Carnivore.

In the ornately luxurious elaborate Nairobi branch, downtown, many of the plates derive from international, including oriental, backgrounds, but the manner of treatment was undeniably English, usually avoiding the essence of the cuisines to convert to bland tastes (especially, but not only, where chilli is concerned), just as do those California-style eating houses I dub "ethnic conglomerate". But the treatment was indeed careful, and the management did a good job in presenting African and Swahili materials with thoughtful adaptation.

My friend had a generous sashimi of red snapper, properly served with heavy chopsticks and soy sauce and thick radish. I had crab spring rolls, full of crab, firmly battered, and a mustard based ginger sauce, served with finger bowls. Possibilities included trout in banana leaves; kizingitini - a seafood mix with coconut, tamarind and coriander; seafood casserole with cognac and coconut; five types of lobster, four of prawn, and salads and meats including venison prime rib with kai apple sauce.

My friend chose a well prepared lobster Swahili, in which the meat is cut out, served with a sauce containing garlic, turmeric, saffron, tomato, coconut and coconut rice -- you had to press deep to find the excellent sauce. I had jumbo prawns piripiri, the prawns large and fresh, easy to get out of the shell, with a side piripiri sauce that was almost totally mild with only the merest hint of chilli (as if the chef felt you didn't really want what you had ordered). Both came served with side vegetables of mostly uninteresting English-boiled quality, quite unworthy of the rest of the cooking. There was an extensive and very expensive wine list.

To go for dinner it was necessary to do so by taxi, navigate barred doors, and be escorted to the taxi for the way home: Nairobi was thought to be dangerous at night.

As might be expected in an upscale expensive restaurant, the clientele during our night out was well dressed and with, I believe, only one exception, totally European. Nearby tables had parties of the safari-rich, others seemed to be diplomatic or business oriented. Yet expense does not always keep African or Indian guests away from good restaurants -- style of cooking can do.

One of the good things about the Tamarind is that the African staff is well trained and polished. Training waiters is extremely difficult -- how can you expect them to be attentive without being over-attentive? How encourage them to watch your every need without over-doing it intrusively? Early in my last trip we christened the over-attentive waiting, in which plates are whipped away before you or especially your partner are finished, in which the waiters warmly enquire after your needs when you are in the middle of an intense conversation, in which they exercise their English by entering into a formalized conversation about what you saw on safari and are you enjoying your stay and where do you come from -- natural and well-meaning comments that are insufficiently spontaneous, too text-booky, to carry the affective meaning that the speakers want -- the Masai Mara syndrome. It often cropped up in Nairobi, where nevertheless we had to admire the way African waiters managed to handle what to them must have been the extraordinary sequence of dishes in the oriental restaurants. It was refreshingly absent at the Oasis Lodge, where the young staff behaved with a natural friendliness, and took well, with some amusement, to our request to leave the plates on the table until both of us had finished.....

Kathy Eldon's book lists several other restaurants that give attention to up-scale international cuisine, but I have not sampled them.

If you want a cross-section of the Nairobi population, including families, tourists, bureaucrats, people from the international community, lovers, African businessmen and women, parties, then go to the better Indian and oriental restaurants. Go there too if you want the best standards of cooking in Kenya, and add to your list the little family run Indian restaurants, of many varieties, tucked away in the suburbs. I have not come across as consistently high standards of varied Indian cooking on such a scale anywhere yet outside of India.

Take the downtown Minar, for example (one of two in the chain, the one Kathy Eldon considered faded, but which I think still feels warm, almost opulent in its dark elegance). The head waiter who dealt with us smiled fulsomely with much rolling of eyes, persuasive about the food.

The food was indeed superb. While the menu lacked variety in small things (no samosas for example) it contained several items which could be used in lieu, plus soups. We did not sample the desserts which are highly thought of. *Shami kebab*, vegetable dumplings, were firm, served with salad-slaw, deliciously spiced. *Murg saagwata* was chicken in a thick smooth easily slipped down spinach puree spiced with ginger -- the menu said tomato too but there was little evidence of that -- and can come with *gosht* (mutton) instead. *Ruganjosh* was a Kashmir plate of mutton hotly spiced with saffron coloured curd. Stuffed capsicum was one of the daily specials, in a delicious sauce, rice and herbs inside. There are several excellent *biryanis*, at least in flavouring. Among the *naan* we chose *naan rogani*, softly flavoured with fruit, jam-style. There is a long list of tandoori-oven preparations, some going well beyond the standard tandooris, such as *kadai gosht* or *murg*, cooked with yoghurt, ginger, garlic and spices in a metal *kadai* container. In short, it was pleasingly varied Indian food of high interest and delicacy of standard. It was one of the two places in Nairobi to which I gave three ticks (out of three) in my last visit.

On earlier visits I went to the Excelsior Hotel Steakhouse, which combined excellent curries and Swahili dishes (though I am not sure it still operates that way.) The Jax cooks Goan foods as part of its buffet, with lots of coconut. The Khyber is said to be of high quality, the small and homely Krishna for vegetarian food. Up the lane from the Kwality Motel is a small room that used to serve the most wonderful Parsee food, but has now, I believe, been converted to Ismaili. Parsee fare is also available as part of the menu of the Maharaja. The Mauriya has Kashmiri entrées, the Mayur North Indian vegetarian. And so it goes on and on.

The Chinese restaurants have high standards too. One we sampled was the Rickshaw, comfortably decorated in a large office building (again you enter from a side door through security guards.)

Since the cooking inspiration is Cantonese, you have to allow for the toned-down tastes, but that having been recognized the blends are subtle. The spring rolls were crisp and thick, with a bland interior and sickly sweet sauce. Hot and spicy chicken, mixed stir-fried vegetables, braised duck smothered in sauces -- the difference in this food, as my companion pointed out, is that the ingredients are sauced heavily, almost like gravy -- not at all unpleasant, but not what we have been used to in Chinese restaurants elsewhere. An English, Kenyan or colonial influence???

Some dishes the menu describes as spicy hot, but the one we chose was weak. The chicken and duck were chopped unusually finely. There is a large selection of prawns on the menu. The overall impression was of a pleasant difference -- a cuisine to be called Kenyan Chinese?

We did not try the Japanese or Korean restaurants, but came across another wonderful surprise, again three ticks on my scale -- the Bangkok, which had not been open long enough to make Kathy Eldon's edition. It was small, elegant, tucked away upstairs in a bourgeois shopping mall in a wealthy suburb, with a well dressed very mixed clientele. And I must say that at the time of my visit it had the most authentic, best cooked, most elegantly presented real Thai food I had so far sampled outside of Thailand.

The Spring rolls were thick with scrumptiously crunchy fillings. The beef salad was hot and smooth sauced with fine-chopped beef for rolling in fresh firm lettuce leaves. Excellently composed and flavoured Thai style curry and beautifully balanced Thai hot soups. Nobody here messes around asking do you want it hot? The appropriate degrees of chilli are built in to the food, not added inadequately at the last moment, as so often happens to "please" the Western palate. And as in any really good Thai restaurant, the menu tells you what to expect and gives you plenty of opportunity to sample recipes where mouth-burning chilli is not appropriate. The menu also had a selection of appetizers, small dishes essential to any good Thai meal, but so often missing from overseas restaurants.

Quite a surprising achievement -- as so much in Kenya can be.

My experience of West Africa, apart from Nigeria, was in francophone countries, and unfortunately far too limited. Throughout these lands the French colonial influence, in every aspect of modern African culture, is noticeably different from that in the anglophone countries. It is a matter of style. In anglophone Africa the emphasis is overtly practical, "business" like, profit-oriented, don't waste money on frills. There was poverty in the francophone countries I visited for sure, and there was no less expression of business enterprise with many well-to-do. But there seemed to be an aesthetic ambience which was hidden elsewhere. And security was not nearly as evident as it was in Nairobi.

Wherever possible in this part of the world I sought out the Inter-continental hotels, not for their *luxe* but because they often served as local modern art galleries and their casual restaurants had local dishes on their menu. They were also good locations to observe the African well to do, who came to sup, play, use the swimming pool, or host weddings and meetings. The one in Abidjan in the Côte d'Ivoire was one of the best from this point of view.

The city itself has a business section on a nearby hill. Residential areas and offices are spread out across riverine lagoons with verdant vegetation. The university is also close to the hotel, consisting of spread out low level buildings for classrooms and offices. It was easy to find my way to the office of Mariba Touré, whose position was described as *Directeur de l'Institut de ethno-sociologie*. Not anthropology which was then still a suspect word. Like so many others in universities he of course had no secretarial or similar assistance and he showed me his papers, typed on flimsies or hand-written. I tried to encourage him, as I did with others, to submit them, but I am afraid it was too difficult and nothing came of it. For one thing the costs of postage were prohibitive. We did not solve that problem in *Current Anthropology*. In retrospect I wonder now whether we could have sent a bunch of postal reply coupons. His position represented such a waste.

Then on to Zaire, emerged from its brutal Belgian colonial regime.[7] The hotel was much simpler than the others and the town, as I saw it, was spread out with an indistinct focus. I have no recollection of the university as such and could not get to Lumbubashi where there was another associate, but was able to call on Kanga Kalemba-Vita and on Mamengi Xlzaxi the director of a small university museum.

The latter directed me to the Institut de Musées Nationaux de Zaire in which I visited M. Cornet and his staff. Their tiny offices were situated on a plot of land within the precincts of the presidential palace. The taxi was not too sure where to go, but arrived successfully at a military guard post. They smiled and waived me on, giving me the totally false impression that this was a relaxed sort of country. The little French run office was struggling financially but engaged in an ambitious programme of recording Zairian traditional music.

Then it was time to visit the Président du Conseil d'Administration des Universités du Zaire, Msgr. Tchibangu, also an associate. The ride to his residence, way out in the suburbs, was an eye opener. The main road was lined for miles with small allotments and modest homes, often of traditional structure, with side roads every few metres. Each allotment had its bananas and papaya and small garden plot. Out of these humble cottages, probably one or at most two rooms, emerged from time to time men and women who were impeccably dressed in city clothes, often waiting at bus stops to commute elsewhere.

---

[7] Now. as the Democratic Republic of the Congo, immersed in vicious internal strife.

The bishop was graciousness itself as we talked about the problems of university finance and curriculum. Then he gave me a book based on his graduation thesis. It was an immense tôme. The theme: the relationship between religion and science, with a thesis that they were strictly compatible.

Perhaps by this time you have forgotten the title of this chapter: *Africa Resurgent*. You haven't seen much of that theme so far. But between the early 'eighties, when most of these visits took place, and 2006 there have bee immense changes in the worlds of Africa. The press is naturally full of the horrors of Darfur, the troubles in the Congo, the tragic mess of Zimbabwe, of violence and famine. These are shamefully there and are international scandals which have to be addressed, especially by Africans. But it must be stressed that, even in war torn countries such as Uganda, there have been enormous positive changes which should not go unnoticed. I did not have the truth of this impressed upon me in Africa itself because I have not been able to return, but rather during a meeting at the Afrika Institut of the University of Leiden. It was both a privilege and an education to be there.

The participants numbered around fifty, drawn from most countries of sub-Saharan Africa. They included archivists, librarians, publishers, all concerned one way or another with the interface between the printed and the digital word. They were professionals one and all, *innovative* and dedicated to their crafts. Their papers are on line at the Afrika Institut University of Leiden website.[8] My own contribution, an excuse to attend and learn, was to compare my experience as print

---

[8] I will discuss the issues of print v. digital in Chapter 43

editor of *Current Anthropology* and digital editor of the on-line *The AnthroGlobe Journal*[9].

I was there to learn, and learn I did. I heard about a publisher in South Africa who issued his books entirely on line, how rural treatment centres in Uganda were all linked to the central hospital in Kampala for real time instructions on how to handle medical issues, of digital access to global publications and the exposure when scholars put their African materials on line, of the explosive growth in mobile phones, of ingenious simple methods of creating power sources in remote villages. Vodaphone is concentrating its business in emerging economies, beginning with India and now Africa for the land line infrastructure is often deplorable and wireless connectivity offers a strong chance to leapfrog over archaic phone systems. It has taken private enterprise to make the promise real[10].

Twenty years ago this meeting would not have taken place. When the internet came along it was difficult for African scholars and others to use it, even in major centres, because pricing was based on tie use and the size of messages, so that to exchange papers was prohibitive. That has changed. Libraries and archives and the publishing industry have taken major leaps forward and the supply of well educated professionals has increased at the same time.

The experience stimulated thinking about the future of a non-violent Africa, with expensive military equipment downplayed, and about the priorities of

---

[9] Continuing under the editorship of Michael Fischer at the University of Kent, U.K.

[10] Not all private. Rwanda has embarked on an ambitious programme to link all villages in the country by oprical cable, with laptops in every school.

international aid. There are major continental infrastructure needs in roads, railways, and communication devices. This is getting attention but not nearly enough.

Countries investing in Africa, including China, identify promising countries according to their natural resource supplies. Some countries, for instance on the edge of the Sahara, have very limited or no material resources.

What every country does have, though, is *people* – highly intelligent people who are not short of enterprise, initiative, and inventive capabilities when the conditions are ripe. Thus I argue strongly that, even in materially destitute countries – or perhaps especially in those –huge investments in education, from primary school up to university research and graduate studies. Those who do have this opportunity are also schooled in world languages such as English, French, Portuguese and Spanish. This gives them the possibility of making their mark globally.

And what then? Research institutes and foundations should re-think their priorities so that they become directed not only to urgent African issues such as malaria, but to fundamental world knowledge. India has done it. Africa can too. Government aid agencies have a hard time thinking outside the box. The huge new private foundations, such as that created by Bill and Marilyn Gates (which has changed the face of malaria eradication) could concentrate at least some of their immense resources on Africa's greatest asset, its peoples and their minds, starting with the countries most beset by chronic poverty.

25. America Latina

On my first trip to Lima, not only did I learn to appreciate ceviche and pisco sour but I discovered the function of military bands.

It was for a meeting of the International Congress of Americanists. This was and is a meeting primarily focussed on Latin America, although Canada and the United Sates are part of its mandate, and it is very much an old boy network. On this occasion the meeting took place in a nunnery in the centre of the city.

The president was José Matos Mar, a distinguished and well respected social anthropologist. The country was at the time a dictatorship. Matos Mar was close to the President of the country and was his speech writer from time to time on Indian affairs and a personal adviser, said to have done much to modify the regime's policies towards the indigenous people.

Just the same there were numerous political and social activists in prison, as was the case in most South American countries. Many scholars had to move from country to country as policies changed, and even sought safety in Europe, mainly France.

The opening plenary took place in the hall of the nunnery, with balustrades above it containing the nun's sleeping quarters. Wives of prisoners managed to occupy the front row or two of the hall. The President himself was to open the proceedings. He arrived, escorted by a military band which played an opening anthem.

The President rose to speak. The wives took up a loud noise of chanting "*Amnestia generale. Anmestia generale*" they shouted. The President was drowned out. But then the band stuck up a raucous tune and drowned out the wives. The band earned its pay.

Matos Mar talked to the President and calmed the shouting down. He announced a deal that the wives would not be prosecuted if they allowed the President to speak and that he would talk with them. There was agreement and the President indeed spoke.

But when he finished military police entered the building. The wives scattered for their very lives and ran up to the balconies, supposedly sanctuary territory. The police followed the flurry of skirts. I don't believe they caught anyone, but I may be wrong.

Lima was not a happy city for me. On another occasion the city grey polluted clouds contributed to my heart difficulties. The well to do lived in suburbs with neat villas which seemed to escape much of the pollution. There I visited colleagues at the Catholic University.

On of the features which fascinated me was the sight of the massive slums by the turgid river on the way to and from the airport. The fascination came from the observation that each time I visited Lima over the decades the slums noticeably changed. The ramshackle buildings of cardboard and flattened cans were slowly replaced with wood or clay bricks, taking on a permanent life of their own. Some added an upper storey. Power lines appeared and the roads looked cleaner and better kept. There were TV ariels and service shops and enterprises also arrived. This of course was from a distance.

Peru is not just Lima. Most tourists spend little time there but head to the uplands. Some walk from Cuzco along the lengthy *alte plano* a land of indigenous villages, llamas and resistance to government. One of the main attractions is Machu Picchu, the dramatic city ruins on a high mountain above a steep gorge surrounded by other peaks. When I managed to get there I wanted to photograph the buildings which were witness to a vibrant society amid the swirling clouds. It was difficult as a result of the pressure of tourism. One could not get away from people.

From Cuzco you take a train to the foot of the mountain. There was a choice of two. One was a tourist train which was frequently held up by brigands. The other was the local train. By happenstance I took the latter. It was "never" held up though after I left the papers reported one such unheard of incident.

Cuzco itself is a charming city enclosed in defensive walls. The centre of the city can be somewhat overwhelmed by back packers and other tourists, especially in the main square.

I decided to walk the perimeter walls. Not long after I began I was accosted by a woman and her young children. "Be careful" she said in English. She then pointed to my back pack which was open and openly showing my camera. "That is too easy to steal."

Lima is typical of much of Latin American lowland cities, but the upland towns, often on the side of dormant volcanoes, can offer a more rustic appearance. Quito's surroundings of open grassland with farmed animals and mountain peaks earns it comparisons, superficial, with Swiss pastoral locations.

Colombia has the advantage of both coastal and high altitude cities and the disadvantage of revolutionary militants and the drug trade. Bogotá is high but is larger and anxious about security. On my only two night visit my colleagues met me at the airport before I could choose a taxi. The motivation was partly courtesy but also because at that time there had been some instances of taxi drivers taking foreigners straight into the hands of kidnappers. They warned me not to go walking around at night alone.[11]

They gave me a lavish dinner. To me the *pièce de resistance* was the enormous fruit bowl in the centre of the table. It had lowland, temperate climate and high altitude fruits of every description, some of which I had never known before. I could not help thinking that they would create a sensation in Canada. Since then air transport has brought Colombian flowers and Latin American fruits to our supermarkets but there are many species which do not make the trip.

Apart from Peru the country I had most to deal with, though still superficially, was Brasil. The country is so vast, so diverse, with such a rich history, so many complex difficulties, and a combination of contrasting energy and lassitude, that its contradictions present an endless fascination and intellectual as well as practical challenge. It is a country seemingly always on the verge of dramatic but elusive industrial and commercial growth, containing on the one hand a major aero spatial industry and on the other the threatened forests of the Amazon, great cities and drug infested *favellas* (slums),

---

[11] Security in the city has improved substantially.

drug lords and industrial barons. If I had had my time over again it is possible I would have chosen to work in Brasil.

The commercial heart is of course Saõ Paulo, though I did not visit that city until the 'eighties, on the trip to drum up participation in the Vancouver World Congress. I was lodged in a hotel beside a multi-lane thoroughfare with no possibility of walking and exploring to find a lively ambience. But my hosts more than made up for it.

A colleague took me one night to the central railway station. The streets around were covered with flop houses and milling groups of migrants from the poverty stricken north. We entered a small room with a long table and bought beer. There were perhaps twenty-five or so men seated drinking and listening intently to a bard at the far end. As he finished his song there was quiet conversation until someone, including ourselves, pushed money to him and gave him a theme in our case Canada loves Brasil. With little hesitation the bard broke into song, to applause as he finished and another theme turned up.

Rio also has significant anthropologists at university and museum, though they were not always welcome in the time of the generals. Physically, Rio does not impress me. The great beaches of Copacabana and Ipanamena and the peaks overshadowing them are certainly as dramatic as guide books and travel publicity would have you believe, and the view from the top of the mountain of the giant Christ statue is breath-taking. But these are only a tiny part of a huge city and do not dominate most of it.

The *life* of the city is something else. The *favellas* are mostly but not all nasty places, though their intimate adjunct to the beaches provides a challenging contrast with the smart jeweller inhabited main street below. They have a life of their own, as studies have demonstrated, with familial support and some entrepreneurial energy.

Their girls descend on the beaches where an uninhibited pride in body predominates. And it is not just girls. Muscular men and middle aged women, the thin and the thick, don't seem to care. They are who they are, and are quite pleasingly comfortable with it.

In the 'seventies and 'eighties I was interested, out of curiosity, in the phenomenon of carnival and similarly structured activities throughout the world. The great Carnival of Rio is the prime example, but it is mirrored in perhaps less dramatic ways not only in Latin America and the Caribbean but in Europe, as I shall describe later. (I have never seen a Rio carnival).

Rio is also famous for its football. Carnival has its samba schools based on social groups and geographical propinquity. The football clubs have parallel and sometimes overlapping organisations and intense rivalries. They serve to give people who are otherwise often alienated from the mass society a focus and sense of value. The work for both goes on for months. No sooner does one carnival explode than work begins again to design and create floats and costumes and music for the next. What is not quite so evident as in European carnivals, is the mocking of an establishment through satire.

On my last visit to Rio I had come via Santiago de Chile and Buenos Aires and had picked up a stomach bug in a hotel in Santiago after foolishly eating seafood.[12] I used to get the complaint from Paris water, now no longer a risk, but kept it at bay by consuming yoghurt before and during the trip – and do the same if there may be a problem in other parts of the world. This time I didn't. So I was feeling quite poorly and the discomfort would not go away.

I was staying in a somewhat run down hotel on the beach and decided to brave it and have a meal down the strand at the Meridien. It was a waste of a meal and I was beginning to need to vomit, but there was enough time to get back to my room.

On the way a woman ran to catch up with me, pass me and confront me. She seemed thin and badly undernourished and offered herself for my pleasure. As she did so and I was protesting she kept looking over my shoulder, almost certainly to a pimp who was controlling her. I could not even summon up any sympathy and brushed her aside. She kept it up for a while before giving up and before I had the relief of throwing up in my room.

Next day was a Saturday and I was no better. I keep up membership in IAMAT, he International Association for Medical Assistance to Travellers, and looked up their Rio doctor. By great good fortune he was, exceptionally, in with his receptionist going over files. He agreed without hesitation to see me. He did not simply give me some pills and send me away. He gave me a thorough examination before he agreed that what I had was what I had. He gave me a diet of: dry toast, apple with the skin, and *overripe* banana with plenty of non-alcoholic liquid and told me the worst thing I could

---

[12] Diarrhea can be picked up in hotels because the seafood is refrigerated sometimes too long at inappropriate temperatures.

do was to not eat. The problem cleared up almost instantly.

I have a yearning to visit Manaus, the once rubber capital of the Amazon, with its opera house and the remains of a commercial aristocracy which in the nineteenth century sent their laundry by steamer to Europe for cleaning, and its wandering waterways of riverine jungle. And the great cities of the northern Atlantic coast. The nearest I got to the latter was a couple of days in Santiago de Bahia. I had a car but my coastal route by barren parched lands was uniformed and a waste.

By the seashore in the evening there was a small procession of candle bearing worshippers. The town itself, above the port which began the Atlantic slave trade, was pressed inward by a press of humanity.

In a hotel I noticed a showing of a local artist's oils. They impressed me and I determined to have one. The prices were possible but I had no money. The woman in charge said she did not have credit card facilities. Then she had a brainwave. Perhaps the hotel reception will charge it on their card f or me. The hotel declined.

As I was leaving the woman ran up to me. "The hotel tells me that there is a meeting upstairs of the regional American Express. They are going to issue me with credit card facilities." The deal was clinched then and there and my pocketbook noticed the transaction for quite a while.

I have mentioned Candido Mendes, the political scientist who was president of the International Social Science Council. Candido came from a wealthy estate background. He used some of his wealth to create a downtown university with a business orientation. One year he organised a meeting of the International Political Science Association in his building. One interdisciplinary session was on the theme of laws in social science. I gave a very much unfinished paper arguing that genuine theoretical law was almost absent in the social sciences except for economics. The participating Danish sociologist rose to the bait. He pointed outside the window where there were traffic lights and chose an unfortunate example. "Look out there" he said. "There is a law in practice. Everyone stops at the red light." In Rio? I did not argue that if it were true, which it isn't, it would be a data regularity, or a statistical probability, not a law that is part of a theoretical structure.

Candido was the perfect Rio host. He had a corpus of beautiful guides and hostesses who made sure we were at the right place at the right time, and sampled the right canapés, and he organised a show from a samba school.

Another but less frequent contact was Roberto Cardoso de Oliveira. Cardoso, an eminent sociologist with anthropological leanings, had been a victim of the generals from whom he escaped to France. As the generals were replaced he returned. I visited him in Brasilia.

Brasilia itself was an extreme exercise in contrast. An artificial city as is Canberra, Brasilia is stark whereas Canberra at least attempts a unity. Brasilia has three parts. There are the magnificent public buildings, each one a major work of art, set way apart from each other. Then there are the extremely ugly brown high rise buildings, stretching out laterally, which contain the apartments of most residents and lower ranking civil servants. They seem devoid of services or interest, but also contain hotel accommodation which I used. And then there is a suburbia with decent homes and mainly small villas.

Cardoso lived in the last. He was an earnest, quiet, modest and retiring colleague with hospitality but few smiles or easy humour. He was named one of the honorary presidents of the World Congress in Vancouver of 1984 but it took major pressure from Lita Osmundsen of the Wenner-Gren Foundation for Anthropological Research to persuade him to turn up.

No doubt he chose an academic life in Brasilia because it linked naturally with politics. It was only a decade later that Roberto Enrique Cardoso de Oliveira was elected, on a reform ticket, President of Brasil. He managed many significant changes but was continually frustrated by the country's archaic, special interest and sometimes corrupt political system.

26. Around the World in Curiosity Mode

You will by now have realised that too many of my experiences were based on very short visits, limited to making contact with *Current Anthropology associates* and other colleagues and talking up the Vancouver World Congress and the International Union of Anthropological and Ethnological Sciences. Sometimes. Nevertheless it was sometimes possible to vacation and take a little time to explore just a little more deeply.

There were many many countries I did not visit, and there were some visits not mentioned in the previous chapters which remain in my mind as a kaleidoscope or slide show of personal impressions. These I will mention here.

For now here we go around the world....... starting in the north.

Before the 'nineties my one visit to West Germany was for a conference of the Americanists, who have very strong European representation, in Stuttgart. Much of the central city was still, in the 'seventies, not rebuilt after he war. I was very much in the company of a Danish group led by Helge Kleiven called the International Work Group on Indigenous Affairs or IWGIA. This was mainly a study and pressure group trying to bring their influence on governments and others who were permitting or executing genocide and ethnocide or similar actions against their indigenous peoples. There were other groups, such as an important one out of Harvard and I was becoming chair or a committee of the IUAES on the same subject, of which

Helge was a member. The IUAES did not want to duplicate the work of other committees and wished to work through them and give them support. A good Netherlands friend, Henri Claessen, was deeply immersed in such issues and was a leader within the IUAES.

In Stuttgart we met in cafes on the street leading to the station, and the Danish and Norwegian delegates naturally congregated in a beer hall. Within five minutes they were needling Germans, who had nothing to do with the conference, quaffing drinks at the same long tables. They were listing nasty incidents during their countries' wartime occupation, the Germans were trying to defend themselves and speak of changes in their country, but the Nordics would have none of it. The temperature, fuelled by alcohol rose and the voices grew very much louder. It was a miracle there was not a brawl, even though the Nordics were far fewer in numbers and would not shut up. All this was in English....

In my late *Current Anthropology* days, in the 'eighties I made a quick trip to Helsinki, Stockholm and Oslo. In Stockholm I met with a local anthropological association. It was meeting in a small facility on the park-like outskirts of town involving a long bus ride. The time was almost midsummer. My first sight at the building was of four men and women playing badminton in the total buff, nonchalantly and easily. Why, I thought, are we so uptight about natural public nudity in other parts of the world?

A colleague took me to his home past a port and fishing fleets.

And then Stockholm shut down. Completely. Everyone disappeared to their cottages to do whatever they did on Midsummer's Eve. I was stuck in my hotel, a well recommended boutique sort of place. My room, a strange elongated affair, was fully exposed to the hot sun. There was no way of getting moving air into it and the blinds were drawn adding to the stifling atmosphere. I sweated night and day. And at night a group sat outside below the window drinking and happily laughing in a loud conversation.

I went outside to cool off and explore. The downtown streets were deserted but I did find a nearby beach, not quite deserted, but not, I thought up to international beach standards, with rough sands and few people. It was not until another visit in 2006 that I understood Stockholm, city of islands and waters[13].

In Oslo it was pretty well all business. The group of Norwegians who met with me were, to me, undertaking interesting work. Some of them were concentrating on studies of Norwegian society itself, rural and working class. It was the sort of thing I really wanted *Current Anthropology* to get into. I don't know what it was, some kind of shyness, some belief that this might not be of international interest, loyalty to local publication, whatever it was the articles did not come my way.

I would usually fly from Vancouver to Europe in those days through either Copenhagen (via Seattle) or Amsterdam. So I saw quite a bit of the Danish city, strolling down the pedestrian streets with relaxed pleasure and sometimes arranging for Danish furniture to or oddments to be shipped home. It was there I developed a taste for the local aquavit and where I lived on open faced sandwiches.

---

[13] Chapter 39

Schipol airport near Amsterdam was a place I knew like the back of my hand. In the 'seventies and 'eighties it had an open feeling with good interior navigation and there were many spaces where you could sit and read comfortably. The food services were good and the boutiques did their job well without overwhelming. Now it is little more than a crowded shopping mall.

Another advantage was that between flights there was often enough time to go outside into Amsterdam itself or, in my case, to den Haag, The latter town had its green spaces and beaches and the lovely Mauritshuis art gallery which should never be missed on a visit to the Netherlands.

Amsterdam itself was always a pleasant break. I used to enjoy the café in the Van Gogh museum, which set high standards, and the brown café across the street. It was possible to dig fairly deeply but as an outsider into the life of the city. The central architecture, the old mansions, the old necessary habits such as hoisting furniture and supplies with outside ropes up to the higher storeys, the flowers, the lace curtains, and boats on the canals.

Casual food in Holland has little to recommend it[14] and some of the restaurants are disappointing. But a handful in Amsterdam and den Haag are worth the visit. Some depend on atmosphere with old basement rooms or the equivalent. Among my favourites were Borderij and Vijf Vlieghen. Naturally it is the place for a decent rijstafel in a place called Bali – or the now defunct Indonesian restaurant that abutted the airport. Near the fish market I could not get a decent fish meal, but there

---

[14] But see Leiden in Chapter 39

is a fine small place in the city centre which calls itself an Oesterbar and serves excellent simple fish dishes.

The Wenner-Gren conferences in Austria I have already mentioned. They brought ne to Vienna on three occasions, once getting to Burg Wartenstein on the usual weekend train packed with hikers bound for rambles in the mountains. These serious meetings were popular amongst anthropologists as much for their styles of operation as for their content. The Wenner-Gren staff, led by the Director, Lita Osmundsen, pulled out all the stops to make the otherwise isolated stay memorable. Spouses were not accepted and the setting sparked a number of romances.

The conferences themselves were limited to perhaps twenty participants around a theme proposed by a colleague who then became the leader of the paper discussion. One which I sponsored was more practical than academic, on the subject of journal publishing. I used the technique which I had learned in the beginning days of the Regional Training Centre for United Nations Fellows, namely basing the discussion on selected themes, overseen by a steering committee, rather than set papers. The participants after all knew their subject inside and out, so why confine them to papers? They shared more wide ranging knowledge and opinions.

We met for meals in the castle. There was a small outside area between the building and a castle wall. There we were expected to come together in the evening for a concert of classical records. At the end of the meeting an um pa pa band came up from the village below and we danced our thoughts away.

It was not until the 'eighties that I spent time with colleagues at the university in Vienna. When I did I decided to invite two friends to dinner at the hotel. They were Annie Hohenwart-Gerlachstein and a friend of a friend whom I shall not name.

Annie was an aristocrat in the Hapsburg tradition and a favourite of Jean d'Ormesson of the International Council for Philosophy and Human Sciences in Paris, himself of the bluest of bloods. Annie had devoted her life to establishing a network of colleagues around the world who were theoretically correspondents on the subject of Urgent Anthropology, that is threatened cultures. She published an occasional journal on the subject, which received significant ethnographic material, though not all articles seemed directly related to the notion of urgency. The journal was for many years the only anthropological recipient of a grant from the ICPHS, which was a bit of a concern to the Union. Annie's family estates had disappeared as Hungary became communist. She was not at all well off.

I did not know of the other friend's activities until I spent time with him here. He was a Canadian Jewish psychiatrist with a good practice in Montreal. He was now devoting his life to entering communist territory and arranging for Jewish refugees to move clandestinely to safety n the West. A dangerous mission.

The dinner began well enough, helped by the refreshingly quaffable Austrian wine. But then the male friend told the story of his arrival in Vienna. He rented an apartment that was inexpensive but luxurious in the older Viennese style. He asked the owner how she had managed to obtain such a place. "We took it over from people who had disappeared" she said. The implication was obvious, and my friend was underlining it to indicate the way in which racial attitudes still persisted in an outwardly smooth city.

Annie froze. What could she say? For the rest of the occasion, shortened as quickly as could politely be managed, she spoke hardly a word.

Italy was very much on my agenda, often for several days, either by motoring from the Swiss haven or flying to Rome or Milan for a meeting. When I motored I could take roads away from the autostrada and find other atmospheres.

One of my favourite towns, in Tuscany, was that of the competitive medieval towers, San Gimignano. It is one of the numerous hilltop towns where originally people congregated to escape both violence and malaria. The towers are symbolic of much of Italy when loyalty to lineages and parishes runs high.

In the main square there is a hotel which abuts a steep slope overlooking lower roofs and gardens. When I first stayed there the restaurant was a draw, featuring local Tuscan dishes carried out with skill. The second visit saw a decline. The room was filled with tour groups and the menu became banal. On my last visit I crossed over the square to the still reputable café.

My last visit in 1998 was a huge disappointment for additional reasons. There is no car traffic in the town, except to deliver baggage to the hotel, a feature I always liked. This time I missed my way from the one way circular road into the square and found myself in the narrow main street. It was totally crowded with Sunday shoppers and tourist visitors through whom the car had to push its way illegally. The once medieval street has been turned into a tourist trap with fancy high priced shops. Added to the now uninteresting hotel it was a place to get out of quickly.

Siena and Firenze attracted me for other reasons. As I have mentioned in relation to Brasil, carnival and its equivalents fascinated me, and both cities have their equivalents, in that high ceremonial events are rooted in defined social organizations of which Siena's violent horse racing is one. The "equivalent" comes from its organisation, based on local identities. The horses are in honour of parishes which stand by them and support them, and indeed take the horses into the churches to be blessed. It is a vigorous no holds barred race through dangerous streets and the plaza, the riders bedecked with parish colours and the square ablaze with banners. Quite by accident I found myself in the wild city on a day of advance rehearsals. One would not have known it was a rehearsal, but would think of it as the real thing. And I did get a seat in a café as the horses thundered by.

In Firenze I had another stroke of good fortune. In Siena I had stayed in a converted convent on the outskirts of the town. In Firenze I found a hotel across the river which had one of my favourite sorts of places, its restaurant on a roof deck overlooking the scene of water traffic. I walked across the famous bridge to find a different eating place for lunch, after the usual sightseeing. The place was a semi-basement with windows on to the street, and close to a small darkly contained square. I heard the sound of a band. Then through the window came the sight of lower limbs marching, clothed in gaily emblazoned stockings.

This was a team for the mighty football competition carried out with mediaeval rules (almost none) in the stone paved square. Again with parish identification. The game is brutal, and the hard field and strenuous play result in many injuries – deaths have not been unknown.

Under Mussolini both events were forbidden. But such is the power and attraction of competitive identity that they revived even more strongly after his demise.

This is a global phenomenon. As people get richer they often pour their increased funds into identification mechanisms, usually as a way of giving individuals a significant role that the national society denies them.

I can find my way around Rome by foot or car pretty well geographically, although I have had trouble entering the city from the autostrada. I can even be at ease driving in the traffic. Each city has its traffic conventions, fundamental to survival. In Paris there is a strict unwritten rule that the car on the right (or is it left. I forget) has right of way. So when cars enter the huge densely populated unsigned squares the trick is to edge your car close to your competitor and slightly ahead. Bingo. In Rome priority is given, reluctantly, to he (or she) who blows the horn the loudest and most determinedly. Geneva is the worst city to drive in. For there the whole of Europe comes driving, each miscreant following his or her own rules of his or her city of origin, resulting in chaos.

Usually I stayed in a hotel, once again with a rooftop restaurant, and with luck, one parking spot usually available outside on the pavement. The rooftop is a compensation for the unhelpful and somewhat snotty reception. It is quite close to the coliseum on a side street. And across a large semi-piazza there is a small café where I fell in love with wild strawberries soaked in orange juice, though there is little else worth eating on the menu.

I never did mange, though, to conquer Italian restaurants and cannot claim good recommendations. There was a place in Vancouver, now gone, which had the same name, Piccolo Mondo, as a highly touted one on the Via Corso. For my money the food in the Vancouver one was superior. And the Roman one treated non-Italians like suspicious extra-terrestrials.

There were two favourites. One was small and open air near the home of the anthropologist Vinigi Grotanelli. It was not great, but the summer atmosphere was superb. After my disaster recounted in the next chapter, Vinigi and his wife invited me to their aristocratic roof top apartment. But I shivered when he drove me. His main idea was to shoot straight for pedestrian crosswalks and make the offending walkers jump for their lives. Vinigi, to put it mildly, was very conservative indeed, had no time for riff raff, and was at painfully at odds with his son who had different ideas. Once, many years before he died he came to Vancouver for a committee and specially asked to see me privately in my home. There he said "Cyril, this will be the last time I see you. I am about to die." He didn't, for many a long year.

The other restaurant was across the river in the Trastevere. There I lunched with an executive meeting of the IUAES including Sol Tax. There I had the most tender and tasty young artichokes I have ever sampled. Despite my ability to walk around Rome I could never find the place again, though I searched several times.

It was easy though tiring, to walk or, in the rain, bus from place to place. I loved going to the Piazza Navona with its numerous though touristy cafes and ice cream parlours, for the life of the piazza was ebullient and unending. It could be especially full of neighbourhood children, kicking balls, riding bicycles, just having a good time.

It was similar in Venice when one got away from the admittedly wondrous palaces and found the other side of the island where people actually live and children actually play.

Back in Rome near the Ostia station and its Roman gate I sometimes stayed in a hotel run by nuns.

Its small rooms were properly equipped with good writing desks. The Food and Agriculture Organisation has its headquarters a few blocks away, so the furnishings were attractive for their visitors. And, unusually for Roman hotels, it has its own open air parking. Its food was totally dreadful, but I found an unpretentious trattoria across the street. One day I admired their carafes for wine. The owner, without a word, sped around the corner and returned with a couple he bought at a simple store, insisting that I accept them as a souvenir of my meal.

Now I fly to the other side of the globe, to exotic tropical lands. The first stop is not the first on a geographical line but is a country which had not so long ago and may still have more anthropologists of every sort than any other country, the United states included. India. So many of my friends and colleagues know India very much better than I do. I haven't even begun to scratch the surface. But hey I've been there (just).

The most enchanting was a visit to Kashmir. Dr. Kohl Bhatt was officially an historian, but his anthropological interests qualified him as an associate. The present tragic violence was only an underlying tension at the time, though there were troops on the streets of Srinagar. Unfortunately I stayed in an Oberoi hotel in an old palace outside the city. The setting was undoubtedly remarkably beautiful, with the famous gardens beside it and a clear view of the lake and the houseboats on the other side. There was a jetty below where I hired a boat and floated on the lake past produce vendors, houseboats, and forests of water lilies.

But the food was not up to standard. In fact it was dreadful – except for afternoon tea on the shaded verge outside with quite delicious pakoras and other nibbles. So one way or another I missed Kashmiri food and did not know of the fabulous competitive feasts in the villages and he high standing of the cooks who led them.

Dr. Bhatt took considerable time to show me around. I fell in love with the verdant picturesque villages and would have given much to spend time in them – many I am sure now destroyed in the current strife. And of course he showed me the vestiges of the occupation by Alexander the Great. I began to realise how deficient my high school education had been when it came to the great dramas which shaped the world. To some extent I have made up for this in recent years, following not only Alexander but other major players in the effervescent world of Central Asia, the Middle East, the early empires and the populating of Europe from the steppes beside the Black Sea. My view of the significance of elements in the current world has too late been sharpened.

The second and last visit to India was to Delhi in 1978 to attend the International Conference of Anthropological and Ethnological Sciences over which Dr. L. P. Vidyarthi presided and where I was to be appointed incoming president. I was staying at a small interesting hotel quite a distance from the conference building which itself was a distance from the centre of town. The logistics for me were not easy. As I had to shuttle from the meeting to the hotel where I was sometimes meeting with groups of colleagues, taxis or motorbike rickshaws were frequently invisible. On one occasion I was due at a reception given by the Canadian High Commissioner for the Canadian delegates. The driver simply could not find he address after we had wandered street after street and I had to miss and convey my apologies. That was very bad diplomacy.

At that time Betty and I were in the middle of our sabbaticals in Montana-Crans. Betty left a message at the hotel in a great state of anxiety. Phoning back I heard her panic. Adrian and his girlfriend were due to visit us for Christmas after a sojourn in Spain. She was desperate because of a tragic train crash in Spain fearing that they had been caught up in it. I tried to reassure her that it was most likely that we would have known if they had been hurt because they had good identification and notes of our Swiss address. They were in fact on a different train. Not long afterwards I had reason to learn that no news is not always good news.

The return to Geneva was by Japan Airlines first to Rome and then with a connecting flight. I had arranged to meet Betty in a café opposite the Geneva railway station. The JAL flight was seriously late and I was afraid I would miss the connection and again Betty would be worried that I had not turned up on schedule. The plane touched down in Rome just minutes before the connecting departure, which had already loaded and was prepared for takeoff. The JAL crew hustled me down on to the tarmac and over to the other plane. No ticket check or gate waiting. Up and into the plane and I arrived on time. Miraculously my suitcase did the same. That would be impossible today with the security procedures. How in this and many other ways has air travel deteriorated.

My first visit to Indonesia, had mixed results. The main contact in Jakarta was the well known anthropologist Koetjarinagrat who for years was the front man for the subject in Indonesia and well regarded. I had left time in case it would be possible to go to West Papua, or West Irian as it was sometimes called. This was of major interest to me personally because of my earlier involvement in what is now Papua New Guinea. I had also corresponded with an earlier Dutch Governor, van Baal, who had strong anthropology credentials. At the time that this part of the island was being officially given to Indonesian rule I was furious at the attitude of the Western powers who simply lay down and let the Indonesian colonial ambitions rule the day. In an Australian journal I had advocated a federation of the whole island as an independent state, possibly including other Melanesian countries. The Australians were as collaborationist as every other government. Since I was now based in Canada I had made representations to the Canadian government to stop the transfer. The Canadian attitude was more or less "Where is West Irian on the map?" It was miles away from their agenda or interest. The Indonesian claim was based on the claims of the earlier Sultan of Ternate, a small island off the coast, to suzerainty. But this claim if it existed in law would only apply to a very small strip of the northern coastline.

When I tried to make arrangements to visit through Koetjarinagrat he merely shrugged his shoulders and said there were no anthropologists there. I knew this to be untrue – there were at least a couple of Indonesians, his protégés. But he refused point blank to assist me, and I would not have known where they were working.

West Papua is now a hotbed of insurrection with the Indonesians using the military and a plan to resettle peasants there from other parts of the country.

There was also a meeting of the Society for International Development in Bali, full of development economists and public officials. Margaret Mead was there. The subject of the meeting included discussion of "social and cultural factors". Three decades before Margaret Mead had written a brochure for UNESCO which made all the points which are relevant today and which had largely been ignored. The participants had belatedly decided that social and cultural factors had to be included in a development model and not merely consigned to the category of "externalities". I was in awe at Margaret Mead's patience. Not once did she say "I wrote this thirty years ago." It was yet another example of the continuing isolation of economics from other social science disciplines, a barrier I had unsuccessfully tried to breach from day one of my immersion in anthropology.

Now I must put such interests aside to enter a world of disaster, the loss of Betty, and immersion in a strange, threatening, and isolated counter-society.

SHATTERED

27. Disaster

In the summer of 1978, for the first time Betty took advantage of her entitlement to a leave of absence from her duties as a Senior Instructor in English, and also for the first time we had our leaves together. Betty, although essentially a Milton scholar, decided to work on themes in the writing of Katherine Mansfield, whose work she had always admired, though she disliked what she knew of Mansfield as a person. She wanted especially to concentrate on Mansfield's reception and criticism in France, where not only was she known, but her stories were often included in high school curriculua. As for me, I had the idea of comparing the Swiss and Canadian constitutions, looking at them not so much as written documents from the top of the political system down, but as expressions of society and culture seen from the bottom up.

We decided that we would spend the first half of our leaves in England and the second in Switzerland. For the first, Rosemary and Raymond Firth lent us their house below Hampstead while they travelled to New Zealand. For the second we would base ourselves in our old haunt of Montana-Crans, and Betty would make forays into Paris to work in the Bibliothèque Nationale.

Betty took her university work very seriously and was dedicated to its responsibilities. Her teaching was of such a high quality, imbued with warmth and no nonsense standards, and at the same time intolerant of laziness and careless work. Students reacted to her style positively and many with great loyalty. She fully deserved the acclamation she received through the acquisition of a Master Teacher Award.

To begin with she stayed in Vancouver to complete the assignments she had of preparing for the next term's student intake. She could have arranged for someone else to do it, but to do it herself was typical of her. I went first to London to see the Firths before they left and then to Montana to begin my research and to find and rent an apartment for our return in December. In London I took the Firths for dinner. Rosemary was in a relaxed conversational mood. She confided that there were two anthropologists she cared for most – Leach, who was godfather to her son, and myself, and that Betty and I were just about the only anthropologists she knew personally who had stayed together *en famille* throughout our lives (this was not accurate – I myself knew of several long lasting and devoted couples). Alas, she was soon to get a serious shock.

In Montana I stayed at first in our old building, Les Mischabels. But its long term rental had inflated well beyond our means. A lady friend, with whom I had been having an affair, visited me. An estate agent showed me around. For a long time the only apartments within our means were isolated on the outskirts of the town. I knew that the comparative isolation would not be right for Betty – she needed to be close to the action, such as there was, and to grocery and other shopping and conveniences. So I persevered and ultimately found something that would suit.

The building had half a dozen suites and one for a manager. One suite was permanently occupied by an elderly lady. Our unit was situated below a steep incline from the centre of Montana with a horizontal path to Crans. The parking was on the road above the roof with a somewhat hazardous walk-way bridge affair descending to the main door. The outlook in summer was across a small lake toward a forest of great trees and the Mischabel alps beyond. More to the point, there was a cross country ski trail around the lake, snow covered in winter. Betty had not overcome her fear of heights which inhibited her from downhill skiing. Cross country seemed to be a good outlet for her. I thought I might at last improve my downhill skills on the dramatic mountain *pistes* promoting myself from low to intermediate.

I had brought my Citroen Maserati, purchased in Europe in 1972, across from Canada and picked it up in Rotterdam, planning to have the bodywork refurbished in Europe, though that turned out to be far too expensive. Betty joined me in London and we took possession of the Firth home. It suited us well, looking out at the back onto a treed garden and lawn, with two tenants in an upstairs flat.

The neighbourhood had its drawbacks. One block away, by the underground station, there was a main lorry route out of London, the trucks spewing black fumes as they started to climb the hill. Black clouds covered the outdoor produce of greengrocers. The journey into London was unpleasant, the entrance to the underground grubby. On a couple of occasions the jam packed riders stood by without turning a hair as men urinated. Thankfully there were the buses, but they too had routes which were far from uplifting.

We could access the Heath and do our shopping from butchers, grocers and wine merchants above it, and enjoy wine bars and other pleasing eating places. We took in a couple of plays and did some pre-Christmas shopping. I found material in the smaller libraries and in the Swiss Consulate.

Betty wrapped herself up in her work: it was her only focus. Although it had improved over the years, and as a student she had written a Master's thesis on Milton she found it very awkward to write. Frequently it was my role to help her with setting out a student evaluation, or some other piece of business writing. Her letters were written with such a tempestuous dash that it was often very difficult to read her words.

She did her research in the British Library, leaving straight after breakfast and coming home perhaps near six o'clock. I did what purchasing and cooking there was to be done, and spent much of my time typing, looking out on the garden.

It was not fun for Betty. She made copious hand written notes [now deposited in the University of British Columbia Archives]. As she did so she found that the Mansfield "experts" had made an astonishing number of errors of detail, particularly in their bibliographies. I myself was astounded at the carelessness in some of the material she found.

This though was not her objective. Betty was one of those brilliant people who are outstanding receivers of knowledge, but who have great difficulty in using that knowledge creatively. Yet they interpret and speak about it with great panache. At this stage she could not see her way to producing written results. We would talk about it at length. One of my suggestions was that she might try her hand at writing some informative notes on her discoveries, before deciding on a major theme. She had no opportunity to do that.

Towards the end of our stay, as autumnal mists started to rise in the British forests, we took advantage of the Firth's offer of their Devon cottage, and drove down for a couple of nights, obtaining the key from a neighbour. It took time to warm up the damp interior, but we enjoyed walks down country lanes beside fields where cows observed us lugubriously.

We snuggled in a cold bed. The next morning Betty could not wake properly. It was as if she were intoxicated. I managed to take a hot dink and spoon fed her our usual breakfast of yoghurt and muesli. She woke gradually, and we walked up an inclined road to the tiny village of local shops. By this time she had become herself again.

When we returned to London it was just about time to depart. Betty did not consult a doctor. She described the incident in a letter to her friend Barbara Scott. Ever since major guilt lies upon me. I should have insisted on a medical consultation. I wondered later if it were some form of tumour or minor stroke

To complicate matters further the bed we were sleeping in collapsed. One of the side slats had a gnarl in it and chose this moment, after years of use, to break. I arranged an emergency repair with the manufacturer (who later denied that his beds would ever have a gnarl) and I wrote to the Firths who by this time were in

Greece. They were having troubles of their own – a theft of passports and money were creating delays.

So we packed he car and drove to the ferry and Switzerland.

Adrian and his girlfriend, as I have mentioned, were holidaying in Spain, visiting national parks, and arrived in Montana to spend Christmas with us after I had made my quick rip to Delhi for the IUAES. We had a lovely, untroubled, totally relaxed time. Adrian even went to the basement suite to learn Croatian dancing from the building manager. We wandered the decorated shops and Betty cooked up her celebratory feast.

Then they had to leave, taking a train crowded with immigrant workers with standing room only to catch their flight in Paris. Every Christmas I can remember left Betty with a depressive anti-climax. The joyful excitement was over and there was a hole left in her spirit. This time it was the same. I remember being with her out on the little patio looking at the night sky as she drew into her sadness. Children grow up and we have to learn to let them be.

We planned to make an exploratory trip to Paris ourselves so that Betty could present her credentials to the Bibliothèque and cast her eye over the relevant holdings.

The weather was foul with heavy snowfalls. [Confirmed by Swiss meteorological records] and to further complicate matters the car battery was dead and it had to be towed for servicing. But we set off late one morning. We chose a route south of Geneva into France thinking this would be easy for joining the north-south autoroute. This was a bad mistake. We did not know that a branch of the autoroute was being constructed to link it to Annecy and Geneva.

Heavy construction was going on. The road was full of slush and snow and vehicles passed each other in both directions with inches to spare. In fact one car driving in the direction opposite to me had its outside mirror clipping mine. Betty, seldom calm when being driven, was tense and I was not much better. So on the autoroute, where the weather and road were much better without snow, we stopped at a motel by a flyover where we could get a meal and recover and spend a little time at a touristic Asterix model village.

In Paris we stayed in a Novotel in Bagnolet, chosen for its parking convenience, writing facilities in the room, and closeness to the Metro, but away from Parisian action and otherwise unattractive. We ate in the hotel.

The next fateful day we had breakfast served in our room and both took the Metro into town. Betty had her usual work satchel, letters of introduction and authentication, leaving the train at Bourse, the nearest stop to the Bibliothèque Nationale.

That was the last time I saw Betty. She was gone from our lives for ever.

We had arranged to meet for lunch at Galeries Lafayette. I did a little window shopping and waited outside the café. Betty was late. After a while I took a table. Still no Betty. She must have been diverted at the library and lost her sense of time. I had a quick meal and still waited. Then I became concerned. Betty was punctual and knew her way around Paris.

Anxious by this time I went to the library and was astounded to find long line-ups at outside desks where staff were processing student library applications and cards for the next session. It was the opening time of university term. Betty would have little patience for that.

Most likely she would have quit, though that did not explain her not arriving at lunch. To make sure I elbowed my way to one of the desks. They had no record of having processed her application. She could not be in the library itself without the required pass.

This was unsettling. As afternoon morphed into evening I decided to go back to the hotel. She was not there. I phoned the front desk and reported her missing and asked what could be done. Who answered the phone was bored, nonchalant and unhelpful. A year later the hotel had no record of my call and no one remembered it. The Canadian Embassy was closed by now but I phoned. The duty officer said it was the business of the consulate, not the embassy, and that I should go there the following morning.

I phoned both children. They were also alarmed and said they would come as soon as they could.

Still no Betty. Alarm bells were ringing loudly and sleep deserted me.

First thing in the morning I went to the consulate. Ironically it was just around the corner from the library – had I known I could have gone there right after my library visit, but then the consul would probably not have been alarmed. I did phone ahead of time and left a message to say that my wife was missing and I would be there next morning.

The consulate was not yet open and the speaking hatch was beside locked doors. Perhaps half a dozen young down and out Canadians were already there. I eventually saw movement inside and banged heavily on the hatch. The consul, a fine man named Nassrallah, was angry. Who is making that noise? It's me, my wife has disappeared. I left a message.

He let me in and sat me down. He said not to go looking myself, he had his routines. He would contact all the hospitals. I should send him a photograph when I returned to Montana. Meanwhile he would phone the police, especially the detachment at Bagnolet and I should go there and file a report and description. In a later deposition Nassrallah said I was calm and did not mention my hysterical behaviour at the beginning of the interview.

I returned to Bagnolet and went to the police station. The police office was in fact just across from the hotel. The gendarmes knew I would be coming. Their quarters were tiny, cramped rooms and there were other worried people at the reception wanting to make statements. They took me to a tiny room just large enough for a desk and a typewriter, where a gendarme took my statement and description using the machine one finger at a time. Later it became a matter of suspicious guffaws that I mentioned the brand of her underwear, Lejaby. But I used to buy her fresh supplies at her request when I went to Paris – It was her favourite brand and the most comfortable for her.

Nassrallah had told me not to be impatient because it was early days yet and there could be many explanations. Missing people usually turned up, and even husbands might no know what had been going on in the head of a missing wife. He would inform consulates and they would inform the police and there would be missing persons bulletins. (One appeared on French TV, but I did not see it.)

I returned to Montana in the vain hope that there might be some message or that she might return there. I overnighted in a motel on the way because in my state I could not face the winding mountain road in the dark. I sent a photograph to Nassrallah and informed the

Canadian consulate in Berne. I sent vouchers for the children's air fares.

There was nothing further I could effectively do except give in to internal tension and wait for Diana and Adrian. Diana was acting in a play but could arrange a stand in. Adrian was attending classes at the University of British Columbia and had a job as a teaching assistant. He was able to make arrangements.

Diana was the first to arrive, but not without incident. I went to Geneva to meet her at the airport, and she wasn't on the scheduled flight. The airline staff were able to check, and reported that her trans-Atlantic flight had engine trouble and was diverted to Glasgow instead of London, so she missed her connection. I stayed overnight in Geneva and picked her up next morning. As I was driving the autoroute she made me stop, took the wheel herself, saying that I was driving erratically.

In Montana we talked it over. But were waiting for Adrian. In the meantime we drove around aimlessly. She noticed a church outside the community and spent some little time there seeking her peace.

One day in the town we ran into Samy Friedman, he Secretary-General of the International Social Science Council, and his lady friend. I invited them for a cup of coffee and later picked them up at their hotel. On the way I asked them to excuse our disorganisation and told them we were trying to cope with Betty's disappearance.

In the apartment they both stood by the fireplace. Samy talked with me about disappearances in general (he did not know Betty), indicating that most were *fugues* – deliberate runaways by children or spouses and nearly all solved within days or weeks. If Betty were found the authorities would not tell me until it was determined that Betty *wanted* to be reunited. She might have had her own reasons for disappearing, and spouses were often the last to know. I said that if that were Betty's motive I could not imagine her leaving Diana and Adrian in the dark.

Meanwhile Samy's lady friend, whose name I never knew, talked sympathetically with Diana. [When the Swiss police interviewed Samy in Paris his signed statement says we did not talk about Betty's loss at all.]

Adrian arrived and the two children were a solace to me as they dealt with their own private pain. We agreed that we would not move from one location to another, even on short trips, without informing the others. We discussed going to Paris but could not figure out where we could add to what the consulate was already doing. Diana washed Betty's clothes.

They both had to return home to pick up the pieces. My house had been let to a colleague coming to Vancouver with his family on his own sabbatical. Adrian was imbedding himself in the small community of Sechelt and Roberts Creek on what is known as the Sunshine Coast, a ferry trip northwest of the city, immersing himself in an alternative lifestyle, and continuing his graduate degree work at U. B. C.

I kept in touch with the consuls in Paris and Berne, especially when I left Montana for any reason. When either called me my heart was in my mouth – where was she? Hopes were always dashed and depression returned. The swings of hope and frustration took their toll on my psyche. There was no one there with whom I could let my hair down and cry in company. There was no word from the police who extended their contacts and enquiries from France to Switzerland. I had asked them to include Britain in their searches, n case Betty had gone there.

I walked and waited, keeping in touch with Vancouver. Sonny Nemetz, friend and Chief Justice, used his considerable influence to maintain a state of alert with the Canadian authorities. The father of a friend of Adrian's was a senior official in the Department of External Affairs. He too kept the enquiries alive. Each day felt disastrous.

Rumours abounded. She had been "seen" in Vancouver and Montana, the latter by the apartment caretaker. She would have had to use credit cards to get to Vancouver and they did not show up on her statements when they arrived in Montana. I took the desperate step of writing to a clairvoyant in the Netherlands who had become famous by locating a plane and its survivors in the South American alps. His brother replied to my letter saying that the clairvoyant had stopped undertaking missions because it created too much strain for his physical and mental system.[15]

I decided to take up at least minimal professional contacts as an antidote to what I was feeling. I gave a talk to the department in Neuchâtel. My staff in Vancouver continued to send me *Current Anthropology* materials about which decisions had to be made.

There was a meeting in York of the Association of Social Anthropologists of the Commonwealth, where I thought to go to talk up the journal. On the way I called in at the Salvation Army which has a good reputation of finding and handling disappeared persons (this is not the case in France). The building was in a disreputable part of London adjacent to a railway station. I had to knock several times before the one member in the building

---

[15] Later the police scorned this action: no intelligent man would do such a thing they said.

came to the door. I told him the story. He looked up his records and did not find a person matching Betty's description but said he would look further. By the time I was taking my leave I was crying heavily. He embraced me as a father would a child. I did not like his physical contact. Weeks later they sent me a letter indicating that there was no result for their searches.

I briefly called on the Firths and we met again during the meeting in York. I was in my meeting when Rosemary came in to say there was a phone call from Paris. Again my heart leaped. Could this be it? The caller was a Commissaire de Police, putting more energy into the search. I asked if there was any news. No no, but would you come by Paris to give more details. Down again with a miserable thump.

Two flat tyres later I went to their office. The French police were responding to more diplomatic pressure from Canada. The Commissaire was a tall man in braided uniform, a look alike for de Gaulle. He was assisted by a younger officer. Both were well educated and perceptive. We had wondered about the likelihood of Betty being in the south of France, searching for Mansfield connections, and particularly about Fontainebleu, near which Mansfield spent her last days and is buried. They said they would check more thoroughly.

And that was it. My depressive feelings returned in spades. Twiddling my thumbs did nothing for my mood. I decided to take a break and go to the famed Carnaval in Basle. This I did and it did temporarily help. The city was in magical mood with spirited laughter, packed cafes and family action. I could get nothing to eat except from street vendors, not even through room service, so packed was the hotel's dining room.

It is so much a satirical family affair. Couples (Spouses? Lovers?) of masked men and women roamed the side streets, softly playing flutes and side drums, sometimes with a child in tow. Great bands deliberately playing out of tune paraded and roamed up hills and especially down – get out of our way or we will overwhelm you. *Wagglies*, clowns satirising the supposedly dim workers from the nearby fields in Germany, with greet red noses and fuzzy heads mingled with the crowds, buttonholing passers by and questioning them about their morals. All the organising *cliques* and their friends packed the restaurants and cafes. And into these rooms came the real satirists. They carried poles with attached huge sheets of drawing paper. Tapping for attention they began drawing caricatures of city notables. All the while they made up skits in the local dialect explaining who was romancing whom, into whose pockets the city money was flowing, and all the dirt they had been able to dig up. The crowds loved it, laughing uproariously, banging on tables, clinking over full glasses.

Yes, I loved it even though unable to penetrate the event. But it was temporary and could not disperse the reality of depression.

The time was steadily approaching when I would have to return home to Vancouver. I could not afford the change in registration of my car and its insurance from tourist to resident and would have to move it home, through Rotterdam. My status as a tourist was coming to an end, though no doubt I could have negotiated an extension under the circumstances. Classes were beckoning.

One day as I was starting to get ready I received a phone call from Freddy Reichen in charge of the police in the valley at Sierre. Could he call and discuss Betty? Of course.

He was uniformed. I showed him some of Berry's things in the apartment. We sat on the patio outside. He took in the neighbourhood and atmosphere. Then he asked me to supply Betty's dental records from Canada. He said if he had to go through the formal protocol, embassy to foreign affairs, it would take unnecessary time. "So do you have a body to check out?" "No, not at all." My heart fell yet again.

But he lied.

The dental chart came. I could not bear it. It would lead to more false hopes. If a dental chart were required it might mean a body, a body perhaps in a state o decomposition after these months. I did not want to see Betty in those circumstances. I wanted her as she is in so many photographs and in her real life and my memory, a vibrant, sometimes happy sometimes unhappy real person. Emotions flooded through me. I was in some sort of denial and I could not stand it.

Almost without thinking I altered the charts, using liquid white paper to remove marks, and black ink to add others. I took the chart to a local copying machine and made a new changed copy. I took this down to the police office, where Reichen was not available, and left a message that in a few days I would be taking a break in Brittany, would return here to hand in my keys and settle my accounts, and then go back home to Vancouver.

The Brittany break was uneventful as I looked at menhirs and stone circles, disconsonently found crepes for meals, noticed signs of close ties with Cornwall, remarked the picturesque homes. But none of this did anything for my mood.

I returned to Monatana and handed in the keys. handed in The car was driven to Rotterdam for sanitizing and shipment, and I left for home from Schipol. In Vancouver I stayed in a hotel for a few days until the renters could leave. The days and nights passed without word.

The university detachment of the Royal Canadian Mounted Police called me to ask for the name of Betty's dentist because the Swiss wanted a fresh set of charts. I told them. Then I realised that there would be a discrepancy and I should do something to correct the situation. I phoned my lawyer, Bill Gorham (Penny's husband) but he was away. So then I called Mr. Poole, my former lawyer who was also a magistrate in the suburb of Deep Cove. He said "write them a letter explaining. I am sure they will understand."

I did. The police[16] didn't understand at all.

Betty's (reduced for leave) university stipend stopped. I protested, saying that this was based on the unacceptable presumption she would not return. I said the true test would be if she did not turn up for classes. If she did, imagine her dismay at the presumption. In the meantime, if they insisted, her salary could be held in trust. Furthermore there had been no dismissal procedure followed, and almost everyone on leave during the summer did not come back until classes began in September. Why should she be treated differently?

Classes did begin. Betty's absence was a very bad sign indeed.

Late one September afternoon I was participating in a Master's oral discussion. Penny came into the room

---

[16] Nor do many members of the public.

saying that the Royal Canadian Mounted Police university detachment was on the line. I excused myself and took the phone. "Come in and talk to us". No please or if you can. "This must be about my wife." "Yes."

I left the exam as soon as I could and reached the little house which the police used as their offices. I was shown into a large room. There was a constable behind a large desk and two strangers on chairs. "Sit down. These are Inspectors Fischlin and Wyss from Switzerland." "I presume you have news of my wife." "Yes, her body has been found." "Where?" "You tell us....."

For the next hour all three peppered me with aggressive questions. I told them about Betty's disappearance. At one point Fischlin pulled out a black garbage bag. "Where did you get this?" "What on earth are you talking about?" I explained the issue of the dental charts as I had in my letter, describing my despair and confusion.

At one point Wyss leaned over close to my ear. "You won't get this kid glove treatment when we get you in Switzerland." I cannot remember whether he said it in French or English. (The main conversation was in English although Wyss later claimed he did not understand the language.)

Then Fischlin said "May we see your wife's jewellery?" "Of course."

I was driving a rented car since at long last my Citroen was having its six year body paint redone. "I'm not sure I can drive properly. Will someone come in my car." The police were only too happy to oblige.

When I got home the drive way was full of police cars and half a dozen constables came into the house with Fischlin and Wyss and myself. I brought down Betty's jewellery from upstairs while the constables spread through every room, upstairs and downstairs. I turned off the upstairs light switch so that they came down. They paid special attention to my study and easily found the file in which I had the dental charts.

I phoned Diana and told her that Betty's body had been found and that they were accusing me and that they would give absolutely no details. There was a bilingual constable right beside me as I phoned. She told me to get hold of Bill Gorham immediately, which I should have done at the outset as soon as I became aware of the thrust of their questioning. Bill told me to tell the police to get out of the house. I turned and said "Every one of you, get out." They did. I was shaking in tears by this time.

They told me to make a written statement next day.

The whole episode was a mass of trickery which I shall describe in Chapter 29.

Bill arrived bringing in tow another lawyer, Harry McLaughlin, whom he introduced as being better versed in police proceedings. We went outside to talk in case the police had planted bugs, though we couldn't see a radio reception van. McLaughlin said that they were on a fishing expedition, and that I should only respond, through him, to written questions. He also said that he would arrange for the house and my university office to be swept for listening devices.

I phoned the police next day to tell them about McLaughlin's instructions requiring questions. The Swiss were angry and before McLaughlin had delivered my answers, went back to Lausanne in a huff after inspecting my car in the repair shop.

Adrian came by and again we talked on the road as we walked. The technician arrived, accompanied by

Philip Hall, a private detective who used to be in Scotland Yard's major crime squad, swept the house and my office but found nothing. McLaughlin urged caution since he felt the police could easily enter and place their devices unbeknownst to me. Philip Hall, even after the trial, expressed amazement at what he described as unconventional and clumsy police behaviour.

The news of the visit was fed to the Vancouver papers which thenceforth carried tid bits of the story on their front pages, often with gross errors as their journalists groped for information.

In due course an autopsy report arrived made out by a doctor in Aigle in the Canton of Vaud. Through press leaks we had learned that Betty's body had been discovered in a wood beside the substantially trafficked two lane road which links Aigle to Chateau d'Oex. The discovery was gruesome, made by roadside workers. The body was enclosed in plastic bags. It was intact, but had marks of rodent bites.[17]

The autopsy report indicated that the cause of death was unknown, without traces of inflicted wounds or poisons. The doctor said it was homicide nevertheless. I took the report to the senior pathologist at the Vancouver General Hospital, Dr. Sweeney. He expressed surprise at its tone and vagueness – he said he had never seen a report written in this way. I asked him if there was any likelihood that Betty had died of a stroke or tumour, citing the episode in England, which might be revealed in a second autopsy. He said he would let me know his thoughts via McLaughlin. In the chaos of subsequent events, this never happened.

---

[17] Some press reports invented even more gruesome details such as dismemberment, which were quite untrue.

I kept on with classes, my mind not on them. Students were supportive. The paper would not leave the matter alone.

Then in November I was to fly to Paris to attend a meeting of the International Social Science Council. McLaughlin was concerned and took me for an interview with a colleague by the name of Braidwood, an authority on extradition. Braidwood was also concerned, but put it in terms of kidnapping. No one expressed a thought there might be a case for extradition. I was foolish enough to scoff. If I were kidnapped, I thought, that would surely be the end of their credibility. Bedsides I was innocent, so why should I let them influence my professional life? I scoffed too soon.

The Canadian Embassy in Berne issued a note protesting because the family, if not myself, should have been apprised of the circumstances of Betty's death and that my interrogation was improper. The Swiss rejected it. The consulate sent me names of lawyers in Lausanne where the action was taking place. I chose Maître Felix Paschoud out of the air, and never regretted it. We arranged to meet in Paris. He urged me to wait for him to contact me, and not to try to get in touch with him. He was quite afraid of something. He had good reason.

I left via Copenhagen. In the plane from that city I sat next to a Danish sociologist also attending the meeting.

In Charles de Gaulle airport I presented my passport. "Just a moment" said the immigration official, and took the passport to a room behind him. "Come with me" he said and took me into the room, sat me down and told me to wait – along with half a dozen others, Africans. "What's this about?" I protested. "We are executing an Interpol warrant on behalf of Switzerland". Telexes flew and a copy of the warrant arrived. Other officials congratulated my gaoler for the warrant had only just been issued.

When I learned this I wondered who had betrayed my travel plans. It was some months before I found out. It was Samy Friedman of the International Social Science Council in a deposition to the Swiss police[18]. I had seriously underestimated the cloak and dagger stuff of legality.

---

[18] I have a copy of his statement which appears to me to have been malicious on several points.

28. Caged in France

An official took me to the incoming carousel to collect my bag and then return me to the holding room. I waited there all day until two plainclothes police arrived. They drove me to a dark and apparently empty police building, saying almost apologetically "It's not our doing. It's the Swiss." They took my personal details, confiscated my passport and billfold. Then back into the car to a massive ancient building on the bank of the Seine close to the Boulevard Saint-Germain. They honked the horn, a gate opened, and they passed me over to a gaoler. He took me to a cell with a filthy straw mattress on the floor. I had my raincoat, laid it over the filth, lay down and slept.

In the morning I looked out the small window and saw the feet of passers-by going to work. I am reasonably sure that few in Paris know what lies behind those small barred windows.

Then I was taken into a large room at the same level and added to a long queue, mainly of Africans, some women, who had been arrested during the night. This was the finger-printing queue. The technology was primitive. We put our fingers on a block of thick messy ink and then on the record pad. We were given a hunk of already dirty cloth to wipe our hands, not very successfully.

Then into a van, noisily speeding to a set of makeshift buildings which looked like old army huts, and which I later learned were close to the old Le

Bourget airport. We were herded into wooden cells just wide enough to take one person, but equipped with a toilet. A policeman came to my door and told me to give him my glasses. I hit the roof saying that I would not be able to see, and he let me keep them. I then demanded to see my consul. He said the consul had already been informed.

At midday there was a ration which became only too familiar to me – a tiny triangle of cheese, a small hunk of bread and a thin slice of salami. There was no liquid – water or anything else. I had nothing to do but stand and wait except for one moment when I was taken to an office where the police fingered my passport and checked my identity.

Well into the evening another van took me to the other side of Paris to the huge prison of, I later discovered, Fleury-Merogis, the biggest in Europe. In a large room a couple of staff members had my baggage on a large table. They were going through the contents, taking out clothes and other material for my use in prison. Curiously they did not give me my underwear, but issued prison alternatives[19].

They had me strip, examined my orifices for drugs and told me to take a shower.

I was already tense. The water was icy cold. The two things together provoked a massive angina. I had to come out and sit, head down to my legs. The staff were concerned and asked what was happening. I told them and they asked if I needed a doctor.

---

[19] I later worked out that this would simplify laundry since the underwear could be received and replaed without having to identify an owner.

For six years I had been having heart problems with frequent anginas and fibrillations, but had never been hospitalised. Often the anginas would last an hour. I had had no opportunity to take my medication – it was still not available to me. But I said no, given time it would pass although this one was the most painful to date.

Then, by now past midnight, I was escorted to a small but clean cell with two bunks one on top of the other. The top was occupied so I lay down on the lower one. When morning came, after a can of milky coffee I was ushered into a small office with a young civilian behind a desk. He was a social worker whose job it was to assess me to determine such things as - was I dangerous, a maniac, dirty or whatever. He was pleasant enough.

Then a guard took me up stairs to a higher part f the building to a cell which would be my home for the next two months. It was quite large and clean with one bed, a place to store clothing, a toilet and wash basin, an electric outlet where I could use my shaver. Above all it had a large barred window where I could look across to another equally huge building over a couple of fenced courtyards, and a writing desk close o it.

Later I was able to read some early volumes about prison reform. Fleury-Merogis was built on the model of the first attempts at reform in Pennsylvania in the late nineteenth century. Each building on several floors consisted of two large wings at an angle. Where they joined there was a kind of a roundhouse, a slightly elevated glassed command centre where guards could observe everything along the corridors and could operate the high tech security system.

That system electrically opened and closed all or individual cell doors with a buzz to tell the occupant the state of the door. There was also a speaker system which could give an order or a message to the occupant of each cell.

The routines, as far as my wing was concerned, was simple enough. Once a day, at varying times to deter helicopter escapes, the wing occupants were sent down the stairs and into one of the courtyards (which also varied) for fresh air and exercise. The courts were furnished with some heavy gym equipment in a shaded area. Some prisoners brought down chess sets, some footballs. To begin with I joined others walking fast around the perimeter to keep up muscle strength.

I met several people. A high percentage were Africans and others who had been caught drug smuggling. Most I knew were amateurs, doing it to have funds while they were in Europe. The system, to me, was weird. Each was supervised by a *juge d'instruction* who handled their case. The culprits were required to pay, not a fine, but the customs duties on the contraband. The prison sentence was for the length of time it took the prisoner to raise this money. How? By remittances from abroad? By employment in the attached prison workshops operated by private companies? By friends, including girl friends or wives working to earn the funds to get them out?

I talked with a Kurd. He had tried to smuggle in order to finance publicity for the hopes of Kurdistan. He was desperately worried about his girl friend who was due to have a baby, and who was working to raise his customs duties. I liked him and my ideas about the validity of the Kurdish position were enhanced.

From time to time I ran across a cheery Australian in the corridor. He did not go on exercise but worked in a private machine shop attached to the prison. His main worry was to keep his situation hidden from his parents in Australia - he wrote to them using an intermediary address. As time went on they surely must have wondered.

The morning after I arrived I was called "*avocet!*" (lawyer) I went down to the semi-public interview rooms. It wasn't a lawyer but no less a figure than Nassrallah the Canadian consul.

"So the police did tell you" I said. "Not at all. There was a tiny paragraph mentioning your arrest at the bottom of the paper." Amazing. I later learned that the police had contacted the *New Zealand* consulate because my Canadian passport noted that that was where I was born. That consulate, however, did not try to contact me. We talked about my situation and he promised to keep an eye on proceedings. That he did, seriously, with his warm and concerned assistant, Madame Lafortune.

And later that day I was down again. This time it *was* a lawyer, a man who worked for and stood by me until the very end, devoting enormous time and energy to my cause, Maître Felix Paschoud from Lausanne whom I had been intending to meet in Paris. He had received a message from the *juge d'instruction* in Lausanne boasting that they had laid their hands on me.

He was serious and questioned me closely. He looked at me frankly and said "Did you do it?" I said "Absolutely not." Paschoud gave a sigh of relief. He said if he thought I had done it he could not represent me, and if he ever were to think I had done it he would resign forthwith. He held on to the case with great personal time and emotional constraints and at the trial testified about his faith in me.

He said he would pass the Paris aspects of the extradition to a colleague Maître Badinter and that I should follow is advice completely. He also said I should go to Switzerland as soon as possible.

He also told me that he and his wife were in a fashionable boutique and by chance were talking to another customer. She learned that he would be defending an anthropologist. She told him the Paris anthropologist community was concerned and hoped he would be successful.

Badinter came a day or two later. He had a different opinion.

Whereas Paschoud was warm and caring, Badinter was sharp and incisive. "I will never knowingly submit a client of mine to the procedures of the Canton of Vaud" he said without hesitation. He described those procedures as archaic and oppressive. "We will fight this extradition, which is totally improper," he said.

He talked about my case. The Swiss were required under the treaty with France to give *"indices"* (supportive evidence) which led them to make the accusation. Badinter was quite clear. The only *indice* the Swiss offered in the Interpol warrant was that I had tampered with the dental charts. "That does not make you guilty and is understandable under the circumstances, and in itself it is no cause for extradition."

I saw Badinter only once more, in court, but in his able and energetic assistance, Dany Cohen, I found a sensitive and intelligent ally.

Then I had a surprise visit from a friend who was announced as "consul". It was Jean Laponce, a political scientist from the University of British Columbia who had been attending the meeting of the International Social Science Council where I was supposed to be. It was particularly good of him because the public transport to Fleury-Merogis was a considerable hassle. The sight of his always cheery face gave me a noticeable morale boost.

Meanwhile life went on in prison. The weather turned bitterly cold and one seemed to feel it more in the courtyards. My coat was a thick winter raincoat but it seemed not to protect me. I wore socks under my leather gloves, extra underwear, pyjama pants under my outerwear and two pairs of woollen socks in my shoes. And I was still shivering. After a while I realised the authorities didn't care whether I went outside or not, so I stopped going.

The meals were sloppy stews for the most part with some decent herbing. It was brought on a big cart tureen and dished out onto a personal platter. Sometimes there was offal to which I am allergic, so I tipped the meal into the toilet bowl and flushed it down. Sometimes it left a stain which had to be cleaned up. The greasy metal plates were hand scrubbed in cold water in the wash basin.

I could use my electric shaver and some prisoners even had kettles or pans which they could plug in. We could buy goods from a commissary, and many bought carrots and potatoes and soup stock to make their own food. I didn't.

I bought pads and stylos from the commissary, an occasional bar of chocolate, and stamps with money from my traveller's cheques which the consulate converted for me and placed in a prison account. And welcome cans of beer although up to then I had not been a beer drinker.

The beer was refreshing and a little calming. Doctors at home had recommended a little alcohol in the evening. Some weeks into my confinement the doctors at the prison hospital had different ideas and my supplies were stopped outright. Protests did not help. Luckily my Australian friend saved the day. He ordered beer and passed it along to me.

I also took a subscription to *Le Monde* ad passed it along to an eager neighbour.

I wrote to the management asking if I might have my briefcase. They called me down and with stern faces wanted to know why. I explained my address book and writing materials were in it. Without a smile they let me have it. I did not know to what extent my correspondence would be censored, but erred on the cautious side, even when writing to Bill Gorham in envelopes marked *avocat*. Correspondence with lawyers was private, but Bill was not registered as such in France. In fact I don't think the authorities in France bothered to read anything. After all I was not their problem, but belonged to those Swiss over there.

On Christmas and New Year's Eve the inhabitants of the building opposite sang carols and then lit the darkness with fiery like streams of burning paper pushed out of the windows.

My staff in Vancouver had spontaneously set up a programme to elicit letters of character and support from about a hundred senior colleagues around the world, including Claude Levi-Strauss in France. They worked frantically over New Year to get them into Badinter's hands before the second session of the court. This was loyalty beyond compare and impressed the lawyers. Not the court however. The issue alas was not one of character but of the cold logic of the law.

It was by no means all fun and games.

Now and again guards would come into the cells unannounced and tap the window bars to make sure they were still firm. One day shots rang out. Someone had managed to get over the walls. There was no mercy. He was shot dead. On another occasion escapees were caught in an external laundry truck.

Sometimes there were desperate screams from neighbouring cells as prisoners had nightmares. A prisoner spreadeagled himself against the window as he screamed until guards pulled him down and put him in a straight jacket. There were occasional films in an auditorium where church service were also held. On the corridor leading to it there was a large unfurnished cage accommodating a muscular "dangerous" criminal pacing round and round like an angry tiger.

On one occasion, coming back from court. I was pulled out of the line taken to a shower room, stripped and had a guard poke around my orifices in a random drug test. I was surprised and asked the guar "Is this normal?" He gave an unemotional "*Oui*" and got on with the job.

Not long after my arrival I was called down quite early one morning and herded with others into a van with rough seats along its sides. It was my day in the *Court de Cassation*, the country's highest tribunal and court of appeal which hears extradition cases. With other courts it heard its cases in the fine *Palais de Justice*.

The ride was fast, the horns blaring warnings to get out of the way. We had a job holding onto the benches. On my second such journey we all fell (we were handcuffed and could not protect ourselves) and I swept from one end of the van to the other with eyeglasses shattered. (The prison hospital later repaired them.)

I was not there to admire the architecture along with the tourists of the day. The van descended into the depths. We emerged one by one, identified, and taken to the tiny individual cells where indeed there was a bench to sit on. It was all very mediaeval. Still handcuffed I managed to eat lunch – the tiny square of cheese, the little piece of *baguette* and the thin slice of salami. And waited until mid afternoon.

Inside the court a case was proceeding. Three robed judges were at one end of the room with benches along the sides for, I presume, the public. My guard had me stand at the back, and there to my delight and surprise, were Madame Lafortune and consul Nassrallah. They gave me greetings and told the guard to release me from the handcuffs, which he did.

Badinter was there on the side of the room where the pleaders simply stood and made their cases. I noticed that two of the three judges were sound asleep – an occurrence which was repeated during my other two appearances.

Badinter did not speak with me, but when his turn came launched into an erudite, low key, analytical but fervently eloquent peroration. Unfortunately I do not have court records, if indeed they exist in detail.

His case was straightforward enough and he was confident. He explained that the treaty with Switzerland requires the Swiss to produce direct *indices* or indicators of the crime and guilt. This he said they had not done. The only support was the accusation of my changing the dental charts which was an offence called *faux dans les titres*[20]. That was explicable because of my state of mind (which he described) and was not a direct link to a crime. Furthermore, in itself it was not an extraditable offence.

---

[20] Falsifying a title which, ironically was later shown not to apply in my cse.

At the very least the Swiss should be required to offer better *indices*, or better still I should be released.

The court agreed to request such *indices* from the Swiss and set a second date.

When that day came the process was repeated. This time Badinter sent Dany Cohen and the consulate Madame Lafortune. The Swiss in their usual arrogant style simply returned exactly the same document. They could do nothing else because they had nothing else. Cohen pointed this out. The court reserved its judgement until a third and final session some weeks later.

Badinter was so confident that he sent Dany Cohen. Madame Lafortune was also there. She had a plane ticket for me at the ready. The Interpol warrant was still in force and would be open in Canada. The consulate had arranged with the RCMP not to arrest me at the landing in Montreal but when I got to Vancouver. There I would almost certainly have obtained bail while yet another set of extradition proceedings took their course.

It was not to be. In a terse decision the court upheld the extradition. The Minister of Justice was at the ready and quickly signed the deportation order. Years later Dany Cohen told me that Badinter was upset and felt it was the worst defeat of his life. Whether or not this was literally true he was planning an appeal to the European Court of Human Rights. But the Minister of Justice got in first.

We drove straight to the border crossing close to Lausanne.

Maître Badinter became President of the French Constitutional Court and under a new government Minister of Justice. Dany Cohen developed his own distinguished practice and lectured in faculties of law.

91

29. Caged Swiss Style

We were met at the immigration island by Inspector Margot. I was bursting but at last allowed to go to a toilet. The four of us sat in a café where we had a meal, like ordinary customers (the police were not in uniform). The French offered to pour me a glass of wine, but Margot said NO. I was to see a great deal of Margot.

We went to the prison of Bois-Mermet on the northern outskirts of Lausanne. I'll say it straight away. That prison was a disgrace to the Canton of Vaud, to whom it belonged, and to the citizens of Lausanne. I am told it was not typical of Swiss prisons, and believe that. And no doubt it has changed somewhat as the time came for its repair, though outwardly it has not changed at all. Its current web site lists its principles of operation, but the fact was that some of them were totally ignored.

A small elderly guard took me to the reception hall. Here he sorted through my bags and carefully hung my business suit on a rack with others – "for the eventual trial". He removed my other clothing and toiletries to be in my cell. I asked for my electric shaver. He refused. (I found later that it could not operate in the cells because there was no electric outlet.). We took the whole caboodle, including me, upstairs to a cell.

Next morning the local paper quoted him as saying that I was more concerned with my personal state than my case. And at that moment I was.

When I went in it was a shock. I asked the guard is this truly whee I will be held? He said yes, and told me all the other cells were the same.

The cell was about a quarter of the size at Fleury-Merogis – just enough for the bed and appurtenances. There was a tiny window near the high ceiling which could only be opened and shut with a special long pole which had to be requested and never seemed to be available. A weak bulb lit the room pitifully from the high ceiling. There was no switch and was controlled by the administration.

The mattress was on an iron bedstead which had bars that rose above it so that it was impossible to sit on the mattress in the normal way. There was a flush toilet but the seat could not be closed. The wash basin had no warm water. Above the toilet there was a piece of scratched metal which served as a mirror.

In a corner by the door there was a huge rusty cylinder which was exuding almost boiling heat in he winter night. It was useful for drying rinsed clothes but unless one could manipulate the window the cell was as grossly overheated as a sauna. I was unable to touch the window for a long time.

The walls had been painted with an inferior water paint which flaked and created sneeze inducing dust. The floor was grubby and any thought I had of lying on it to exercise was a non-starter. Every now and then the prisoners were given a dirty mop and bucket with a disinfectant like Jeyes Fluid and given ten minutes or so to leave more grub from the pail on the floor.

The bed was furnished with coarse sheets – fair enough – which were changed frequently, and a rough blanket which was changed every few months. There was a small hard wooden table with a hard wooden seating block, both fastened to the wall. The seat was extremely hard on the bottom and caught the tendons of my thighs by the knee.

I learned that there was communal electrical shaving time every morning in a shower area after breakfast where we used electric shavers one after another.

Breakfast consisted of weak tea and a hunk of bread. We were allowed to purchase a thermos which the kitchen filled with hot water which we could use to make our own drinks such as Nescafe or hot chocolate. As the thermos went down to be refilled, it often got mixed up and I was often handed someone else's which could be cracked and useless.

One gets used to everything.

The morning after my arrival I was called down and led into a well furnished even elegant public reception room where I was confronted by the senior *juge d'instruction* of the canton. This was a well dressed man with the aristocratic name of Chatelain. I only saw him once more near the end of the investigation, but heard a lot about him. He was a colonel in the Swiss army and had taken over the case from the first magistrate because of its diplomatic implications. He was suave as he read my rights – to such things as silence, and the use of my own language – rights which were observed by their absence in practice. I had the status of *détenu*, someone not formally charged but held in preventive detention until the enquiry was complete and I was formally charged.

Why preventive? Goodness only knows. To prevent flight, though I had no passport or credit cards and any money was in the hands of the prison. To inhibit finding defence evidence (serious in my case since I could not get material from my files at home or from my office). To prevent an excess of positive morale – rather to undermine one's spirit.

It was a day or two before a voice on the cell speaker, crackling and indistinct and very hard to understand, called out *"En ville"*, a command I would hear day after day. A guard unlocked my door and told me to go downstairs. At the entrance to the prison there was a small van. Other prisoners and I loaded into it. The van was quite different from those in France. Its body was divided into cubicles with wooden seats, just large enough for one person to sit in each. It did not use a siren but took us to the centre of the city near the railway station. Except sometimes for someone who had to go to the hospital, we dislodged, passed through the door of a stone building which I am sure the good *Lausannois* hardly ever notice and were ushered into solitary waiting rooms.

Then Margot would come for me and take me to a specialty interrogation room, where he was joined by Inspector Wyss, the weasel who had been in Vancouver. And the interrogation would begin, sometimes for a morning or an afternoon, sometimes throughout the day. Sometimes I would wait the whole day without anything happening.

The prison food was rough and, mainly at dinner, pasta, which unfortunately makes me throw up. Except for what sauce I could retrieve it went down the toilet. Lunch might be bread and cheese. *En ville* I would be given the routine triangle of cheese, hunk of bread. And *maybe* a slice of salami.

We were able buy our own food, though not for cooking and it was even possible to order dishes from downtown eating places, though I never did so and only one or two ever did for it was naturally costly. My salary was for the time being continuing, though it went to paying down credit cards and mortgage. Bill Gorham and Adrian had powers of attorney and looked after my

Vancouver obligations. It enabled me to put small sums into a prison account, and use these to create my own food intake when the prison stuff was inedible. In fact for months I lived on yoghurt, fruit juice, and chocolate.

The procedures guaranteed prisoners one hour of fresh air exercise a day. To begin with, on the rare days I was not *en ville* I went into the tiny exercise yard, where prisoners walked round and round in a tight circle, sometimes chatting, often silent. The grass had been worn into a dirt path. Mud would be tramped into the cells. At least it was not as cold as in Paris. When summer came Adrian sent me a large parcel of light clothes and Maître Paschoud measured me up on one of his visits and bought me light pants from the city Co-op store.

But at weekends we were completely shut down for forty-eight hours, except for those who attended a church service (in some cases just to get out of their cells) as the prison staff was on short shift. On civic holidays, including Easter, the complete shutdown could extend as much as four days.

En ville there were no such exercise breaks, though regulations required them. Paschoud complained and pointed to the rule book. His intervention was scorned.

There were interesting and sometimes very sad characters. One fellow had a fetish about cowboys. His cell was festooned with photographs, posters, cowboy hats and belts (a bit dangerous that) like a teen ager's room.

One day I noticed during the walk that there was a new prisoner with a bottle strapped to him and a tube inserted into his body. He was an English chronic offender who had been wounded in a gun fight with police as he was holding up a car on the freeway. He was the kind of prisoner the police loved to have; not interested in getting off, easy confession, treating the police as his friendly enemies. He had published a book on *How to Survive in Prison.* A tall sophisticated Middle Eastern medical student became his close friend. The latter had a typewriter which he was using to finish his thesis, and was released on bail.

Police were theoretically not supposed to enter the prison premises, but there were interview rooms which looked out on the walking ground and sometimes they would be looking out on us and notice who was talking to whom. The Englishman mentioned that one of the onlookers was his own inspector and that he had old the prisoner that there was in fact no case against me.

A young man named Roland, who worked in the kitchen, was accused of murdering his girl friend. She was hooked on drugs and alcohol. He tried desperately to get her off her addiction, paying good money. One night she had passed out and he shook her vehemently to pull her together and found she was dead. Curiously he had the same prosecutor and judge as I was to have, and both were gunning for his conviction. The jury ruled otherwise, holding that it was accidental.

I had a call down to the kitchen, an unusual occurrence. There I found Roland in a highly emotional state, collecting his things after the verdict. The director of the prison had allowed him to see me. He hugged me in tears and said he wished they had found him guilty. He didn't know what to do with his life and was hoping to emigrate to South Africa. He wanted o see me and say goodbye because, he said, I had helped him to survive and hold on to the future. I was touched and completely ignorant of any way I had helped him.

Sometimes there were desperate scrams in the night.

At the end of the summer the police enquiry was finished. So too, in July, was my university salary. I set in motion the sale of my house and vehicle.

In my next cell there had been a corpulent man who needed continuous medical attention. The prison doctor who visited me (once) was aged, incompetent and useless, but my medication was served with the evening meal and the guard watched me swallow it down. My neighbour, though, required hospital supervision and, though convicted, was placed in Bois-Mermet to be near the facilities. He had work to do as librarian, grocery coordinator, and meal deliverer. He had the run of the prison with his door unlocked except at night. The time came for his release and he recommended me for his replacement.

All year Paschoud had been visiting me at least once a week and sometimes more as we would go over developments, especially after at long last we gained access to the police files. I wrote him long commentaries in my terrible hand which must have been a trial for him to understand – incidentally he insisted that we communicate in English because he wanted me to keep my language up! His own English was perfect.

He agreed to my taking the job. In a way it was a relief because other jobs involved prisoners sitting for hours at their awkward tables putting charity cards, like those of Save The Children Fund, into boxes, rewarded by a few francs of *piculet* (minimal income) per hundred boxes. I would get a similar *pecule* which I could use for my purchases and letter mail. But I would also have the freedom of the prison. Paschoud also had the romantic idea that I would be able to exert an educational influence through the supply of books to the inhabitants.

I heard that my neighbour was overcome by anxiety when he left the prison walls and had to face traffic. I had my own minor anxiety out of my cell. The job was not without its difficulties.

Some of the prisoners did get up to tricks and one or two tried to escape. For a while a couple of men quartered in the wing above the women's cells managed to use sheets to get from their small windows to visit the women and have their fun. I simply don't know how they managed it for I could not imagine myself getting through the cell windows- their joint cell must have had a different format. It was put a stop to, and would have been dangerous at night. In the dark, with the prison closed down, there was a patrolling guard, dressed in black, with night goggles and a night operating rifle who, when he talked to me, indicated he was just itching for a chance to use it.

Nevertheless, escape attempts were not illegal, on the theory that to try to escape was natural to humans, *provided* no illegal act was performed during the attempt. I witnessed the results of two escapes, where the prison exercised its own privilege of punishment. In each case, when the culprits were caught and brought back, the giant cook transformed himself into vindictive mode. He knocked the culprit to the floor and bound his ankles. Then he and other guards dragged him to the iron stairwell leading down to the basement. As he was dragged his head banged heavily on each metal step so that he was certainly unconscious before he reached the lower floor. There his feet were unbound and he was thrown into a windowless padded cell for a week or two, where his cries if there were any would not be heard. He was totally incommunicado, without access to lawyer or doctor save for when a tiny hatch opened and food was thrust in to him.

Twice a week each prisoner could order supplies which were provided by a monopolistic corner store owner across the street – a political perk I am sure. They were delivered in bulk to a small room near the entrance. There it was my job to reconcile the delivery with individual orders. Then, while the prisoners were on exercise and their doors open I would make the deliveries.

Fortunately only once did I get into trouble, though the possibility was always there. For example something could be missing from a cell – and I would be the suspect, incurring the wrath of the prisoner. One day I delivered an order which the recipient thought was deficient. He was ballistic until I was able to show him the order slip.

The same thing could happen with laundry. Some of the women in the lower wing earned their *pecule* by doing laundry for the prisoners. There were no other facilities and they did a good job. But sometimes I would get someone else's underwear – it always took time and uncertainty to clear up.

The other two jobs required the presence of a guard to open and shut the cell doors, as was the case if grocery delivery did not coincide with exercise time. There was an ancient elevator which operated between the basement and the two main floors. Meals were assembled on a heavy cart for delivery.

So too with the "library". This was located in a spacious attic room. It had large windows which looked out over the wall with views of grass and trees which gave some meaning to the outside world. There were several hundred books almost all of which had been given by other libraries in the early or middle twentieth century. There was not a modern publication amongst them. Perhaps a tenth of them had been crudely catalogued in a large folder. I continued entering items into the catalogue but with half a heart it seemed so pointless. Various prisoners had left behind a large number of comics *s*.

The procedure was for me to load material onto the cart which I could not get into the elevator by myself. So I had to wait for an often reluctant guard to help. He would then accompany me around the cells, unlocking doors and offering books to the occupants. They could look through the catalogue and order what they wanted, but they rarely did so. If they did, the choice would nearly always be a grossly out of date technical book about which they later complained. For the rest, they thumbed through the *comics* trying to find something they had not already read. The whole exercise was disheartening and led to many complaints, but it also said something about the level of interest and literacy amongst the prisoners. I hope matters have changed since then.

I took some books out myself, but all I can remember were ancient tomes about prison reform.

One day when I was coming out of the library I heard a call from the basement (where the kitchens and some cells were located) "Hullo Vancouver." I blinked and saw it was coming from a fellow going to his cell from the kitchen. He shouted he had lived there and had a story to tell me.

We did meet up. He was a cheery rascal who lived on credit card fraud, which was relatively easy to do in those days. He had been caught using his card to buy jewellery. At the time he was living in one of the posh hotels in Geneva. His mode of operation was, when in liberty, to steal a card and live the highest life possible until he was inevitably caught. (Jewellery ho obtained was pawned or sold.) His term in prison he regarded as the business cost of the job.

However the Vancouver connection involved he theft of paintings from an Amsterdam museum, which hit global headlines. He and his accomplices took them to Vancouver where they lived in a rented house in Surrey, an outlying suburb. Disappointingly I did not hear what the outcome of the heist had been.

Apart from Maître Paschoud and, later, Maître Stoudmann when he was added to the defence team, I had one other regular and very welcome visitor, the consul, T.L. Mooney, from Berne. He was disabled, in a wheelchair, but pursued his interest as conscientiously as had the consuls in Paris. He also had another colleague from U.B.C. on his list, hospitalised after a heart attack. He would talk and bring me day old papers from the consulate, which I read avidly.

There was a psychological anthropologist in Geneva by the name of Cleopâtre Montaudon who wrote to ask if she could visit. When she came she told me the reason was that she had just come back from a meeting in New York at which the local anthropologists had asked her to enquire about my well being. Her visit had an additional interest in that she was investigating the use of psychiatry in the penal system. I told her about what I had observed in Bois-Mermet. I was in fact disgusted with the way the psychiatrists behaved. They met with the target prisoner once or twice for very short periods. They had at their elbow the official police record of the prisoner's presumed actions and some background. They based their analysis on that. The prisoner was thus categorised *a priori* without any thorough knowledge and he psychiatrist pocketed his fee. Cleopâtre was well aware of this situation.

A friend from Vancouver passing by also came for a visit. Each visit of course had to be individually approved by the *juge d'instruction.*

And one day there was a visit from Eric Sunderland, the Secretary General of the IUAES, from England. At that point in the late summer I was thinking about what I would do when I returned home, as I felt pretty sure I would. (It helped enormously to know in myself that I had done no harm to Betty.) And I was opting for the simple life, getting rid or responsibilities, including those of the Union. Eric was warm and told me he had been consulting with others. Another member of the executive had stood in to take decisions if they were needed and I could respond to queries by mail. But neither she nor anyone else was willing to take over the presidency or run the forthcoming world congress. He urged me to stay on. I said I would hold on until this matter was finished, and then we would see what the circumstances would be.

I did get some correspondence from the other organisers of the congress, but fortunately there were several years before it would occur and there was no immediate rush.

It was different with *Current Anthropology* and the university. Class students rallied at the beginning and sent messages of hope when I was in Paris, but their sense of urgency naturally waned and there was nothing they could do. One graduate student continued to send me drafts of his thesis, as much as anything to provide evidence that I could handle some university matters. It was generous and loyal of him and lifted my spirits, but of course did not count with the university in the end.

The Vancouver staff of *Current Anthropology* loyally continued their work. They were used to my periods of absence and knew exactly what had to be done, though in this case they were aware that I would be unable to return heavy manuscripts readily. Jacqueline would let me know the referees and commentators she had chosen for a particular article and Penny would send me the referees' reports for my decision. Barbara Metzger in California continued her highly professional editing and I don't recall her ever having to refer some author's disagreement to me.

The mails provided a headache for Margot. His English was that of someone brought up during his school years in the English Midlands (he had an English wife) so that was not a problem. But the sheer volume took him a great deal of time to carefully censor. Every bit of correspondence passed through his hands, except that to and from Paschoud and Stoudmann and he took his duties seriously, looking for passages which might give me support or hints that he could use against me.

One such incident occurred when the university decided to stop my salary. He brought the letter, written by a bumbling professor, assistant to the President, a physicist by the name of Eric Vogt, into the interrogation room, waving it in triumph. "You see, even your friends are turning against you" he actually shouted in triumph.

I was furious at the university, not so much at the cessation of salary, but of the way it was done. It carelessly contravened the agreed procedures, sending the correspondence directly to me, with predictable consequences, instead of to my solicitor, Bill Gorham.

105

The abrupt termination also contravened the clear procedures agreed with the Faculty Association. They would have led to the same result, but what the university did implied that salary interruption could be done simply at the will of the President (in this case severely constrained by the Board of Governors) without due process. There was no way I could continue to pay my mortgage so I gave instructions to sell both house and car.

From time to time Paschoud considered the possibility of arranging bail. This involved a submission to the Tribunal d'Accusation, which also had every few months to approve my continuing detention. He wanted me to be in a downtown room where I could look after myself, and where it would be easier for us to communicate. Although such things as my passport and credit cards were in police custody the Tribunal ruled that it would be too easy for me to escape from Switzerland and refused. If I had done such a thing it would not only have jeopardised my whole position but it would have totally ruined my career. The tribunal did not think of that!

A few days before the end of my residence I received a strange call to go downstairs and act as an interpreter. That had never happened before.

In the small interview room I found the *juge d'instruction* of Aigle, the man who had started proceedings when Betty's body was discovered. He was accompanied on the other side of the table by a boy of maybe thirteen or so. He asked me to translate for the boy spoke only English. He had other resources and had no need to do this. His motive I believe was simply to take a look at me out of sheer curiosity.

It turned out that the boy, an Iranian, had been at a private school near Chateau d'Óex. He was friendly with an older German boy. They went downtown to Vevey and, perhaps as a lark stole a few things from a large store. They were caught. The German boy was as it were racked on the knuckles and sent back to school. The younger Iranian boy was arrested. He had no lawyer and was in tears. The magistrate revealed to him that he was being sent back to Iran next day. I tried to be gentle in my interpretations, but I was disgusted and shocked. The boy's parents had left Iran when the royal family was tossed, and were living somewhere else in Europe.

Imagine, this kid, alone without family being abruptly sent to a country where he would be marked as part of a subversive family, without any formal procedure of defence whatsoever. And his older companion getting off with minor if any punishment.

I received notice of the trial date, the 3rd December 1980, my birthday and a notice that it would take place in Aigle, the small town at the eastern end of Lake Geneva near which Betty's body had been found. The charge was deliberate murder of the first degree plus *faux dans les titres (*falsifying a title document*)*.

There were two padres for the prison, one Catholic and one Protestant. The Catholic priest was a small white haired gentle man. The Protestant was large and burly and outgoing. They each called on me from time to time although they knew I did not share their faiths. I found it welcoming to talk to them about my issues, as individuals who were not part of the process, and in confidence.

107

Imagine my surprise when, the day before the trial, the Protestant pastor came to me in the evening and surreptitiously passed over a mickey of scotch!!!!!

30. "Impeccable" Police [21]

I was learning a great deal, not only about prisons, but the way police work. They are to a great extent an international fraternity. The Royal Canadian Mounted Police, few of whom have ever looked a horse in the eye, and the Vaudois police worked hand in hand. Their loyalty was to each other, and in the case of the RCMP there was no question of preserving the rights of a Canadian citizen if they were in conflict with the wishes of the Vaudois police.

There is enormous pressure on police forces to get their man. That is what they are paid to do and that is what society expects of them. In doing so they can operate in dangerous circumstances, but even if they don't, if they can manage a short cut successfully they will use it. If they make a mistake they will do their best to avoid its becoming public and they will stand together in doing so as a close knit fraternity. I can understand, even sympathise, with the motivations behind that. In their minds they are doing their duty.

However, let me be frank. Maître Paschoud, who was strongly conservative, had worked *with* the police – indeed with Fischlin - on the case of the theft of the Charlie Chaplin body - told me repeatedly "Never forget. These men are your enemies. They can and will use

---

[21] In every case in which I refer to police actions it is recorded in the official evidence file, unless the context makes it clear otherwise.

every trick to get you." To this day I cannot excuse some aspects of police behaviour. I committed an unethical act in a state of emotional turbulence. Everything they did was in cold blood and deliberate.

It is possible that in my case their sleights of hand were more frequent, even more blatant, than in many others. The easiest way to resolve a case was to get a confession and that is what they could not get from me because I knew in my mind and heart that I had not harmed Betty. This was all the more significant for them in that there was *no* direct evidence of any criminal act by me. In the end the case was totally circumstantial and involved a certain amount of fantasy. I believe they knew that shortly after my arrest, but having taken that step they could not back down. In Swiss law I could have sought damages. Determined tunnel vision and a lack of psychological insight dominated their actions.

The errant tactics began from the first moment the Swiss police arrived in Vancouver to harass me, with full RCMP cooperation.

The interview was secretly taped: in law I should have been informed.

Press releases from Switzerland. Quoting the *juge d'instruction,* stated in clear words that I was *not* a suspect. Yet Fischlin and Wyss were formally instructed in writing to undertake what is known as a *commission rogataire* in Canada and that I **was an** *accusé.* In Swiss law the moment one is accused he or she must be informed of that and read their rights. Neither of these things happened until I met Chatelain weeks later in the prison. There was deliberate misinformation as well.

When the Swiss arrived the RCMP sought legal advice in order to obtain a search warrant for my house.

They were told that an application would not succeed. So they resorted to the trickery I described in Chapter 28.

Twice during that visit I was directly threatened, again contrary to procedure. One was during the taped interview when Wyss hissed at me that I would not get kid glove treatment in Switzerland, a threat made when his face was turned away from the hidden microphone close to my cheek. There are several places in the transcript where the typist notes "inaudible". No doubt a technician could reveal the words, but that was not done when the tape was transcribed.

The second was when the RCMP corporal in charge of the house invasion turned to me as he left my home and said "You would be better off if you confessed. Because otherwise we will turn your whole life upside down and reveal everything about you." They certainly tried to live up to this promise, but of course I cannot prove that it was voiced.

The official Swiss police record consists of two parts, with the pages carefully numbered. One part details the legal proceedings such as arrest warrants, interactions with lawyers, tribunal decisions, authorisations to enquire in other countries and he like. The other consists of evidence gathered, including records of my interrogation, also sequentially numbered. Every act of obtaining or trying to obtain evidence should b e recorded. The defence may also insert documents. Some of my letters of protest to Chatelain are in the procedural file.

One early evening shortly before the Swiss visit my lady friend phoned me from the university after an exam in which she thought she had done badly and asked me to meet her at her car in the parking lot, only a short

111

distance from my home. I did so. She drove around nervously and we ended up outside the physics nuclear laboratory, which, for security's sake, was lit up with powerful lamps. We started to check the examination papers in the light. We noticed a police car pull up behind but thought nothing of it until the constable tapped on the driver door and demanded to see the vehicle licence. My friend could not find it. I then piped up and gave my own name, unasked.

When the Swiss came the constable suddenly became interested and reported that he had seen us in suspicious circumstances and that our clothing was disarranged. McLaughlin, when told of this, was rightfully scornful at the convenience of the report and of the unlikelihood of (a) our choosing such a place to play sex games and (b) the unlikelihood of a constable finding disarranged clothes under such circumstances, plus other considerations. He never got a chance to cross examine in court.

When I retrieved my vehicle from body repair in Vancouver the mechanics amusedly told me that Fischlin, Wyss and their RCMP counterpart (Corporal Smith) had visited them and taken samples from the boot. There is a note in the evidence file that they did visit and that the car had been scratched (it was seven years old) but there is no record of samples having been taken, presumably because they yielded no evidence against me.

The police dossier has a drawing of the car I am supposed to have used and a note that a policeman managed to get into the boot. The car used, however, was a Citröen CX, not the same as the one they inspected in Vancouver, which was a Citröen SM Maserati, a much larger car. The error was not corrected. The only point here is the continuous lack of precision.

The RCMP put out a press release urging anyone who had information to contact them. They received only two recorded answers.

One was from a colleague[22] in the English department at the university. He was not someone with whom we socialised. The essence of what he is said to have said, (t is in a police report which he did not sign) was that I was a "womaniser". When Paschoud ultimately read the statement he puzzled mightily over the precise meaning of the word. It is true that late in my adult life I had come to value conversations with women, whose take on life I found to be more interesting than the perspectives voiced by most men, and it is true that this sometimes led to intimacy.

But the point is that the so called witness had no direct knowledge of this and that his word was taken literally and without the slightest corroborative evidence. He was never asked "Back up your accusation with facts".

The second report coming all the way from Quebec, was in my view vicious. According to the RCMP record one Pierre Maranda, whom I had initially appointed to the department of anthropology at U.B.C. and nominated for Fellowship in the Royal Society of Canada, took the trouble to phone the police long distance. He noted that I had been elected President of the IUAES. This would never have happened, he said, if an incident in the Solomon Islands had been known –

---

[22] I do not name him only because I may confuse him with another.

namely that I had sentenced a native on the island of Malaita to be judicially hanged. The story was complete balderdash. I had never been responsible for anything on Malaita and I had never judged a case of murder – indeed my magisterial powers did not permit it. Maranda went on to say that if Betty knew of this, she would have been distressed at my election, and that this would have caused enmity.

Later on the Swiss police decided to pursue the story. They interviewed Maranda in Quebec, where *he repeated it.*

When Paschoud and I read this in the account of the police second visit to Canada I could not believe how anyone could invent such a fiction. And then by a stroke of good fortune I received a letter from a Solomon Island colleague, Dr. Allen Rutter, a former Methodist medical missionary who had been the Chief Medical Officer in the Solomons during the latter part of my tenure. He had just heard of my troubles and sent a note of condolences.

Paschoud immediately wrote to him, reporting what Maranda had said. He replied to say that it was impossible. He as medical officer had to attend any capital punishment and he could verify that never once had I appeared at such events. His letter is in the record.

Despite this the police decided that a search of the archives would help them. The sheer difficulty of going through archives of forty years ago and working from the records of the disbanded Colonial Office in London, then the Western Pacific records in Suva, and then records which had been deposited in the independent country of the Solomon Islands eventually deterred them. To even think of such a process is an indication of their naiveté on certain matters.

I later tackled Maranda about this, by mail. He provided two excuses. (a) He heard it from some (unnamed) person and (b) – believe this! –he had no idea it would do me any harm.

The police knew that I had had an affair, and they had a pretty good idea with whom. During interrogation I consistently refused to name her, citing the anger of her husband and her own embarrassment. So the RCMP used harassing tactics. They drove marked cruisers into her driveway and sat there for a while. They knocked on her door for an interview at the very time her husband, no longer in ignorance, was due to come home. She refused.

The Canadian Broadcasting Corporation planted a television crew on the boulevard median in front of her house. This led to fears of other journalistic prying. The family children went to school climbing over the back fence, and teachers promised to watch out for any strangers trying to talk to them. As the old adage says, *cherchez la femme* and it is the woman who pays the price.

My friend got fed up. She decided to make a complaint to the RCMP headquarters in the region, on the grounds that their mandate was to protect, not harass, citizens. The brass listened to her and then sent a cable to Switzerland. The lady has admitted the liaison. There was no longer any reason for me to hold my tongue.

Interrogations took place for most of the year on average three times a week. Wyss sat close to me at a table where he finger picked on a typewriter when called upon to do so. He never posed a question although he occasionally prompted I could not take to Wyss. He was a plump man with a walrus moustache, round face and small eyes, to me the very embodiment of nastiness.

Margot turned up in a style which never varied. He wore grey flannels and a dark blazer looking very much the English sportsman. He had been educated in the English Midlands where his parents were established, and he had an English wife. Thus his English was perfect, spoken with a Midlands accent. From the outside he looked straightforward – which helped him when he interviewed Anglophone witnesses – but he was quite capable of ineffectual bullying, and, above all, lying.

At our first interview he announced that we would be speaking in French since Wyss, he said, did not understand English. (This condition had a bearing on the validity of Wyss's two visits to Canada). I knew I was formally entitled to speak in my own language, but I did not try to exercise that right. It would have no doubt involved an interpreter (unless Margot did it) with major possibilities of distortion and slowed proceedings although they were certainly cumbersome enough as it was.

Margot never sat but stood before me. His style was sometimes matter of fact, sometimes angry and aggressive. He would start with a discussion of issues he had decided to press. After that had been done for an hour or so he would announce, now we will take this down.

Out of the conversation he chose questions which Wyss typed as such. Then I gave an answer.

Instead of writing down my words Margot rephrased them. He said it was to correct my French. He took the opportunity of course to put words into my mouth which I never uttered. I was told to sign which I did. Very occasionally I would say, no that's wrong and they would add a correction. However if I had pursued such a stance systematically pretty well the whole document would have had to have been corrected.

After a while I got angry at this and insisted that my objection be written into one of the interrogations. I said that the words could not and should not be taken as mine. If I had refused to sign, said Margot, they would simply write up their own version of what I had said. Nothing changed. It was in fact an indication of their handling of witness statements that permeated the whole enquiry, as we shall see. Later I wrote in the strongest terms I could muster to Chatelaine. He replied that they were doing their duty. Paschoud knew about it but could do nothing.

Sometimes I would sit in the arrival room all day with no interrogation.

Fischlin had remained in the background. He had dark inset eyes and a facial structure which reminded me of a death camp guard stereotype, though I am sure he was a good family man. Once he came into the holding room and harangued me about my Christian duty. He was, I discovered, in charge of the technical branch with its laboratories.

He had also worked closely with Paschoud – Lausanne was full of such connections, Paschoud and Willy Heim my trial prosecutor, for example, meeting for tennis. Paschoud was the legal advisor for the Charlie Chaplin family, and sometimes told me about Oona Chaplin. When Chaplin's body was taken from its burial place and held for ransom it was Fischlin and Paschoud who devised and executed the sting operation which caught the culprits.

Another time Fischlin came in and made me take off my laced shoes. Then he made me re-tie them. Presumably he wanted to see if my knots matched those which tied he bag in which Betty's body had been found. There is no mention of the experiment or its results in the official record. As with the vehicle dust samples, presumably nothing incriminating was learned.

During the Vancouver visit Fischlin held out a black garbage bag. He maintained that it was of the type used to hide the body, with identifying manufacturing marks, and that it was only distributed in Montana-Crans and neighbouring areas. There is indeed a note from a company employee on file making this statement. However a more senior employee certified that it was much more widely distributed in Switzerland, even as far away as the Ticino.

Fischlin also queried me more closely about the dental charts. He visited Montana, tried to find matching paper and ink and an equivalent copying machine. He could not do it and discussed his problem with me. I told him exactly how it had been done, but he still could not do the match up and apparently could not find the right copying machine which was there front and centre in the Co-op store. Maybe the store had changed the machine in the meantime. The irony is that without my admission the police could not have pinned the act on me and might even have been led to believe that the act had taken place elsewhere, even in Canada. There is no mention of this in the record.

Fischlin did not have much luck.

One day Margot and Wyss collected me from the transport van outside the railway station. They took me to a filthy and dilapidated windowless cell in the station itself. This was a cell where suspicious characters were hauled off the trains, a very frequent occurrence.

The morning passed. "You see where you could be. We're treating you very well." It was their lunch time and they had nothing for me so the three of us, me handcuffed under my jacket, made it across the street to the MacDonald's where they bought me a hamburger. I hope they were reimbursed for their extravagance.... (At the beginning they used to say "Come on confess - then we will go to a bar and drink together.)

After that the exercise of the afternoon began. We walked up a cobbled lane in the old quarter, Margot in front, Wyss behind, and me, still handcuffed, in the rear. I could not help laughing to myself. There was Wyss in front of me, his gun on his wobbling behind in an open holster which it would have been so easy to pull out and create a disturbance, even with handcuffs. Of course it might have been a deliberate temptation.

The objective was Lausanne's main department store. I had mentioned in my disappearance report that Betty had her favourite Samsonite satchel with her where she kept her papers. They took me, joined to Margot by the handcuffs, to the luggage section where there was an array of travel ware including many specimens of this well known marque, common in Europe.

"Now" said Margot, "Which one was your wife's?" I do not joke. I said that none of them were like hers. They expressed disbelief and made me look through a catalogue. They completely ignored the obvious reason. One, Samsonite markets different products in different countries. Two, Betty had had the bag for years: it was almost her trade mark. It was almost certainly not still in the market.

At least I got a hamburger and some fresh air and some amusement out of it, and learned more about what happens to immigrant interlopers caught on the trains. This incident is not recorded in the police dossier. And behind my wry amusement was the thought that the police bumbling was preventing the conclusion of my case.

Of course the police scanned my credit card and Vancouver telephone records. They found nothing of interest, but I was curious as to how the companies responded to the request, executed by the RCMP. When the companies identified one of my charges they supplied the *whole page* on which the item appeared. Most of the other entries were by other people. Out of sight went the privacy of others.

I had told the inspectors of my meeting Diana on her visit and that I had stayed overnight in Geneva waiting for her. That encouraged them to access the hotel's record of my stay and charges. When they had found what they wanted Margot burst into the interrogation room waving the paper, a favourite trick of his when he though he had found something juicy.

"Who did you phone in England from Geneva?" he demanded loudly. I was quite puzzled. "No one" I said. "You did, you did. Why are you covering up? Who was it? Look here."

I could hardly believe how careless they were. I had NOT made the charge. It was made by the guest who next took my room, as clear as could be. The charge record is in the dossier but not the inspectors' discomfort, nor the explanation.

When they checked the motel and hotel Betty and I had stayed in on the way to and in Paris they found that two breakfasts had been ordered at each place (the first one at a comfort stop over the autoroute plus one double dinner at the hotel. The staff at both places had no memory of Betty – very significant until it turned out they had no memory of me either. On the other hand the hotel front desk denied having received a near-hysterical phone call from me on the evening of Betty's disappearance asking if they had heard anything and what could I do? Admittedly the staff were not particularly interested at the time.

The motel register showed that I had unusually entered M. *et Mme.* Belshaw. This seemed suspiciously like some sort of crude cover-up. In fact Betty had teased me. Why was it only the man and not the woman who was registered??? It was nothing more than a feeble joke.

Much later Eric Stoudmann visited the motel and asked if there was any record of the linen used. This would have shown that linen respecting two persons had been used. The motel kept daily records of linen removed from the rooms for a considerable amount of time. *But the relevant records had been garbaged about two weeks before Stoudmann's visit.* They were still presumably available when the police visited earlier, but the police did either not check or did not want the result to be known. We just missed out.

Margot and Wyss made two more out of country visits. What they found should be interpreted in the light of what we discovered happened in the second; in fact the second casts light on their whole system of gathering witness evidence.

In the first instance they went to London and interviewed the Firths. Rosemary gave them the copy they wanted but Raymond stayed silent. Rosemary mentioned two "incidents".

I have mentioned the collapse of the bed when we were saying in their home. The police went to the manufacturer who repaired the bed. He denied that there was anything wrong with its structure. But one of the wooden supports had a noticeable gnarl in it which decided the time had come to break completely. Had I known that months later the police would interpret this as some kind of foul play – what? – I would have taken a photo. We are not gifted with second sight and thus I cannot prove the truth of what I say happened.

The second thing which troubled Rosemary was the arrival in the post of a risqué lingerie catalogue. It was in fact addressed to Betty who had obtained a copy, not fully knowing its content, from the classified section of the very proper *Times*. Apparently after we left London the catalogue continued to arrive and Rosemary held on to a copy. The police found this only too revealing of strange habits, in these days of *Victoria's Secrets*.

When Margot returned he entered the interrogation room brandishing Rosemary's testimony and shouted "Now tell me what happened in London". I hadn't a clue what he was getting at. He threw the bed and the catalogue, figuratively, in my face. I laughed and spoke an explanation into the *audition* (interrogation record) statements. But the police continued to think of this as prosecution evidence.

The second was a further visit to Vancouver, Toronto and Quebec City, where they took a considerable number of statements, all but one in English. It should be noted that Wyss continued to adopt the position that he knew no English, yet he signed the transcript of the oral statements.

Not a single statement bears the signature of the witness. The statements, put together in one document, were signed only by Margot and the non-English speaker Wyss.

When I read them I knew immediately that they were, at least in some instances, false, though it would take a contortionist to use them against me and indeed they were not presented at the trial.

My doctor, Melville Shaw, was reported to have said that he "feared for the safety of Cyril's children". There was simply no doubt in my mind that Mel, whom both Betty and I had known for years, would never have said such a thing. McLaughlin contacted Mel, who said it was a complete corruption of what he had said. He swore in front of the Swiss consul in Vancouver that what he said was that, *if I were found guilty* he would then fear for the safety of my children. And the open conduct of Diana and Adrian was clearly not one in which they felt threatened.

Bel Nemetz, the wife of Nathan the chief Justice, reused to testify on the ground of illness. Our neighbour is said to have given the opinion that when I cam back from Switzerland I had behaved somewhat grossly, a statement recorded without any supporting details.

They went on to talk to Diana in Toronto by appointment. Friends had been warned to make statements only in writing and in the presence of a witness. Diana followed this procedure, though no one else did, and had her lawyer attend. Margot and Wyss and the RCMP corporal Smith turned up much earlier than the agreed time, presumably hoping to catch Diana unawares. Instead she gave them coffee and refused to talk business until her lawyer arrived.

When the interrogation began the police accused her of incest with me with a resulting abortion in New York, where Diana at the time was working to earn money for her education at Yale. Now Diana did have an abortion, the father being a fellow student. As a result of this insult she wrote to the father, who gave an unequivocal statement that he was indeed the father. My only contact with Diana in New York was on a visit for *Current Anthropology* where on Betty's insistence, I bought her a warm raincoat! Paschoud was totally outraged. To this date I do not know who was responsible for the tale, and if the incest twist was an invention of the police of not. In any event it reinforced Diana's disgust at police methods. There is no record of the origin of the slander in any of the testimonies or anywhere in the evidence book.

Next stop Quebec City. There they interviewed Pierre Maranda, who repeated his misinformation about my supposed responsibility for a judicial hanging n the Solomons, and Betty's reaction to it, the falsity of which I have described earlier in this chapter.

Thus they collected "evidence"

The original autopsy had failed to show *any* cause of Betty's death. Chatelaine ordered another to be conducted in Lausanne to resolve this central issue. It yielded one further result, in that there were traces of what was known as "pink teeth", a slight coloration at the tooth base. This became a matter of discussion during the trial. It confirmed that there were no wounds indicating any form of assault. According to some authorities, but disputed by others, pink teeth could be a sign of strangulation, but there were no neck marks whatsoever

Among the many other statements in the record, apart from the Canadian ones, several are of significance and several imaginative.

Madame Wuest, the *regie* who had let the apartment to us gave evidence that a lady friend had visited me when I was looking for the apartment. So did Madame Nanchen who was the caretaker of Les Mischabels (Madame Nanchen was a fine woman and a significant socialist politician, rare in the canton of Valais.) Madame Wuest however could *not* identify the woman from a driver's licence photograph the police had obtained.

A retired International Labour Organisation director of finance, a New Zealander by the name of Ritchie, who knew us, wrote a letter stating that he had seen, from a tram, Betty and me walking arm in arm and laughing at the time the police were contending we were in a state of enmity.

A woman Madame Wuest employed to clean apartments when residents left deposed that she noticed signs of blood on sheets from the apartment we used. (She later changed her story saying they sheets were probably from another unit).

The caretaker of Jolilac testified that he had seen Betty in Montana *after* the date of our travel to Paris. This deposition was not believed and no one took notice of it. (Earlier there had been a "sighting" of Betty on the campus at the University of British Columbia which the RCMP investigated without result.)

The police requested the New Zealand police to interview Betty's siblings in Auckland. The elder, Joan, had nothing but good to say. The other, Shirley, was a little more nuanced but still positive.

Around the date of our departure for Paris, there are meteorological reports of heavy snowfalls in Montana. These contradict a statement by the caretaker of the building next to Jolilac where we were living. It was his task every morning to use a mechanical snow blower to remove the snow from the driveway to his garage. It was annoying because he managed to eject the snow against Jolilac and our apartment windows. He testified that there was no problem with the snow, and in particular no build up of snow between the two buildings.

The significance of this is that I might have been able to carry a body between the two buildings and load it into a vehicle. The only other alternative would have been to carry a body up three flights of high angled metal stairs to a vehicle parked on the road in full public view. The meteorological report gave the lie to the caretaker's testimony. When Diana and Adrian visited to join me in our despair I took a photograph of them outside the apartment. This clearly shows in the background the wall of snow piled up shoulder high. When Adrian was asked to find it and submit it to Paschoud, he could not find it and thus it was never entered into evidence. (t was found later.)

I used to take the vehicle to the Garage du Lac when it had difficulties. It had quite a few of those – punctured tyres and discharged batteries being the main ones. I had no covered garage access so the car was parked on the road above the stairs subjected to the elements. The day before our departure to Paris the battery failed and the garage had to tow it to their premises to have it re-charged. The garage confirmed this in detail in a statement made at Paschoud's request, together with the dated billing note. This, together with a deposition from an optician that Betty had picked up a pair of glasses she had ordered before going to Paris support the truth that it was unlikely for her to have died and been hidden in the days before the trip.

European procedures suggest that there be an on sire visit. This was undertaken with the prosecutor, Willi Heim, police, Paschoud and myself. We drove first to the spot above Aigle where Betty's body had been found. It was calm autumn day with no passing traffic. There was a pull-off at the side of the road with a light grove of deciduous trees on a steep incline to a substantial stream. The body had been found by road workers in the copse, not difficult to spot. Heim and the others talked quietly while Paschoud and I took in the atmosphere. It was strange, unreal, almost ethereal, difficult to relate to anything else.

We then drove to Montana where we were joined by Reichen, the Valais policeman. I was put in a cell below the Montana police station which I did not know existed, while the others went off to lunch somewhere. I had none but Paschoud did not know this. Then we went to the Jolilac apartment. It was almost as if I had never left, that Betty might still be there. I doubt it had been let in all the months after my departure. I can't remember why, but I had an argument with Heim's insinuations so that Paschoud had to shut me up.

And that was that for the on site visit.

At the end of the investigation I was taken to Chatelaine's office. Like other police locations it was in the old part of the city up almost mediaeval stone stairs. The room was large and almost empty except for the senior magistrate's desk and a smaller one slightly behind for a stenographer. Chatelaine and the well dressed matronly stenographer were the only others present. The magistrate proceeded with an audition. The subject was pretty well confined to my financial situation and other personal details, which I found would have a bearing on the details of the final judgement.

At one point Chatelaine left the room without explanation for about ten minutes. The stenographer and I made polite conversation. In my state of paranoia I wondered if this was a sort of temptation for me to try and flee. Probably not, but there you are. The atmosphere during the audition was coolly formal.

There is one thread which might sound strange to those used to anglophone style policing and evidential proceedings. Throughout, time and again, the police relied on hearsay evidence, without backup or checking for sources or reliability. This seemed to be acceptable in the Canton of Vaud and was not queried during the trial.

31. How the Vaudois Conducted Trials

The *code pénale* which defines crimes and authorises punishments is an institution of the Swiss Confederation, uniform across the country. Not so the procedures of the courts, which are the responsibility of individual cantons. When Maître Badinter said that he would never allow a client of his to be subject to the procedures of Vaud, he meant just that and was careful not to say "Switzerland". The cantons of Geneva and Zurich are more in keeping with international standards.

Maître Paschoud did his best to give me insight, but when the day came it still seemed strange - no doubt a Canadian court would also have seemed strange in the circumstances, but this was something else again. He told me that the tribunal had been set for three days of debates beginning on my 59th birthday on 3rd December 1980. To introduce material that called for further attention would irritate the judge and jury, so we had to confine ourselves, as did the prosecution, to essentials agreed between the parties. He said, and this turned out to be vital, that any appeal could *only* be on procedural matters, *not* on the facts or so-called facts set out in the judgement. "The judgement may say that black is white and white is black" and there is no appeal. He also said that the President of the Tribunal, one Jean-Pierre Guignard, himself a former prosecutor, was notorious for the illogicality and errors of fact in his judgements, but that there would be nothing we could do about it. There were other strange features about which I was about to learn.

Prior to the trial the prosecution and defence were provided with a list of lay jurors, citizens of the commune, one of many which make up the Canton. We were each entitled to reject two of six, who would then be replaced. All lay jurors were selected from lists provided by the main political parties with the official selection based on the proportion that each party gained in the cantonal election. As feminist observers were to point out they were all men. We knew they were small businessmen and farmers but not to which party they belonged. Otherwise we knew nothing but for form's sake arbitrarily exercised the veto.

Diana and Adrian had come for the defence. In an unusual act of clemency the judge (who now had taken over from Margot the reading and censoring of my mail, since I was formally under his direct supervision) authorised them to visit me at Bois-Mermet. I was warmed and encouraged by their presence. Diana had been take in hand by the Paschoud family and Adrian by Stoudmann's. Adrian and Stoudmann had much in common and ran an exercise route together every morning.

On the morning of the first day I was accorded a special shower and shave and taken to the basement room where my baggage and my dark suit were secured. The suit had been pressed and hand cleaned. When I put it on it hung baggily over my now smaller frame.

Two uniformed police put me in a station wagon without handcuffs and drove the autoroute to the town of Aigle. The day was clear with light snow. When they arrived at the rear of the courthouse they released me and told me to walk to the back door across a small lawn. I was unaware that a free lance photographer had stationed himself on a nearby roof. The resultant grainy photograph of a distant little baggy man with clipped moustache was widely used, sometimes touched up (or down?) to make me look a veritable evil criminal.

A *huissier* led me into the room. It was rather like a lecture hall, with perhaps something over a hundred spectators. I sat against a lower wall between Stoudmann and Paschoud.

We faced rising tiers of seats. In the centre, half way up, sat Guignard, the President, a small sharp faced man. At his sided and slightly below were two secondary judges and below them in an arrow shape, the members of the lay jury. *The judges and lay jurymen together constituted the jury and made their private deliberations together.* There were also a backup judge and two lay jurymen in reserve, attending all the proceedings, and ready to step in should anyone become incapacitated.

There was no court stenographer nor any sign of microphones to permit recording and transcription. In fact there was **no official record** of the proceedings (except for such statements as "the tribunal met on such and such a date and heard witnesses"), what the witnesses said, what the cross examination revealed, whatsoever. This gave a fee hand to the eventual judgement to write what it liked. The only record consisted in press stories from Swiss, French and Canadian journalists present. We will see what that meant.

The President called the Tribunal to attention and ironically congratulated me on my birthday. There was some discussion as to which papers in the dossier would

131

be made available to the jury. (The President himself saw the whole dossier including the undebated items.)

In Swiss law there are three degrees of murder: *assassinat*, where the killing is marked by aggravating circumstances, ("in circumstances or with a premeditation indicating that he is particularly perverse or dangerous" (according to article 111 of the Code pénale, as Heim quoted it); *meutre*, otherwise intentional killing, implying premeditation; *meutre par passion*, implying uncontrollable passionate actions on the spur of the moment.

Prior to the trial Heim, the prosecutor had created the formal charge. This accused me of premeditated murder that is with "intentionally killing a person", implying premeditation without aggravating circumstances or spur of the moment passion. He came to this conclusion because "*one does not know how or why he should have killed his wife*" (my italics!) and therefore a charge of *assassinat* would be unjust!

The prosecution and the defence agreed before the trial that certain matters would not be raised. These included Maranda's allegation that I had been involved in a hanging and the police insinuation that I was the father of Diana's baby.

The President read the charges: that I had deliberately murdered Betty by unknown means about 13th January 1979 and for unknown reasons and had falsified a *titre*. Then Heim rose to abandon the notion of murder with premeditation and argued instead for murder with passion.

I pleaded "not guilty" to the murder charge and "guilty" to the falsification charge.

Margot and Wyss had seated themselves in the front row, even in front of the jury, looking straight toward the defence team. Immediately Stoudmann asked if they were witnesses or spectators. They were witnesses. Stoudmann then pointed out two things. He argued that their official role was to exercise all the powers of the *juge d'instruction* and to act as if they were him. The *juge* is excluded from attending the trial: thus they should not be here. Secondly if they were witnesses they should be treated like all other witnesses and kept out of the court room until their turn to speak arrived. The President denied the motion, so there was at the beginning one clear indication of a breach in procedure, and the leanings of the President, modest though it was and even a possibility of some sort of appeal.

Stoudmann then requested the removal of the transcript and tape of the RCMP, Fischlin and Wyss recording of the very first interview they conducted in Vancouver. This was not because of anything damaging in the material but because it was contrary to Vaud and presumably Canadian procedures for the suspect to be taped without his knowledge. The President denied the request. Stoudmann then had the matter put to the jury. The jury agreed with his request and that part of the record was removed. It was a Pyrrhic victory. Stoudmann wanted to lose since he then might have grounds for appeal if the case went against us.

The prosecution began with its witnesses. The autopsy doctors simply described themselves as totally mystified as to cause of death. There was discussion of the "pink teeth" phenomenon, in which pinkness at the roots of the teeth has been said to be caused by lack of oxygen, and hence possibly strangulation. But the expert did not have to be prompted to indicate that research showed that this was far from proven and furthermore there could be other causes of lack of oxygen than strangulation. (There were no neck marks indicating strangulation.) Of course traces of certain drugs such as barbiturates could easily have disappeared over time.

Professor Thelin, who conducted the second autopsy and has respected status in the pathology community, stated that he could not swear that the death was not *from natural causes*. This enormously significant point was almost totally ignored in the development of the trial. Could it be that we were not dealing with murder at all (though certainly a criminal disposal of the body)

Among the "denouncers" ("*dénonciateurs*" -- the formal legal term which the President used in his announcement of the trial) was Chief Inspector Fischlin, who had led the first team to Vancouver. He was among other things in charge of what the forensic laboratories and bureau and attempted to describe how the odontogram was falsified. The combination of my own memory uncertainty, the failure of lab tests, and the failure of identifying and technically proving which photocopying machine was used led to totally inconclusive results.

At this point the President turned on me and both he and the prosecutor grilled me on the odontogram falsification, the kind of back and forth, disconcerting, departure from strict procedure that would not be possible in Anglo-Saxon courts, yet, I must say, having an element of natural justice to it. The President was clearly going for my jugular.

I endeavoured to explain my psychological state in altering the dental chart. As the press quoted me, "It was an act of moral weakness, and I make no excuses for it..... The act of falsifying the documents weighs heavily on my conscience.......I was in an irrational state of mind, almost crazy....... All the beauty of the countryside without Betty.... I wrote mechanically, without reflecting. I was alone....I wanted to think of my wife living..... I could not take the idea that something horrible might have happened..... I must tell you I have not killed my wife." The quotations are from the press. In fact I also described the ups and downs of my emotions as a result of incidents of false expectations, much as I have described them in previous chapters.

There was testimony about the finding of the body and the state of snow at the time.

The policeman from Sierre in Valais, Freddy Reichen, who had, with a Vaud colleague, called on me in the apartment prior to my departure to England and subsequently back to Canada, gave a reasonably accurate account of our talk which departed significantly from his written deposition. He had deliberately hidden from me the fact that there was a body to be identified, and that his companion was from the canton of Vaud where Betty was found. Yet, in retrospect, the presence of his colleague was some indication that the police were speculating that it might be Betty. Yet Reichen specifically denied to me the existence of any specific body under investigation. On an indicative point, Reichen's written testimony says that I took the initiative in getting the odontogram myself. Reichen honestly admitted in questioning that it was very possible (it was indeed a fact) that *he* had asked *me* to do so, to circumvent troublesome international bureaucratic procedures.

Inspector Margot summarized his work and his views of me -- as being almost totally incomprehensible and uncooperative. The defence attacked his status as witness without success, and also his behaviour from the point of view of procedure, again, as we shall see, without success, although a higher tribunal had criticized it stating that it would be the responsibility of this trial court to evaluate further.

Madame Wuest, the real estate agent who had let the apartment, testified that she had met a woman with me when I was searching for the apartment in the summer of 1978, but could not recognize the photograph which the prosecution presented to her (taken from a driving licence). She had met Betty during the Christmas period *but had not said anything to her about my companion.* She said Betty and I seemed in good spirits.

The concierge of the apartment block who had, in October 1979, told the press that he had seen Betty in Montana with a red purse in February was called, despite the fact that the prosecution itself paid no attention to his still determined statement. He said there was noise from time to time in our apartment (immediately above his), and that he was away visiting family in Yugoslavia at the critical dates in January. (The noise, I believe, was probably Adrian practicing his folk dance steps during Christmas, when he actually visited the concierge to talk about Yugoslavian dancing!)

A cleaning woman who was employed by the real estate agency to clean the apartment after my departure said it was dirty and that there was a spot of blood on one of the sheets. But she couldn't be specific about what apartment she was talking about, admitting it could have been some other. A laboratory report stated the spots could have been animal. And there were no violent lesions on Betty's body anyway.....

Jeannine Hurlimann, a young Swiss woman who had been a graduate student in my department at U.B.C., testified that on her way from Vaud to an appointment elsewhere she came to my apartment in February to take the opportunity to discuss further studies with me. We had a meal in a restaurant and she stayed overnight in a separate bedroom. I "behaved like a perfect gentleman".

The prosecution also called Anne Badcock. She was a Swiss woman living in Crans near Lausanne, the widow of an English agricultural officer, whom Betty and I had known in the Solomon Islands and in England, and who had visited us in Vancouver. We had visited Anne on previous occasions in Switzerland. Nervously, she told of the close relationship between Betty and myself and reported that I had contacted her, upset about Betty's disappearance in Paris. She had received a letter from Betty at Christmas which sounded happy.

These were *prosecution* witnesses! What did they say about the manner in which I was supposed to have committed murder?

The press dealt with a few of these points.

Colette Murat wrote at the end of the first day "No proof. There is not a single proof that.....Cyril Belshaw.....killed his wife."

Anne-Marie Burger wrote under the headline "An Enigmatic Accused" "(The court is) not at the end of its troubles. Nothing more enigmatic, more difficult to discover (*cerner*) than the accused of whom they must say, after three days of proceedings, if yes or no he killed his wife....... The accused hardly resembles the photographs which appeared at the time the affair broke. One imagined an athletic man with a large moustached face and one sees a small frail man with the head of a Presbyterian pastor....and something tense and severe in his expression. (He) expresses himself in very correct French with a very British accent........his fashion of expressing himself, as do his manners, reveal the cultivated man that he is, the *savant* of whom no one contests the value and authority." Not quite the way I see myself, but still....

Why mention such points? Because, as Myriam Meuwly wrote just before the trial, "At the time of the process, there is a lack of material proofs against the accused. In the absence of a new element brought into the debates, the judges and jurymen of the Tribunal of Aigle will settle the question in virtue of their deep-seated conviction".

Indeed, the use of their deep-seated conviction (*intime conviction*) is built into the Swiss law as a formal instruction to the court, which is bound by that, rather than by the evidence *per se*. Hence the case rested almost entirely, pro or con, on psychological understandings and interpretations, reached in three days of proceedings. Hence impressions of who I was, based on testimony and my own behaviour, in and out of court, became the determining factors. And no doubt much of what journalists saw and thought was passing through the heads of members of the court.

Canadian journalists sometimes saw things differently from their Swiss colleagues, at least insofar as their understanding of the court itself was concerned. At the beginning, Swiss journalists did not comment with surprise on what went on. One Canadian reporter, however, wrote, after this first day,

"Today's opening session.... demonstrated that Swiss justice is a free-wheeling affair, in sharp contrast to the staid tone of Canadian legal proceedings. The judge shouted at the lawyers and prosecution and defence lawyers screamed at each other.

In the middle was Belshaw......who for the most part sat impassively......

The trial was so tumultuous that one Canadian observer said at one point: "I don't know why they even bother to have lawyers here."

While such a reaction was natural, I think it was exaggerated. Perhaps I was too wrapped up in my own thoughts to notice the histrionics, but I didn't really feel that anyone was screaming....

Nevertheless, the proceedings were indeed without the kind of order that one would have expected from the meticulous scheduling. The judge arbitrarily, it seemed, altered the sequence of appearance of witnesses, and frequently addressed me even though I was not on the witness stand. Lawyers and court did interact without strict protocol. But there were methods and understandings which at least the official legal participants knew about, and Maître Paschoud restrained me from time to time when I would dearly have loved to enter the fray myself.

There was a break at midday. The defence and myself (accompanied by a pleasant if sombre gendarme in uniform) met for lunch in a room with white tablecloths! I was confronted by the first true meal in thirteen months. But we did not indulge in wine.

At the end of the day I was whisked off to a small prison in Vevey, nearby, which was my sleeping place for two nights. The difference with Bois-Mermet could hardly be imagined. It had been a nunnery before. The nuns' rooms had been converted into cells, and the whole place was redolent with colour. It was in exquisite taste like a small private hotel and there was even an electrical outlet for a shaver. As far as I could see I was the only occupant apart from one guard who let me in and brought my meal.

The second day took on a somewhat different tone. Much of it was taken up by my own cross-examination, and then witnesses for the defence, questioned by both the prosecutor and the President, who left no doubt in anyone's minds that he had already decided that I was guilty. Yet the journalists realized that the prosecution did not have the answers and their reports changed in tone.

Two developments affected the audience. One was my own defence, which I cannot judge for myself -- indeed I have little memory of this traumatic time -- but was set out in detail in the papers. The other was the testimony of my children, and in particular some of the surprising new information that Eric Stoudmann elicited I am sure by accident from Diana.

My own testimony dealt with my relations with Betty, my affair, whether Betty had been to Paris, my reactions at the time of disappearance, my subsequent behaviour and movements, my dealings with the authorities -- all points which I have set out in earlier chapters.

My interactions were entirely in French, though a sympathetic interpreter helped out occasionally, and sometimes I was not sure that I had accurately understood the drift.

The Swiss headlines conveyed the new atmosphere. *Gazette de Lausanne* carried the caption "Accents of truth?" Colette Muret wrote (all this is in my translation): "Interrogated without intermission, yesterday, during the major part of the session, Cyril Belshaw at last could explain. He did it with clarity, firmness and intelligence. At no moment did he give the impression of being on his guard, nor of betraying the truth".

L'Est Vaudois carried the banner "The Duel Heim-Belshaw: Match Nul". Michel Huber wrote: "Second day of this extraordinary criminal trial at Aigle.......At the end of the morning he responds to the questions of President Jean-

Pierre Guignard. It is an advance taste of what awaits him in the afternoon. In effect, a pitiless duel between two men. The *procureur* of the canton, M. Willy Heim, defends the interest of society, while Belshaw fights for his liberty and his honour. Small in size, his looks sometimes piercing, Belshaw never panics. Supported by gestures, he furnishes all the information requested. However, the prosecutor forces him into his final trenches, under a rolling fire of questions. But Belshaw keeps a remarkable sang-froid, never does he lower his head. At certain moments, he even mounts the barricades when Willy Heim goes into a long digression, then he says without irritation: "I am very pleased that you have at last arrived at a question." "I do not permit that, above all from your mouth" exclaims the representative of the Ministère Publique. At the end of 65 minutes, things have not advanced. In boxing, the tally of points would have certainly resulted in a drawn match. With this difference: Willy Heim had yesterday the great role, when Belshaw was a man under attack, pushed into his trenches. And then, after that sustained exchange, the two children of the accused have come to bear witness. Diana, a pretty actress, and Adrian, teacher also, have enabled us to arrive at an impression of this family, welded together and always united, despite the tragic death of their mother, united for the better and for the worse."

La Suisse had the headline "Bewildering, troubling: but who has killed Betty?" Anne-Marie Bruger wrote: "At last the real trial has begun: Cyril Belshaw was yesterday all day on the mat and he has come out of it unbelievably well. He had a reply for everything. Never have I seen an accused handle himself with such an assurance so calm and natural, also with dignity. To the point that one sometimes asked if one was dreaming. If one was truly in an assize court with an accused, a president, a prosecutor, so much of the tone on one part or the other was courteous, so much emotion also was shared. For Professor Belshaw, let free to explain himself, related with a circumspection and a delicacy which is not habitual from the floor of the court, his life with his wife whom he loved with a profound tenderness and to whom he was equally linked by a large intellectual understanding..........The President Guignard, like the prosecutor, could not shake him; if they saw him weep when his daughter, for example, came to bear witness, they could never see him weaken from the extremely sharp questions with which they barraged him. They had in front of them a man who obstinately, calmly, said to them: "It is not possible that I killed my wife. I could not even envisage doing harm to her. I loved her." And with that tone so sincere and convincing, at the end of the session everyone was troubled. But then, who did kill Betty?"

As the press reported (there is no other record), the substance of the questioning ran the gamut of detail, seeking not to prove with material evidence, but to show me up as some kind of hypocritical immoral cretin behind the façade of respectability, and to show presumed inconsistencies in my testimony, thus, presumably, shaking belief in my truth.

Thus: the prosecutor said that I had stated to the Swiss police that I could not recall what gold fillings Betty had, whereas to the French police I had given a detailed account of her clothes and the even the brand of underclothing. My reply: You confuse different kinds of intimacy. I actually bought lingerie for my wife, and thus knew her preferred brands. But no man can state precisely the state of the teeth, even of his wife. (At this the men in the room laughed -- some starting to check out their own fillings.)

Thus: But then you falsified the schema the dentist sent you. My reply: You confuse two things. The act of falsification and my state of mind. My state of mind led me to refuse the thought of the death of my wife. The falsification was a consequence of that.

Thus: Madame Belshaw was formalist, conventional, but at Vancouver did not know anything of your private life. At Montana a dispute would have broken out [in connection with my affair]. My reply: My wife was not intolerant. She was intelligent and did not attach great importance to a physical act, - she had already pardoned me for one - as long as I kept my affection for her. If a dispute had been possible, we would have used our usual language. That would have consisted of a quarrel with words, the use of arguments.

Thus: You flaunted your affair when (the lady) came to Switzerland in the summer -- I'm surprised you would take this risk unless you were indifferent to Mrs. Belshaw. My reply: I thought the risk was very small.

Thus: The plastic bags that wrapped the body it seems were only in the Montana shops and thus you would have had a supply. (They were in fact, as written evidence from the manufacturer states, distributed over a much wider area.) My reply: But I only bought small ones to fit the apartment equipment. I'd have to have a reason to buy large ones. (It seems I omitted to point out that the bags were available all over Valais and elsewhere, not just in Montana.)

The President made much of me fighting extradition, and of the course of my controlled response to attempted police questioning at the time of their aggressive visit to Vancouver in 1979. The notion that this was normal behaviour, that I had every right to behave as I did, that it was the result of legal counseling, was totally absent from his assertions).

From the President, in mid-course of his interrogation: There are three results possible from your trial: a condemnation, a liberation, and an acquittal with benefit of doubt. Could a man of your quality support the third solution? My reply, as quoted in the *Gazette de Lausanne*, "No, the scholar replied firmly. Only a total liberation would be satisfactory. And, emphasizing his words, because I had nothing to do with the death of my wife".

Betty's letters were read, describing the pleasure of Christmas. It was noted that she often took tranquillizers.

Prosecutor: You could have suggested she take something to calm herself after the departure of Adrian at Christmas, sleeping pills. My reply: No no, it's too extraordinary for me to imagine something like that. The paper said I laughed heartily at such an idea -- that happened from time to time in the session.

After I had said that I rejected the idea I could have killed Betty, the President interjected: "What credit can we give to your replies if your whole psychology refuses that eventuality?" In other words he was convinced from the start that he would find me guilty, an attitude that pervaded his control of the trial.

After my own grilling, it was the turn of the defence to produce witnesses.

My daughter Diana used the interpreter, though Adrian I think spoke directly in French. Probably because she was a woman, young and professional, her impact was immediate, and reinforced by the modest conviction and assurance with which she spoke. The prosecutor sensed that to hassle her would be counter-productive with the jury. Diana said it was not possible that I would have killed her mother; that, totally upset by her disappearance I was lost, and cried continuously. She said that Betty would have been wounded in the heart, disappointed and angry if she had learned of my affair. "My mother loved my father a lot. My father loved her a lot too........."

Adrian said, in response to the same question "I don't think she would have been happy, but I don't think it would have been impossible for her to accept." He also said we cried when we were together. But we showed another face before the world.

Diana said that we expected for a long time that each day Betty would return. The isolation, the idea of protecting Betty from scandal, could well have pushed me to falsify the odontogram.

Maître Stoudmann, cross-examining Diana, asked her what she did when she visited me after the disappearance. She mentioned unpacking Betty's suitcase from Paris and washing the soiled underwear. The audience gasped.

This spontaneous piece of evidence, heretofore unmentioned because of its seeming unimportance, emerged as a major new fact in the case. Here at last was some more tangible evidence that Betty had been travelling, had been on the move. The effect on the courtroom was dramatic.

A Swiss colleague, Professor Pierre Centlivres of Neuchatel, told of our discussions, my visit to his seminar in March, and my general probity.

My collegial friends Barbara and Tony Scott and Kenelm Burridge came at great inconvenience all the way from Vancouver to testify. They spoke warmly of our relationship. Barbara was taken aback when asked what would Betty have done had she discovered my affair. She had to say, truthfully, that Betty would have been upset and angry. Tony and Ken gave character support but of course no material details.

A colleague, Professor Vinigi Grotanelli, of aristocratic manner which was not easy for a jury to accept, came from Rome to testify. Only these words of Grotanelli were reported: "I cannot believe he could have killed his wife."

As far as evidence is concerned, that was it. There was absolutely no material evidence of any kind linking me to Betty's death, nor even that it was murder for sure. The court, apparently, did not have to bother itself with the technical details -- how in material detail the supposed killing had occurred, when, where or how or why.

The final day was given up to pleadings.

Colette Muret in the *Gazette de Lausanne* said that Willy Heim gave one of the most remarkable indictments of his career. The idea that Mme Belshaw had returned to Switzerland without my knowledge, found someone and had repulsed his advances, then falling victim to his aggression, was absurd, he said, advancing alternative hypotheses of his own making, not of ours. Only I had the interest – (undefined) -- in disposing of the body. That led to the falsification of the odontogram. And what had led to it? A scene in which the faithful loving wife confronted me with my infidelity. And if the philosopher Althusser[23] was

---

[23] I was not aware that just a few weeks before Althusser had strangled his wife in an uncontrollable outburst, resulting later in his confinement for psychiatric treatment for a serious mental disorder.

able to strangle his wife, why could not Belshaw, in a moment of aberration, do the same? (There were no strangulation marks in the autopsy) Don't let good lawyers allow this man to escape punishment. I want imprisonment for twelve years, he said.

Implicitly, Heim had moved the accusation from deliberate murder to murder of passion -- and he told the jury **don't let the lack of evidence get in the way** of *intime conviction* (strong belief).

The defence summation had two approaches. Maître Paschoud took the human angle. He described his admiration for his client, clearly good and honest, human, with the heights and weaknesses which that implies. That he could kill was totally unbelievable. "At our first meeting my first question was, 'Are you guilty of your wife's murder?' He looked into my eyes with tears in his and said, 'It was not me.' We grasped hands and I agreed to take the case and I said that if I ever thought he was guilty, I'd drop him. I've never doubted him." The falsification of the odontogram is totally contrary to reason and logic, but highly explicable in view of the state of weakness and abandonment that he was in. It was absurd to posit the idea of a scene leading to strangulation, between people such as Betty and myself.

"The prosecution has no confession, no witnesses, no material proofs, no motivation. They cannot even tell how Betty died, nor when, nor why. They base everything on one fact, the odontogram" But my comportment after the disappearance was totally normal. I alerted and even harassed the police and embassy. The odontogram? The desire to know is not the desire to see. The liaison was not of the kind to produce murderous effects. How could I have taken a rigid body into the boot of a car, some distance from the apartment, a car which had not been functioning?

147

It was not strange that nobody could recognize Betty's photograph in France -- they couldn't recognize Cyril's either.

Maître Stoudmann told the jury to look at me. Could they imagine this small man knocking his wife to the ground, strangling her, pulling her body around in the snow? The case has its enigmas, but don't get rid of the mystery by inventing a rational explanation for what does not exist. Which is what the prosecution is trying to do. We don't (in this court) have to decide who killed Betty? All we know is that we know nothing, and you can have no certainty that would allow you to convict Cyril Belshaw. In honesty, it is impossible to arrive at the conclusion that Cyril Belshaw killed his wife. At the very least, you must give him then the bitter victory that will be acquittal with benefit of doubt.

And whatever happens, he said, Belshaw can never live as before, so true is it that the justice system never leaves intact those whom it has disturbed.

He also raised a major question about the odontogram and the charge of *faux dans les titres*. To my great surprise he argued that the falsification was not a criminal offence at all. A *titre*, he pointed out, was a title to property in the form of a contract. An odontogram had nothing to do with such matters, and was therefore not a *titre*.

And the journalists, as representatives of the audience?

Colette Muret in the *Gazette de Lausanne*. There is no convincing evidence to enable us to affirm that Cyril Belshaw killed his wife as a result of a jealous scene and carted her into the boot of his car. Since the prosecution has no direct proofs, the prosecutor assembled indices. But there was the indication of Betty's clothing, giving some plausibility to her presence in Paris. For the court, the whole is a matter of personal conviction.

And the Canadians? The *Vancouver Province* headlined one edition "Belshaw at mercy of complex Swiss system of justice: jurors listen only to their consciences" and in another "Christmas at home or lonely jail awaits Belshaw". The *Vancouver Sun* "Theatrical summing up." Wrote Marcus Gee in *The Province* "If Belshaw were being tried in a Canadian court he could be confident that the judge would tell the jurors to base their decision purely on the evidence. But in the oath they took.....the jurors swore to listen only to their consciences........Even if four of the six jurors and three judges believe in his innocence and the other five think he is guilty, Belshaw will be found guilty.......only a simple majority is needed.........it is the presiding judge who leads the case against the defendant. At times Guignard seemed to drop all semblance of objectivity, voicing open scepticism at Belshaw's testimony."

So where indeed, did that leave the Tribunal?

It is important to understand that the President and two other judges were full members of the jury. The judge did *not* instruct the jury in open court as is the Anglo-Saxon custom but gave whatever instructions and opinions he might have had in the secret of the jury deliberations. Weeks later lay members of the jury leaked to the defence lawyers that Guignard was quite determined to convict but the lay members, far from being powerless, refused to agree.

After the proceedings terminated on Friday night, the jury adjourned for dinner and deliberation, working to 9.30 p.m., and then "separating" to permit the President *himself* to write the judgement. The judgement states that the tribunal came together again on 8th December at an unstated time, to approve the judgement, which was signed by the President and the Clerk, but *not the other court members*.

I returned to Bois-Mermet prison, where I faced a weekend of isolation, calmly weighing the options with a kind of fatalism, since there was no way anything I could do could influence any outcome. My children waited too, unable to visit, in the company of the lawyers who had become friends, and who had adopted them almost as family. And so too did the Scotts and Ken Burridge.

At 5 p.m. on Monday 8th December the court reconvened in Aigle for the reading of the long 15 page judgement. For the most part it was a simple summary of the procedure, a record of who was being questioned at what point in the proceedings, but *with no reference whatsoever to what was said* or what cross-examination if any took place, nor what records were read into the proceedings and which omitted. For example an item reads "Reading of four items from the dossier." Period. Or "The accused is questioned". Period. Names, including those of my own identification, are miss-spelled, addresses are erroneous.

The judgement itself begins on page 4 (in English translation) with a description of me:

"He is an intelligent man, ambitious, proud, calm and reserved in his social life, not lacking humour and imagination, poet at times, but very conventional in the conduct of his private and professional life.

His wife Betty......had a lively, expansive warm and sensitive nature in all her personal relations, very attached to principles, quite dependant on and particularly faithful to her husband.

The Belshaws formed a united couple if one puts aside some non-serious incidents, showing to others a united front. We know, just the same, that the accused had several adventures, notably a liaison with a professional friend and neighbour....." There is then reference to my friend's visit to me in Switzerland for a short while in June 1979.

The judgement records the beginning of the sabbatical year, and refers to Betty's amnesia in England, although the details are not totally accurate. The judgement then refers to the warm Christmas we had together.

The judgement records the difficulties with the car, my account of the journey to Paris, and Betty's disappearance, and then my subsequent movements. It records the cancellation of my subscription to the Valaisan newspaper *Nouvelliste* prior to the mention in it of the discovery of a body of a "young woman", which later turned out to be that of Betty. It describes the actual discovery of the body, the visit of the police to my apartment, the request for the odontogram, my communication with the dentist, and my letter to Diana interpreting the police visit.

It then refers to the falsification of the dental chart, my admission of that act, and my explanation which "remained consistent throughout the enquiry".

The Swiss police were instructed to visit Canada and the judgement notes that "I refused under several pretexts" to explain myself even though I was unaware of the taping. A marginal note later made by one of my lawyers carries the words "without the presence of his lawyer". The fact is that I talked a great deal, heatedly and in emotional confusion, and only later, *under legal advice*, held to silence until matters were addressed to me in proper form. The judgement does not mention the fact that I should have been warned of my rights at that time and appears to hold my right to silence, enshrined in Swiss law, against me.

The R.C.M.P. report of the incident with my friend on the U.B.C. grounds was accepted as truth, dismissing both our denials. The judgement then says, wrongly, that both she and I denied our liaison, though we finally admitted it. Neither of us ever denied that there was a liaison, though for months, until my friend herself said what she had to say to the R.C.M.P., I did not reveal her name.

The judgement states that in my interrogations and in the trial I declared that everybody knew that Betty suffered from depression and amnesia, and the court says that this could not be verified. This is erroneous. I did not ever say that "everybody knew this". In fact, Betty went to great pains to keep her depressions family-oriented, private between herself and myself and her doctors. Unfortunately it is correct that the two doctors who had most to do with her extreme depressions were not available for evidence. But her current doctor did refer to them in a soft way. And the only case of amnesia which ever occurred, and the only one to which I referred, was that prior to our leaving London for Montana, which is on the record in Betty's own letters.

The judgement says that I did not advance any hypothesis, reasonable or irrational, about the disappearance of Betty. Again, not so, though it is correct that any alternative hypotheses are at least as unsubstantiable as those of the prosecution, and Paschoud told me time and again it was not our business to advance alternative hypotheses.

The judgment also says I did not explain myself about the disappearance of the certificate from Dr. Nishiguchi accompanying the odontogram. I don't know what it was talking about here, since there was no separate certificate whatsoever -- what would such have served? What was it supposed to have said? Perhaps the President confused the matter with the disappearance of the X-rays, mailed separately, about which I did in fact have much to say. In any event, having avowed the falsification of the odontograms, there was no need for me to be secretive about some other act connected with that, had there been such.

Those were the only substantive points adduced. The judgement then moves into a section entitled "discussion and law". I summarize.

It states that I gave a detailed description of Betty, including a photograph, that I was not asked to identify a body in a morgue, and nobody with an elementary morality at the level of the Paleolithic would wish his wife, thrown down a cliff in garbage bags, to remain forever anonymous.

My contradictory attitude (according to the authorities) justified the opening of the enquiry and its presentation to the court. The system of "free conviction" of the judge imposed on the cantons by article 249 of the *Procédure Pénale Federal* does not require the accusers to prove all material circumstances; the tribunal's conviction can rest on circumstances exterior to the act itself, whether objective or subjective. Where there is uncertainty, the defence has the obligation to contribute to the establishment of facts and to collaborate in the creation of proofs. (This is getting very close to requiring the defence to prove innocence.)

In this instance the process comes up against the obstacle of the character of the accused which is contrary to our (the court's) mentality, and his conceptions of justice, founded in Anglo-Saxon procedures. Thus the absolute conviction of guilt, in the presence of constant and firm denials of the accused, so suspect in the light of major and immediate facts, comes up against a very light doubt. So the court "refuses to recognize the accused guilty of murder", even though it is convinced of disloyal and shocking manoeuvres.

In addition I am accused of "*faux dans les titres*", i.e. falsification of certificates. In the *Code Pénale, titres* are defined as any writing destined or appropriate to prove a fact that has a juridical significance and all signs destined to prove such a fact. An odontogram not accompanied by a written description or commentary permitting the deciphering of the signs is not a writing but a collection of signs. These signs are undertaken in order to justify professional honoraria. They are not yet the universally admitted mode of identifying citizens or bodies.

Thus the false odontogram did not constitute a *titre* and the accused is not guilty of that charge.

The costs of "justice" (undefined) amount to 34,791 Fr. 75 centimes. The process of enquiry was proportional to the gravity of the charges, conducted with diligence, essentially founded on methods that conformed to our law and "handled by policemen behaving perfectly correctly". This decision ruled out an appeal for damages which would otherwise have been possible, if not perhaps successful.] Because he is acquitted on the charge of *faux dans les titres* a proportion of the costs remains a charge on the State.

On the other hand, the accused provoked the enquiry by his behaviour at the time of his first contact with the police. Alone, he bears responsibility for a detention that was relatively short, given the extreme complexity that his attitude imposed, and his refusal to appear before Swiss justice. [Despite this being the consequence of Wyss' threat to me in Vancouver and the firm opinion of Badinter in France that "he would never let a client of his submit to the justice system of the Canton of Vaud'] It is thus, says the court, equitable that he pay a part of the expenses of justice, which the court determines to be 30,000 francs.

"The presumption of innocence is reinforced by the court's decision. In the absence of an express request from the Ministère Public, it appears to conform to the fundamental principle of modern law to order the liberation of the accused, his detention being justified by no legal cause."

The President closed the Tribunal and left the room. He could not have done more damage.

Thus the judgement.

Because of the differences between Swiss and Anglo-Saxon law the judgement is difficult to interpret in English. It refers to doubt, so that it resembles to that degree the Scottish verdict of acquittal for lack of evidence. Such a verdict is not possible in other Anglo-Saxon jurisdictions which require "beyond reasonable doubt". Either a jury cannot agree on a verdict and is thus "hung", leading to a re-trial, or it acquits, whatever doubts may be within the minds of the jurors. The Aigle court, however, was a little stronger than a Scottish verdict. Despite the existence of the doubts, it refused to, that is did not, find me guilty, and stressed the "presumption of innocence".

Theoretically, acquittal is supposed to mean that henceforth the accused, having stood trial, is found innocent. This is certainly supposed to be the case in Anglo-

Saxon acquittals, without reservation. It is also legally true in this instance. For the court explicitly stated "the presumption of innocence is reinforced" by its decision. Because that sentence is separated from other parts of the judgement, it is easily lost sight of, and has largely been ignored by some commentators.

That is in theory. Because since, unlike Canadian counterparts, the Aigle court referred to its doubts, those doubts remain. Even in Canadian cases of pure acquittal, members of the public often retain their doubts. Hence, in society itself, the very fact of being charged, of facing trial (unless there is overwhelming contrary evidence) means that the acquitted faces doubt for the rest of his or her life.

In addition, the levying of monetary charges cannot easily be understood in Anglo-Saxon countries, where no such provisions exist in criminal cases. On several occasions the Canadian and U.S. press, for example, referred to the charges as "fines". Fines imply punishment on the basis of a conviction. These were not fines but civil costs.

A young Canadian reporter tried to speak with me as I left the court with Paschoud and Stoudmann. I would have liked to vent my opinions, even though I was in a state of confusion myself, but Paschoud wisely pulled me away.

He took me back to Bois-Mermet. I cleaned out my cell and collected my belongings, took leave of the warden. Paschoud had booked a room for me and also for Diana and Adrian, in a luxury hotel in which he had an interest. He told me to have a bath, change, and he would pick us up for a reception in his home.

I found myself in a huge room and ran a foam bath to get rid, bodily, but not mentally, of the stench of prison. I knew the other prisoners in Bois-Mermet hoped I would find a way to reveal the misery of that prison. It has taken me until now to do so. I hope it has changed. I have seen its image on the internet (and also that of Fleury-Merogis) and suspect that any changes have been minimally cosmetic but you never know.

The Scotts and Ken Burridge and McLaughlin (who attended the trial) were part of the reception. To my shame I was not wide awake enough to then thank Paschoud and Stoudmann properly for the support they had provided. The one person I missed was the consul in Berne who had visited regularly and kept me in touch with Canada and attended the trial.

Badinter in France sent a telegram of congratulations to Paschoud.

The next day the three Beshaws met for breakfast. Someone in the room snitched to the press that we were laughing. The press took it ill. How could we not release our tension with laughter for once, especially with a noisy humorist like Adrian in our midst?

We went to an agency and booked our passage for the next day and I visited a pharmacy to pick up some oddments. Nobody blinked.

Early in the morning I paid our bills – my credit was still good –and we took the limousine to Geneva airport.

I had been told not to go back to Vancouver for a while and the university would not expect me until the start of classes in January and would resume my salary then. So Adrian took a plane back home, and I joined Diana to return to her own home in Toronto.

It would soon be Christmas. But the events of Betty's death were not resolved and still have not been.

32. Confusion Abounds

And there it remains to this day. Betty has gone, we know not how. Nothing new has emerged except one unreliable rumour, and it seems unlikely that it will. Each of us in the family has to come to terms with the unknown. Betty's loss and the manner of it is etched deeply in our lives, our thoughts and our emotions. Objectively we can say What a waste of a woman, a mother, a friend, a lively person. That is true but it does not deal with the intimate feelings. Time and again I see in the media a plea from someone in a similar situation: "Tell us. We need closure." Closure? Baloney. Even when the circumstances of death are clear and uncomplicated there may be acceptance. But there never is closure. Memories and thoughts remain for the rest of one's life. And quite often, as now, the mind asks the foolish but real question "What if?" "What if I had been more aware, had done something differently?" I go through the details time and time again, and that will never stop.

Felix Paschoud some years later became the victim of Alzheimer's and died. I have kept in touch with Eric

Stoudmann who is a major figure on the Swiss chess scene. McLaughlin died not long after. Bill Gorham has retired and is a good friend whom I see frequently.

On the initiative of Bill Gorham, the lawyers put their heads together and decided to charge me half their normal fees. This was a generous act. Imagine the time they had spent on me – particularly Paschoud who had visited me at least once a week, and sometimes more than that, to say nothing of his office work and contacts with the authorities and correspondence with Canada and elsewhere. It was extraordinary dedicated support, well beyond the call of professional duty. The sale of my house brought in a goodly sum but half of that went into payments.

Current Anthropology was still working without a hitch in the Vancouver office. My right hand lady, Penny Gorham, booked me into a hotel with a small kitchen on Denman Street in Vancouver. No one there raised an eyebrow or bothered me, and I must have been there for a month at least. It was a helpful location on a lively almost seaside street with many cafes and some superior restaurants, not far from famed Stanley Park between the beaches of English Bay and the yacht clubs of Coal Harbour.

Douglas Kenny, the President of U.B.C., received me. Once again the only thing that worried him was the odontogram. He was cautiously accompanied by his faculty legal adviser, a somewhat pompous professor of law. They asked if they could have a copy of the judgement. I still found my head buzzing and foolishly gave it to them without commentary or pointing out the conditions under which it had been constructed. Foolishly because they has no context and did not begin to understand the Vaudois judicial system. They could not reasonably under the circumstances. I was no longer a sought after member of university committees, which suited me as *took stock*.

The Department of Anthropology slotted me into a low teaching load for the remainder of the academic year. Slowly I managed to loosen up in the classroom but my heart and mind were not in it. I was looking forward to retirement in four years.

Walking across the campus was interesting. Old friends would stop and say hullo, but it seldom went further than that. Many who knew me from my earlier public appearances gave a startled look of recognition and turned their eyes away.

It was clear that many readers of the newspapers had formed their opinions on their own *ultime conviction* – after all they had been given very little of the evidence as such.

I searched for modest housing and found it on the shores of False Creek, an inlet of the Vancouver Harbour close to downtown, with handy public markets. It was centrally active and I realized how therapeutic that was by comparison with my former lovely but isolated home.

When I was settled Betty's ashes arrived. Diana and Adrian came. Adrian was living on the Sechelt Peninsular a ferry ride north of Vancouver and Diana in Toronto. They took the opportunity to vent their feelings and castigate me. I had no response but to weep. We decided to float Betty's ashes at a beach below our former house where we had had many a family gathering. Her remains were on the wide Pacific, the ocean which connected her to her birthplace and which had been so important in her life. We each privately communed.

Barbara and Tony Scott came to visit. Barbara in particular let loose her feelings. She had felt betrayed at the trial because it was the first time she had heard of my affair, was totally unprepared for it, and felt the lawyers should have warned her. I was too confused to be helpful or rational, much more confused than in police interrogation. My answers were bumbly and unhelpful. I failed also to make it clear that it would have cost the lawyers their licence to practice had they issued such a warning ahead of time. This would have been totally against procedures. Nevertheless her feelings were fully justified. And they had the honesty and courage to let me know.

Not so Audrey and Harry Hawthorn. They shunned me and would not communicate, though I tried to contact them. From now on I didn't exist for them. To grapple with the issues would be too much.

The lady whom the police had delighted in pursuing as they pruriently *cherchaient la femme* moved out of the family home to establish an independent existence. Her children remained close and provided comfort since she was the ultimate devoted mother, and she had some good supportive friends who were steadily behind her. Our sense of isolation, though, brought us firmly together again, independently, for mutual succour, which lasted much of the decade.

My official positions had to be talked over. Lita Osmundsen, the Director of the Wenner-Gren foundation for Anthropological Research in New York, which owned and sponsored *Current Anthropology* and who stood by me, called me in to the University of Chicago Faculty Club. Sol Tax, the first editor, was there and joined the discussion. Whatever they thought, nothing further was said and the journal went on superficially as if nothing had happened.

The Presidency of the IUAES and the forthcoming World Congress in Canada presented other problems. An

Inter-Congress and meeting of the Permanent Council had been planned for Amsterdam. The Executive met, and on the motion of the Royal Anthropological Institute representative asked me to leave the room while they discussed the situation. When I returned they confirmed me in the Presidency and announced their decision to the applause of members of the Permanent Council. This was not the relief it should have been. I was grateful for their trust, but that did not resolve my doubts about my ability to carry out the work.

For the immediate future that was well and good, but I had serious misgivings. It would have been strategically difficult but by no means impossible to have replaced me. But the Congress depended on donations and government subsidies to meet its costs. Would my involvement raise destructive questions? If they did they were not voiced and we received reasonable grants.

Although my head was clearer by this time I was not truly up to the job and allowed bad mistakes to be made.

Braxton Alfred, a physical anthropologist in the department, who had close personal ties to the RCMP, had acted as the conference general secretary during my absence but decided he did not wish to continue. Fortunately the interest of Bjorn Simonsen, a private archaeologist and efficient administrator saved the day. To do this he took a loss of income and commuted to Vancouver from Vancouver Island. The positive results of the meeting owe much to him.

We had a national committee which met in various parts of the country. One of the first things we had to decide was how to react to a request from our colleagues in Quebec to have the meeting there! That would have required a fresh decision of the Permanent Council which had specifically chosen Vancouver and would have jeopardized our local grants; but we agreed that a part of the Congress should be held in Quebec. There were precedents for Congresses to be held in two cities, but as in the Tokyo-Kyoto meeting the locations were quite close together. The University of Laval in Quebec City was by contrast a continent away.

That was a huge mistake. Participants went to *either* Quebec *or* Vancouver, seldom to both. That undermined the financial integrity of both locales.

In addition this was the first Congress in which participants were faced with the raised hotel charges which applied at the time, and many potential participants were not willing to do so. Those who still decided to come found alternative simple accommodation on the outskirts of Vancouver rather than staying in the central city itself.

Thus we over-estimated the number of people who would be staying in the host hotel and others where we had obtained free meeting space on the expectation of patronage. The result was financial chaos since the hotels demanded compensation. No additional revenues could be found to cover this.

After the Congress Bjorn had the embarrassing task of calling a meeting of creditors. I re-mortgaged my home and put $10,000 into the kitty. It was not enough but all I could manage, and the creditors had to accept part payment.

Our colleagues in Quebec, who worked on a separate budget were also unable to meet their financial obligations.

This began a long financial slide for me. I could not meet the mortgage payments and had to sell and from there on live in rented accommodation. Over ten years later I filed for personal bankruptcy not by any means contributable to this alone, but to other bad financial guesses connected with writing which went sadly wrong, and miscalculation of taxes. I was in fact living on unreal anticipations and paid for the misjudgments.

I could not forget what to me was the treachery of Pierre Maranda and Samy Friedman and the colleague in the English Department.

I wrote to Pierre and demanded an explanation. As I have noted responded by saying that he had "heard" the story from an unnamed someone else and *did not think it would have any bearing on the police investigation.* He never named the ephemeral "someone else". And if he did not think it would be relevant, why did he tell the story to the police or make it clear that it was hearsay? I felt particularly angry about this because I felt I had dealt with him generously in the past, and he was a colleague.

When I took up my seat again in the International Social Science Council I found it amusing to see Samy's embarrassment and discomfort. But I let him search his own conscience and did not cause further trouble by confronting him. Nor did I express my contempt to the English department colleague.

Many friendships remained in limbo. Sometimes someone would say to me "There are many people on your side you know". Yet I felt it not quite right to press myself on others, and left it to them to approach me if they wished to do so. Most did not.

Many years later I learned on the internet that Jonathan Bentall, the Director of the Royal Anthropological Institute, had mentioned to an interviewer that he felt I had done irreparable damage to anthropology. Yet before the interview he was affable and easy going when he visited Vancouver for the Congress.

It was by no means all suspicion and distance. Except for the Scotts, those who had been at the trial maintained their understanding and friendship. The Pacific Science Association even awarded me an Honorary Fellowship. And I have mentioned in Chapter 16, the Spanish Commission for UNESCO co-opted me for their several year examination of the future of that organisation. (Ironically one member of the panel was a legal authority from Lausanne; but we never discussed the trial events.)

These did much to allow me to retrieve at least an academic confidence. I wrote a number of articles which were published in reputable but, to anthropologists, out of the way journals.

At the end of the decade I visited Africa and France with another friend and wrote a 400 page account of my story. The agent did some good work but she had the idea of a film which the family were extremely cautious about. She came to Vancouver for a meeting and missed our agreed appointment. Tragically, she was in a literary meeting when a stranger entered and shot someone in the audience. The police had held her as a witness. Eventually we terminated our contract and the book did not get published. What I have written here is the basic summary.

But others did have a go. A writer in Victoria attended the trial and wrote it up in a book. She made one unethical mistake by saying that she had consulted Felix Paschoud. This she did, but he wrote to me saying that he made the condition that he should not be named. She did name him.

Apart from that she tried to be fair. Unfortunately she made numerous errors. At the time I was still uncertain of myself and accepted advice not to take legal action, which might have re-run the trial. I was advised that I would likely win the case but be awarded minimal damages. So I let it go.

Perhaps that was another mistake, though seemingly sensible at the time. The book has been used extensively in other accounts, resulting in similar errors which I missed openly correcting.

In a later chapter I will be describing my entry into the world of restaurant appraisal. The first step was to write a guide. Stimulated by interest at the Congress, on Vancouver restaurants which was well received.

Of course there was publicity. Don Stanley who wrote for *Vancouver Magazine* and who later became a friend, asked for an interview, which I gave him on the verbal condition that it concentrate on the book, not on the trial. When the article came out it was all about the trial with smaller references to the book. When I tackled him he simply shrugged and said "You should have known better". To rub it in, when a reader wrote a letter castigating me for using the tragedy to sell a book, not only did the magazine publish it, but no one corrected the record.

On the other hand an interviewer for a radio station was totally upright and honoured such an agreement.

Then a TV station wanted an interview on the book. This turned again into a discussion about the trial – I showed my weakness once more – but it was direct and not tinkered with. They refused to give me a tape of it however.

There was a production series aired on the Canadian Broadcasting Corporation dealing with controversial trials, produced with the aid of a trial lawyer. The format was a docudrama with actors in the roles. Some years later they decided to do one on *"L'affaire Belshaw"*. Diana in Toronto herself and close to the acting industry learned about the plans.

The producer, as was his wont, contracted me and offered to involve me. The conditions were quite clear however. I would be named in the credits, but the producer would have no obligation whatsoever to build my comments into his actions. In other words, I would have given my name and authority to whatever he chose to say or do. Diana and I protested vehemently and I turned down the approach.

This led us to examine the nature of docudramas and the inherent falsity of their interpretations, however well meaning and accurate they tried to be. We communicated our views with legal help.

The Corporation's administration is highly protective. It hates being crossed, let alone sued, and when threatened, even on apparently clear grounds never openly admits it is wrong and fights to the last ditch. Of course they refused to meet our requests or deal with our observations. In fact they went a step further, publicizing the programme widely and touting it as including new facts and data. The team had a good trip to Switzerland and included photos of the apartment (from the outside) and a version of my car. Eric Stoudmann was observant and noted that they had tea with Margot and his wife. I think that Heim had died by this time, but am not sure.

In the event the script was based almost entirely on what was in the published book to which I have referred. There were no additional details of substance whatsoever. There were acting scenes of the trial. Bill Gorham was of the opinion that it would not alter the verdicts of the public one way or the other and reported a neighbour's family as sating "Of course he didn't do it."

Nevertheless the Corporation may have become concerned about the dangers inherent in docudramas portraying the lives of living people. There were no further episodes in the series. Of course I have no proof of this speculation.

Eric Stoudmann also told me that prosecutor Heim, when he retired, gave a series of interviews on TV Suisse Romande which included an account of my trial. I have not seen it and would be surprised if it were objective from my perspective.

He also reported that a woman from the Valais had come to see him to state that she had been abducted and abused by some prominent men on the same stretch of road where the body had been found. She had not reported to the police, she said, because of the status of the men involved. Stoudmann was not impressed with her reliability and was clear that there was no chance of the police re-opening the case. For us to investigate was not likely to penetrate the group if indeed it existed.

These events kept the wounds open and when they occurred raised emotional troubles. Fortunately they were not totally dominant in my life. While hardly a day passed when my mind did not turn to Betty and the emotional traumas which followed her death, most of my days after retirement in 1986 were peaceful and I was able to think of some creative things.

It was fortunate the early morning depressions were counterbalanced as the days went on by the eruption of a sense of irony, of laughter at the tragedies of the human condition, of humorous and ironic despair at the ineffectiveness of humankind to put its world to rights. This gradually coalesced into a plan for a book about our destiny, though with the humour removed.

My first apartment right on the banks of False Creek had a lovely outlook of water, a promontory, and vistas of city and winter snow-capped mountains. In front of it there was a small spot of garden. Although it was north-facing, in summer the western sun played upon it so that I was able to nurture gigantic dahlias and chrysanthemums, which became quite dramatic.

In addition the condominium garden bordered the west of the apartment. I sneaked plants close to my wall and then worked with the strata council to develop and plan the rest of their soil, including the installation of a Japanese style waterfall.

When I later moved to another unit in the same complex I had one of the most impressive views in the area. Furthermore there was a south facing open deck of substantial size and a glass covered extra room which encouraged tropicals. The living space was tiny but the garden space provided a wonderful challenge. I could even plant small trees including a fig and grow vegetables outside and put on a show for passing people. And the inside room became crammed with everything from flowering cacti and bougainvillea to bananas.

Thus I was able to find some peace and tranquility talking to the plants, nurturing them, and enjoying.

There was a large pine close to the glassed in window. There it was possible to hang numerous bird feeders for several species. A neighbour's cat discovered the scene and hunkered down to seize his chance. He made a couple of lunges and fell to the ground but it did not deter him. He had more than nine lives. After I had sneaked up on him and doused him with a water spray he eventually decided it was not worth the effort.

The time came when the owner wanted to repossess and I had to leave, knowing that I could never find or afford such territory again, and I adopted a totally different downtown life style. This was not until the late 'nineties.

After the Congress I decided to make a stab at some field research. The ambition was to return to the Solomons. Major changes had taken place with the return of plantations, agriculture, forestry and fishing, and a serious number of islanders were getting university degrees. I was fairly sure that such developments were influencing the people unevenly, that many communities were changing more slowly, and I wanted to find out what and why.

The first attempt was not too ambitious. I approached National Geographic, setting out a plan of action with a photographer, emphasizing the areas where I had been involved in the 'forties. The idea reached a final selection but was beaten out.

Then I became rather more ambitious. My totally abstract and theoretical book *The Conditions of Social Performance*, published in 1970, had some impact on sociologists but next to none on anthropologists. It contained numerous propositions which were logically argued but had little empirical verification. So why not see if I could test the propositions with Solomon Islands data?

I produced a mammoth proposal to the Canadian funding agency. Naturally, the bureaucracy needed assessments. When they came in and were anonymously communicated to me, my mind boggled. To be turned down was almost expected, given the sums involved, with assistants and logistical complications. But not the way it happened......

One of the three referees though it was the chance of a lifetime and enthusiastically recommended support.

The second said that a man with my kind of career should be in a financial position to do it himself without a subvention!

The third – read this! – said that there was no *theory* in the proposal –which I had written to test explicit theoretical propositions!

I am not sure which of the two suggested that the money would be better spent on younger applicants. This last may or may not be reasonable, but there was nothing in the conditions of application which mentioned such a criterion and in an individual case like this might well have been contrary to national ethical law against age-related discrimination.

I should have challenged the bias of the two referees. But once again I gave in and let it be. I even doubted my competence to carry out the research, and never again applied for a fieldwork grant.

Anyway, the heck with it….. Why should I bother about another contribution to anthropological research? There were other things to do.

TRAVEL AND FOOD – PART TWO

33. Gastronomy and the Digital Universe

You will have noticed that in the chapters on France and Africa I recounted food experiences in some detail. After my return to domesticated life, and particularly after the Congress in Vancouver, I devoted more time to observing and informally studying the way food was prepared for the public in differing cultural contexts. Thus those descriptions were made *after* the mid-eighties. How did I get into this?

Certainly not during my New Zealand upbringing. My mother was an excellent cook. Her lamb, beef, mutton and pavlovas were truly excellent. But to me food was to put in mouth and digest. One thing, unfortunately, I did learn – to dislike certain foods. Offal did indeed make me sick. My mother made me incredible pasta sandwiches for school, so that even now I gag on pasta and can only sample small bites. In the Solomons curries were the order of the day, English style with lots of fruit. In student England there was not much else at the time but pies though Betty did wonders with the foods on the rations, and, except in Switzerland where we did not stay more than a couple of days, French food was still limited and under rationing. I could in no way be counted as a foodie.

When we *lived* in Switzerland, though, matters changed and in our visits to France and Italy the whole family began to delight in food subtleties. Wherever I went I began to search out local foods, as distinct from globalised menus. Still I did not make notes or see the value of what I was doing.

Colleagues noticed my interest. In advance of the Congress coming to Vancouver I made sure that the executive committee members would sample some of the different ethnic styles, still in their infancy, in the city. They were even slightly shocked (Annie Hohenwart especially) when I took them to an adventurous hamburger joint using unusual fillings.

It was then no surprise when they urged me to furnish a list of good restaurants for the Congress participants.

It was early days for digital functions. I had the idea though that the list could be digitalised and thus furnished in specific formats for other congresses as well. It could also be printed with updates issued for a few cents through the supermarkets. The congress public relations volunteer found that a printer was willing to create a directory for the congress without charge, and then make it public as we had conceived. Just before the congress he bankrupted. Instead we produced lists for the participants in rough format.

I had put in quite a bit of work on the idea and was reluctant to let it go. Digitalising was out of the question for practical reasons. Over the next two years I expanded the data to include evaluations. I needed an occupation to raise my spirits and visited every major street in the metropolitan area, taking notes and sampling food. Harbour Publishing which specialised in local books published the result, which was uniquely organised street by street. A journalist for the *Vancouver Sun* gave the book his "fast food of the year award".

After that I kept my eye on Vancouver food, which was a bit of luck because in 2007 and 2008 The *Chicago Tribune* and the London *Times* independently cited Vancouver as one of the top four restaurant cities in the world, by then a well earned and justified reputation. That standing however was not achieved until the turn of the century. It was due in major part to a Provincial policy of giving immigration priority to executive chefs, first attracting major oriental chefs and then French, Italian German Latin American and British as well as many others. The scene is now of extraordinary quality and ethnic diversity, based on exceptional ingredients and the almost continuous opening of new places of high standards. Local chefs represent Canada in major competitions such as the Lyons d'Or, where they perform honourably.

After the appearance of the book Don Stanley who had written the article for *Vancouver Magazine* I mentioned earlier became the editor of two local magazine projects. The first was in newspaper format and didn't last long. The second was the brainchild of a European couple. It was a pocket format entertainment magazine and lasted a year or two, but its data were in direct competition with a popular and everlasting thick paper called the *Georgia Straight.* For both I ran weekly food columns. One of them, which I shall print below, was nominated for a West Coast magazine award. I also wrote a few pieces on both food and gardening for regional magazines.

I was getting more interested and especially enjoyed comparing restaurants representing a variety of cultures with the genuine foods of their origins. In the late 'eighties, in France, I wrote a combined travel-food book, excerpts from which I have entered in some of these chapters. My agent at the time, though, did not want to pursue it, saying that "only celebrities can get a publisher's interest". I didn't believe it – celebrities have to start somewhere, and many whose primary characteristic is that they just love food get into the trade.

I had all along been of the opinion that printed guide books were out of date by the time they reached the book sellers. By the mid 'nineties the internet was coming of age, and the food scene in the city was maturing fast. It was time to show that an internet guide had the advantage of being up-to-date continuously in a way that was impossible in printed format.

My first idea was even more ambitious. I wanted to develop a multi-media magazine that show cased *everything* that went on in the city, a kind of continuous ethnography. The content would be produced by local writers. It would be multi-media with music, videos and interactive participation. It would thus be a view of the city created, not by a corporation in the usual sense, but by locals expressing themselves. And then, thought I, when this is successful, why not establish the same sort of magazine in other cities around the world: Buenos Aires, Rio, Nairobi, Delhi, and so on. Each would be created from a local point of view. When that was done, the whole web would be put together in one international magazine representing the perspectives of people, globally, from the ground up.

A group of interested young people met with me and we discussed the scope of the project. I then approached a web designer to seek technical support. Their fee to set it up was modest but way beyond my means, at least until I had acquired advertising. My own energies went into content, and though I had a worked out business plan I could not attract help to get the advertising without initial operating capital.

One media company expressed interest but backed off. The company decided to do its own local but severely limited project, which was frankly a mess and didn't last long. I approached a television baron, Izzy Asper, who had the philosophy of basing programmes on public interaction and street reality in a number of countries. I thought it would be a natural for him, but he didn't reply. I simply didn't have the business contacts to make it work, nor the business savvy.

Fortunately long came the software FrontPage in its early form. When I experimented I found that I could use it and didn't need a professional, although the design was amateurish

In a bloody minded way I decided to go it alone. A major part of the magazine, named Enjoy Vancouver Electronically, was a restaurant review section known as Adam's Vancouver Restaurant Guide. Other sections dealt with classical and pop music, theatre, dance, clubs, festivals, opinion and quite a lot more. Now and again I advertised for volunteers whose only reward would be to put something on their resume and gain experience. I learned from one of them how to put videos from a camcorder into the content, and one or two volunteers took the camera away and filmed festivals and events.

The site was successful, though the coverage was limited, in every way except the crucial financial one. Artists subjected themselves to video interviews showing how they conceived of their creations and carried them out. It was stimulating for me. I needed company and found it through bright young people, mature artists and musicians, event organisers, and many others. Messages from other parts of the world carried the refrain: "I wish we had something like that here". I had at least proven my point. The concept could work. And I knew how to get the advertising even if I could not do it myself.

But as the 'nineties approached their end I began to get agitated. I did set aside some time for personal writing, but it was not enough. I had to cut back or the writing would never get done. I could not go on paying the costs without satisfactory revenue and I could not afford to pay those who would attract the revenue.

So I stopped everything *except* the restaurant guide. It became the most visited food site in town and topped the Google searches, except for those sites which had paid good money for the privilege. Concierges told me that if they looked up a restaurant, that place's own site would top the list, but my review or note would be right underneath. Always.

Even that had to go. I had two major book projects that I felt had to be done while I was still on this earth and in sound (?) mind.

At one point when I was writing for Don Stanley, my grand-daughter Eleanor came to stay with me for a few days. I wondered what would be the best way to interest her in good food. This is how we embarked on our adventure.

Eleanor was a young lady aged nearly six. She sat busily at a chair in Settebello's on Vancouver's chic Robson Street, working her way through profiteroles resplendent with cream and chocolate sauce. Alas, it was the last dish of the last meal of her ten-day visit to Granddad, a visit in which she consciously joined me in putting to the test the suitability of restaurants for children. We had worked our way up from our first trial at, of course, McDonald's.

Adult restaurants like Settebello[24] (which produced chic gourmet pizzas and light food for a yuppie crowd) can be a strain for young ones. Menus are not easy to interpret, and there is a distinct impossibility of sitting still on a chair, feet forward. On several occasions the young lady had to get down and move around, or sit sideways, fortunately without noticeable interference to waiter movement. But the menu proved to be as close to the ideal for this purpose as you could expect, with its appetizers, pizzas and pastas, to say nothing of dessert.

In fact we let our hair down. She ate most of a plate of shared salami, enjoyed an appetizer of mozzarella frittata (she liked only mild cheese), though wisely said she wouldn't eat it all so that she could leave room for the main dish of spaghetti and tomato-basil sauce. The waiter, with excellent understanding offered to produce a half-plate order, not indicated on the menu, now a common enough courtesy in the better restaurants. Mostly the choices are made because the words are familiar, or the adult host can translate the meaning. The bar was excellent at producing the numerous glasses of milk any good meal demands. She would have enjoyed other dishes too, but the names raised questions prompting insecurity.

Security, simplicity of presentation, perhaps a visual idea about what you will get (as with buffets), are essential to the success of a Young Person's Eating Out -- from which a gentle venture into the unknown may be possible.

Settebello and Kamei Robata (now called Kamei Sushi and Robata, part of a high quality Tokyo controlled chain) were the best meals of the lot, from both our points

---

[24] Now alas departed this life.

of view. But to get there we built on the familiar, starting with McDonald's on Main Street one Sunday evening. The place was crowded and bouncing with parties. Eleanor's attention was on the carousel and ball pool rather than on the food, and she raced through her choice of fish burger (fillet of fish) and chocolate shake in anticipation of a lovely active time. Big Macs and such were of no interest.

Later on we went to Chuck E Cheese[25] in Burnaby, thank small mercies the only one of its kind in the Lower Mainland, but, according to my guest, "bigger than Toronto". Visions of the Twenty-first century. The Japanese owner runs a couple of delightful view restaurants in Vancouver, but uses this one as a demonstration project for his range of mechanical and arcade electronic games, which have cornered the North American market. The place was full of wildly playing juveniles (some well into their adult years), concerned looking parents many puffing on cigarettes in nervousness, more than life-size robots pumping out rock music, birthday parties hysterical and otherwise. Food was trivial in such circumstances, limited to pizzas and hot dogs (Eleanor chose a hot dog which was on an elderly tasteless bun) and drinks. An experience to be checked out once, and, for me, never again. When I published this opinion in a Vancouver magazine, the German manager dressed down the magazine's staff, including the receptionist, and accused me of being "anti-kids".

In between there was a sentimental visit to the Broadway White Spot[26], where we used to drive-in with Eleanor's Mother when she was a little girl. White Spots are

---

[25] A wild supposedly child-oriented U.S. chain
[26] An iconic Vancouver chain still operating, which all Vancouver adults remember as the treat of their childhood.

the original British Columbia created drive-in fast food outlets, once the only place where families on a budget, and young people, could get decent food and service. Alas, although there are still a number of outlets, only two are still drive-ins.

Sitting in the car we summoned the waiters with our lights, an experience not easy to find in Vancouver these days; and we had an enormous range of choice in both the adult and children's menus. The young lady opted for fish and chips, pumpkin pie, and tried a cola float which she didn't like very much. But the fish and pie were just the job, well produced, and brought in a fold-out cardboard boat which found its way back home. It was a good time, and we didn't have to worry about people at other tables.

Then we went to Uncle Willie's, where you paid a fixed price for the enormous buffet, for children 50c per year of age, so that it cost $2.50 for Eleanor plus 25c for a small carton of milk. Uncle Willie's[27] was down-grade unpretentious food produced in a small chain by a Swiss entrepreneur who used to be partner in some of the fancier restaurants in town. Unfortunately Eleanor was not in an experimental mood that night (you can't be on show all the time), and limited herself to spaghetti and soft ice cream, though there was a wide range of vegetables (something the fast food chains ran short on) and many other entree choices. I think we should have taken a little longer to decide, but there was pressure from the line-ups.

With cousin Juniper, then two, we all three went to Isadora's on Granville Island, which did excellently well by children. The $3.95 children's menu included a choice of clown pizza, chicken drumstick, cream cheese bagel, beef

---

[27] Gone.

or nut burger with fries and raw vegetables, the price included a drink and cookie or ice cream. Both children had a good feed, and the place was deservedly popular with mothers and many many children. Space was tight, furnishing minimal, and the waitresses kept their cool with steady plates; high decibels indicated fun was being had. In summer it was even better, with the adjacent water playgrounds outside, most children in bathing suits.

And finally, Kamei Sushi and Robata. That was our most daring, and with Settebello the most successful. The two adults won centenary door prizes (the firm in Japan was celebrating), which helped set the tone. Deliberately we sat on the bar stools, and Eleanor was stiller than at any other place. The chefs behind the bar, who do the grills and fruit plates as well as the sushi, delighted that a young lady should be there, gave her special attention.

I had felt that the ability to choose a grill would be closest to her previous experience and help her into the atmosphere, and so it turned out. She was not too keen on the raw food laid out but the chefs showed her some ribs, which she chose, and they came back well cooked with a delicious sauce. She sampled in and out of our other dishes -- a couple of pieces of sushi, but soft rice quickly dulls a young person's appetite, and pieces of fruit, topped off with a mud pie.......

The next night, after week-long visits to Lighthouse Park, the Aquarium, the bead shop on Granville Island, markets, an emporium called Kids Only, the beach with dogs, we were home latish and I opted to rustle up some food at home. Eleanor was occupying herself, then came up to me and said "Grandad, I thought you said we would go to a restaurant tonight." So we did. Then she said "Don't forget your notebook." And much later, "Write down 'My grand-daughter likes mozzarella frittata and salami and for

181

her second course spaghetti with basil sauce and then the best of all she also liked profiteroles with ice cream."

So that's what I did.

34. Iberia

My first visit to Madrid, drumming up interest for *Current Anthropology* and the Union was not particularly successful. My hotel was not far from the main plaza which was a construction site at the time and inhabited by touts. I did manage to walk to the Prado and some of the leafy side streets. I did learn more, but most of my enjoyment cane from other towns and the countryside of Spain.

You may recall in the United Nations chapter I referred to the Avila group, organised by the Spanish National Commission for UNESCO headed by Luiz Ramallo its chairperson and Secretary-General of the International Social Science Council. We met for three years in a variety of Spanish towns and in the course of our meetings we had privileges, always for example, meeting the mayor at a reception in his rich ornate quarters. Ad the only trans-Atlantic member I made it my habit to arrive a day or two early.

The first meeting was in the hill town of Avila from which the group took its name. Outside the meeting it was a relief to walk around the massive stone ramparts with wide views of lower farms and woods.

The second was in Segovia, and by then I was getting accustomed to the note taking aspect of exploring food.

Within minutes of landing from the overnight transatlantic flight a taxi sped me through Madrid to the northern railway station, full of bustle as commuters headed for trains in mid-afternoon. Blearily I noticed that within half an hour there was a connection to Segovia and that I could buy a ticket with my credit card in a machine that spoke half a dozen languages. But I couldn't get the thing to work, in English or in Spanish -- as I found later, in both France and Mexico, there were critical times when Canadian cards were not tied in to the right network.

So it was line up time, efficient service that was better than the machine, and the trundle of my bags to the platform. The train was a packed local, wending a gentle way through soft dry open hills, in what seemed to me in my disoriented state completely the wrong direction. For much of the two-hours I stood, gratefully, on the outside platform of the carriage, breathing in the air, assimilating the sounds, if not the meaning, of the language and the people. The old lady with mountains of city shopping bags, joking with the youngsters who teased her affectionately. The precocious high school girls stepping aboard, hair dripping from a swim, flaunting their torsos at spotty boys, clapping rhythmically at their lively songs. Small stations and large. Suddenly Segovia.

The map indicated the Los Linajes hotel was almost within walking distance -- but with these bags and up a steep hill? A taxi eventually came after numerous phone calls, though it took three quarters of an hour for one to arrive.
The taxi passed through the main square of the old town, Plaza Mayor, where life seemed to be booming this spring Saturday night -- band stage and huge carnival like constructions, the arcades filled with tables and people, young and old.

184

I freshened up, and, as usual until I obtained other sources, consulted my Michelin. Indeed, nearby there was a restaurant that seemed promising, the José Maria, three crossed forks. Maybe I could survive a few more hours without sleep.
So off I went, a ten minute stroll through lanes of bars, young men lounging in doorways, babies and prams, tiny squares, to the centre of noise.
The night was hot, the arcades crowded. I was excited by the atmosphere, a mixture of the sensual absorption of sound, the proximity of humanity, the smell of popcorn no less, the realisation that here was another kind of life. Women past the full flower of youth showed confidence and pride in short bright skirts to become seductive or titillating. An Englishwoman with Oxbridge speech pulls up her Australian boomerang blouse to show off her Marbella sunburn to her red-haired partner. A grandmother with daughters and baby in a pram objects vociferously to the prices; a daughter shrugs to the tuxedoed waiter, who shrugs back. The drinks of families, men together, women together, lovers, husbands and wives are, against the stereotypes of Spain, quaffing beer and Coca Cola and artificial lemon -- not a glass of wine to be seen.
On the stage a trumpet warms up, a drummer plays with his battery. On a small platform to the side, not far from parents, young girls from three to five, in beautifully ironed pink dresses, pretend to dance. It's test, test, test, eh eh eh eh eh, si si si si at the microphone. In the arcades couples touch hands and fingers, indulge in deep Norwegian kisses. Then the combo explodes, the woman lead singer tall, provocatively dressed in Spanish style, sinuous within the rock. I work my way close; although you would not know from a distance, she is past her prime and the makeup thick, not to touch. But she is effective.

Through eyes still a little bleary I notice the word Bar José above a popular watering hole, with a sign indicating dining room upstairs. Here we are, I conclude. Time to experiment. Total mistake. I was the sole diner and should have been warned by the decrepit atmosphere. The food was overcooked, canned, and thrown together. Mistaken identity.
Next day, recovered from indigestion, I find that José Maria is quite a few yards away from Bar José, though still by the square.
Like so many European fortress cities, Segovia is built atop cliffs, the story-book Alcazar fortress-palace constituting a defiant prow of some fantastic man-o'-war challenging all comers to defeat. In form it is the model for all those cut-outs of mediaeval castles beloved of children, with tall rounded turrets and be-flagged spires that speak of lovely wimpled princesses and gallant knights. There are churches in their squares and the great cathedral and the homes of aristocracy. The small intimate hotel, perched above a cliff, looked down on fields and watermills, and across to the super-modern Parador (government run inn) on a hill beyond the Rio Eresma.
And the great Roman aqueduct, stretching from the walls to the south-east, dividing the picturesque city from the banal industrial-commercial-residential area below.
Despite my first disillusion the menus I later chose were basic to the Segovian "typical" cuisine, presented by every worthy restaurant. Since I went to the three most famous -- Mesón de Cóndido, Duque, and of course José Maria -- both by myself initially, and with my colleagues later, there was plenty of opportunity to observe variants.
Mesón de Cándido is of these the most famous, the dramatic showcase (though not necessarily the most exquisite food) of traditional Segovian cooking. In a centuries old timber-framed building at the foot of the old

town, abutting the aqueduct, founded by the royal innkeeper to Enrique IV, traditionally known as the Mesón de Azoguejo, Cándido devotes himself to the old traditional roast cooking which has survived in Segovia as perhaps nowhere else. This he developed with his wife, Patro, to whose family the enterprise belonged in 1931. As with the great chefs of France, he has produced the classic book on Spanish cooking, and in the course of time has been accorded several score of gastronomic honours. His competitors recognize what he has done to keep Segovian cooking on the map, to make it the basis of the huge dishes that fill the tables, great and small in his dining rooms and banquet halls, according him the proud title of Mesojero Major de Castilla (roughly, Chief Innkeeper of Castile). The building itself is classified as an artistic monument and has been restored under the auspices of the Director General of Architecture and Fine Arts. The rooms are ornate, elaborate, mediaeval. Merged with artifacts of brass, copper, pottery are murals and paintings of foremost Segovian artists, such as Lope Tablada de Diego and Telesforo L¢pez Sanz, and of course the autographs of aristocratic and famous men (women are notably absent).
I can remember the *judiones del Real Sitio con oreja y pie de cerdo*, a heavy dish from the appetizers, served in stoneware platters, a regal plate belonging to the royal palace site of La Granja. The large red beans came casseroled with strips of pork back, sausage, peppers and tomatoes. And a massive omelette, *tortilla Mesón de Cándido*, softly filled to overflowing with peas, ham, tomato. And *liebre con judjas al vino tinto*, hare with beans and red wine, a bit salty and served with spinach. And the menu presents so much: calf's sweetbreads in a green sauce, pork loin with sweet peppers; medallions of wild boar with apple; pickled partridge; fish offerings.

If you walk down from the Plaza Mayor or up from the aqueduct, you are most likely to follow the climbing streets of Calle Cervantes and of Juan Bravo, the latter named for a famous Segovian patriot. It is a place of boutiques and fashionable shops, a walking street that is the chic shopping place of the city. The houses on the southern edge are on a rise that overlooks the roofs of the lower town. And one is the restaurant Duque.

Chefs and entrepreneurs being human, Segovia being a smallish city, it must be the case, I surmise, that Julián Duque and his Master of the Kitchen must have a collegial and rivalrous relationship with Cándido. The Duque building features stone and plaster, and polished wood ceilings, which gives it a somewhat more luxurious and bourgeois air, and its hangings are more restrained. One room has tables close to the view windows, so there can be more light.

Duque too has a small-type page full of honours, and he bears the title *Maestro Asador de Segovia*, Master Roaster of the Town. His *cochinillo asado* is done totally simply but accurately, with salt to tighten the skin of the sucking pig, a fierce fire, and sprinkled water for humidity. The art is in judging temperature and time for the crackling to be perfect, basted if necessary with fat, but also allowing just the right amount of fat to escape so that the pig comes to the table un-greasy yet juicy.

The enormous kitchens do not figure in the tourist pamphlets, which is a pity. They are worth the visit. Down in the basement, in caverns that are shored with brick and stone, their immensity is unrivalled. The Master of the Kitchen is assisted by a Roast Master and a bevy of cooks of seemingly a dozen grades.

Lamb and sucking pig are there waiting the time of no return, trays contain them in their marinades where applicable, the great furnaces open their maws to receive them; water, or wined and herbed liquids, designed to crackle the skin or add taste to the lamb *fume* in the heat. Yes indeed. The *crema de cangrejos*, crab soup, smooth, smooth. One of the best fried pepper salads, served with onion, I have ever had. *Carnejo* = *carnero* = mutton *asado* was totally fork tender, accompanied by its soup marinade of wine and garlic. How I wish I could get mutton in Canada. On another occasion, with the group, *pastel de verduras*, a vegetable pie served with a creamy spinach sauce on top, *perdiz estofada*, stewed partridge, wonderfully tender. I could have chosen *truchas frescas Gan Duque*, fresh trout, cooked with slices of Serrano ham, garlic, laurel and parsley. Or the famous *crema de nueces*, walnut soup, with cinnamon, sugar and milk....

I did of course ultimately find the famous restaurant José-Maria. Not nearly as splendiferously "typical" as the other two, it is nevertheless an honest open dining room with a very similar basic menu, but with its own selection of Segovian dishes. There is an immense mural of festivities, and proudly displayed cartoons with coats of arms, castles and costumes, place by place throughout Castile.

My first visit, to change my pace, was for fish. The *bonito en escabeche* y *pimientos asados*, announced as an appetizer, consisted of immense filets of bonito covered with a layer of brown roasted pepper, then another layer of marinated red peppers, then anchovies, the whole garnished with black and green olives and onion, and soaked in oil, with no hint of countervailing lime or bitter orange, as there might have been in Mexico. Again, smooth and soft.

The main dish was baked *besugo*, sea bream, served on a sizzling stoneware plate, firmly yet tenderly presented in a sauce with chopped vegetables, herbs, mild garlic and a light tomato theme. And here I had a real *ponche*, so-called Segovian "punch", in fact a dessert made with its layers of differing cream-cheese like textures, a touch of sugary sweetness but not over-done, accompanied by vanilla ice-cream.

On my second visit with the group I had *gambas a la plata*, succulently grilled with a soft marinade, *sopa Castilliana* of red peppers and garlic, served summer-lukewarm with dunked bread, and then raspberries. And there could have been *anguilas de Aguinaya*, eels, *again* presented with peppers, which are a well-deserved favourite element in the cooking of José-Maria.

When my colleagues and I went to the Parador of Segovia I was high in expectation, so excellent can be the regional food found in these establishments -- and then disappointed. Alas, the *perdiz escabacheda* was tough and unsubtle, although the garlic Castilian soup and the *ponche* were minimally passable. Perhaps a different choice might have been tastier -- I did not sample my friends' plates -- such as the *cazuela de merluda* (= merluza) <u>con gambas</u> (hake stew with prawns) or the *judias verdes salteadas con jamon* (green runner beans with ham).

Segovia of old Castile is no place to hold back on grounds of weight or diet. Simple though the menus seem to be, the difference between great execution and banal is considerable -- it pays to go for the best....

And finally to Barcelona itself. I had time to explore the way out fantasy architecture all over the city and explore byways where buildings were being taken down and cats prowled.[28] The *ramblas* with their trees, musicians, and kiosks are something I want for Vancouver, but our city fathers have lost, it seems, their bold concepts.

---

[28] Barcelona has of course changed enormously since its World Exposition.

I was quartered in the luxe Princesa Sofia whish unfortunately was on a traffic boulevard a good walk from the city and somewhat sterile. We met in an old classic building by the offices of the Mayor and the President of Catalunya, who gave us a reception and my first taste of sparkling *cava*, which now I often prefer to champagne (as I do the Alsace *crémant*). Here I note, only for the record, El Gran Café, a great watering hole, and my enjoyment at the Agut dÁvignon. There were actually a couple of places I did not like at all.

In Barcelona the group was given more of a cultural tour. It included a chamber music recital of Catalan composers, long frowned upon, as was the language itself, but Spanish centralism and only since the fall of Franco coming back into the mainstream. We had a visit to the great monastery of Montserrat on its bare mountain away from the city. There in its great library I found they had an offprint of an article by my friend Ken Burridge By myself I paid a visit to the Picasso Museum. Foolishly I did not purchase a print of one of his early still lifes of food, prints I have not found anywhere else.

Some years later I was charged with escorting a friend's daughter, just graduated from high school, who was filling in time over Christmas before setting off the mandatory back packing to Greece. We started in Paris, she by train, me by air to Malaga. I had been there before and was impressed by the sumptuous meals in the local Parador, situated on a hill overlooking the city and the harbour and I was familiar with the narrow Mediterranean streets of the city. Before leaving Paris there was an argument at the train. The young lady was refused boarding because although she had a ticket she did not have a seat reservation, a requirement neither of us had thought of. I was ready to rush and get one, but the strong willed young lady refused and insisted on travelling. In the end the conductor let her ride in the baggage van.

I hired a car in Malaga and we arranged to meet at a specific spot on the harbour's edge. The rendezvous was precise and we drove off straight away down the coast to Marbella where we hoped to find warm Christmas sun. Marbella most certainly did not impress me, with its large Middle east owned estates and a predominantly English and German tourist trade. The ideal of eating was in English style pubs and down grade fast food cafes.

Instead we shopped the supermarkets for trinkets that would pass for a Christmas tree, ate prepared foods with an occasional meal in the hotel's dull restaurant. We were not splurging in the search for good food. There was a path to the beach though the temperature was not inviting. We had a little feast of tinned food and cake for Christmas and drank *cava* and my friend phoned home to her parents. I am sure she wondered what she was doing in Europe.

We did do excursions. My friend enjoyed the open air markets en route where she bargained for clothes – and sometimes missed out on a sale because she bargained too far and face would not let her give in.

The most dramatic was to the hill town of Ronda. The road has stunning views down to the coast and the town itself is cut in two by a vast chasm. I hope it never feels an earthquake. Ronda is noted for the inauguration of bull-fighting, perhaps flamenco, and Moorish history.

We also had an adventure in Morocco – but that belongs in the next chapter. I dropped the young lady off at the youth hostel and she went her way.

I had been to Lisbon to visit colleagues and was entranced by the city. The main boulevard was as full of life as the *ramblas* of Barcelona, though on a more compact scale. I had a hotel at the foot of the cable car which rode up to the top of a high bluff which borders the boulevard. My contacts were most generous. After cocktails in their apartment they asked what I would like to see in the city. I said without hesitation that I was intrigued by *fado*, the sad sentimental music of Portugal. And hey did not hesitate either, phoning to check the availability of a seat in one of the great *fado* houses on the bluff.

The place was small, perhaps not more than eighty or so seats, arranged simply around a series of long communal tables. The fado singer must have been one of the most outstanding. She was breathtaking. Tall, blonde, in a shimmering off-white beaded gown, she walked among the tables. I found it quite ravishing.

And I learned a little. We had been served a plate and drinks, but there was no eating and absolutely no conversation during the singing. In between the singing you could have heard a pin drop.

They told me too of the differences between Lisbon *fado* and the more intellectual style of the university city of Coimbra, and that of Cape Verde.

On my one free evening I decided try a restaurant, called the Conventual famed for its medieval recipes. To get there I had to go up and over the bluff starting with the cable car. It is run by nuns and has a lovely sienna-coloured room. *I was the only guest there.*

The nuns had no English and I no Portuguese. The menu listed specials of the day, so I chose that.

It consisted of a large loaf of freshly baked bread. Inside was a major feast of meats and beans and vegetables, beautifully stewed together with herbs during the backing. Rather like an Italian *calzone* but much larger and more flavourful. A feast for two. It was difficult to walk home.

When I had a car I was aiming to attend a meeting of Basque anthropologists in San Salvador-Donastia with some personal time along the way. Time was short so I did not explore Sevilla as I wanted to, but had a fabulous over night visit in Granada.

The Alhambra is a sheer delight, a wondrous compliment to the brilliance of Moorish royal palaces. The whole complex on the highest spot in the city exudes peace and quiet through the juxtaposition of open courtyards, scented planting, and the movement of water – yes, this high.

My hotel was in a narrow hot city street just below. I puffed my way to the gates, past the elite Parador inserted into the very walls. It was a whole day of relaxed wonder. I wandered past roses, jasmine and myrtle. The last impressed me so much that I tried hard to obtain suitable specimens for my home in Vancouver with little horticultural luck, though varieties of the plant do grow successfully. In the balmy air I took photos through curved doorways and arcades. On the other side there was a broad vista of a deep gully and the view of the tiled roofs of a supposedly unsavoury and poverty stricken district.

I want to return and stay in the Parador. And again breathe the air of the scented flowers.

I had received notice of a meeting of Basque anthropologists to take place in San Sebastian-Donastia on the northwest corner of the country at the French border. I had to go. Only specialists knew of their existence, almost like a lost tribe. It might have been a coup to bring them to international notice through *Current Anthropology* – one of the objects of my visits.

I pointed the car to Portugal. Time was short and I didn't yet have time to explore another city of my desires – the university city of Coimbra. I headed fast up the northern coast taking in just a little with peripheral vision. Night fell. I had not done my usual trick of phoning ahead for a room. As a result every place I tried was full to the rooftops. At last I came to a building that looked more like a shed than a hostel. But they let me in. There was a barn of a dining room full of a party of happy guests. They let me sleep in a storage room.

On ward through the winding mountain roads and dark forests which lead from northern Portugal into Spain, finding only one town with a café, and then ultimately to San Sebastian-Donastia.

I found the meeting, was acknowledged, and then almost totally ignored. There were passionate debates, I could tell, but all in the Basque language, Euskadia. I was at a total loss since no one offered to give e me a summary, let along translate. The Basque anthropologists were simply not interested in wider exposure; they wrapped themselves, at this time, in the clothing of their own warm arguments.

My hotel was on a huge cliff overlooking the city and harbour, a dramatic sight. In the evening I wandered down in the city and found a good looking seafood restaurant. What better than seafood in a thriving fishing port? I don't remember the dish.

But that night, all night, I was trembling and throwing up mightily. In the morning it was over but I was still weak and shaking. I drove to the little airport, turned in the car and flew to Madrid where I caught another plane – onward, onward, onward this time to Africa!

There are many parts of the world I want to visit, for the first time or again. I want to go back to San Sebastian-Donastia which has become, I hear, a major and inventive gastronomic centre, one of the best in Europe.

And I want to spend time in Sevilla. Everywhere you go in Spain, even at the slightest road café, there are tapas. In North America and other parts of the world, the word *tapa* has a thoroughly distorted meaning, being little more than a humdrum appetiser. But tapas are an important institution in their own right and not to be bowdlerised. The word comes from the Arabic meaning a lid, that is a saucer which a bar tender places on top of your drink, complete with his very own delight, cooked or cold. By its very nature it cannot flow over the edge of the saucer, though it may be piled high. Usually it is eaten with fingers. There are certain classic dishes such as *patatas bravas*, *tortilla esnpangol* (a slice of potato pie which should be cut into tiny squared to be popped into the mouth), or grilled sardines. But good bars produce an array of delicacies that demand you drink to keep up with them, all produced by one of the barmen from a tiny cooking counter with a grill that would hardly grace a North American student kitchen.

And you do not normally sit down art a table to consume. You stand elbow to elbow as the other drinkers ignore you. After an hour or so of this you proceed to a nine o'clock dinner upstairs or at a nearby restaurant. If you go from bar to bar you are known as a *tapeador*.

Sometimes restaurants do serve a plate of tapas in advance of the meal. I fell into this trap, not knowing the etiquette. It was at an unusually dull Parador outside of Madrid. Tapas were on the menu so I asked for them. At least thirty delicate beauties came on one big plate. I slowly tucked in. In retrospect maybe I was supposed to select a few – I don't know, because communication was minimal. In any event there was no way |I could consume the main dish afterwards – a redolently flavoured chicken. I had to cancel. The chef came to the door and scowled. Without doubt the dish was already cooked. I found my way out of the room. Everybody, without exception, was scowling.

So I want to spend a month or so in Sevilla. I will not have dinner. I will become a true *tapeador,* moving from bar to bar which huddle together in street after street, but then I will not be a Spaniard, for whom the night is just beginning, but humbly find my bed. The main cost will be for the drinks, since individual tapas cost a fraction of that price.

35. Croatia

After I stepped down as President of the International Union, the baton was picked up by Yugoslavia. The rules of the Union named scholars of *countries*, not parts of countries, as hosting Congresses. This was still the communist federation, which did however give a certain amount of local authority to its parts. The Croatians were very keen to do the job themselves, but we found face-saving devices – at least they acknowledged Serbian colleagues.

Hubert Maver was the new President. He was feeling his age and had bad eyesight. I think he thought the post was largely honorary and did not realise that direct action on behalf of the Union would be involved. To some extent this was true because the energy and drive behind the scene was in the hands of Pavao Rudan, a much younger forceful and ambitious colleague. It was Pavao who organised the Congress.

I had the ex-officio position of Vice-President which in the normal course of events would indeed have been that of a figure-head. But when Hubert had to chair committees and run the public business, he frequently asked me to take charge for him.

There were also other Union meetings which took place in Zagreb, the locale of the Congress. Thus I found myself visiting the city on average at least once a year for four years. The visits coincided in part with my retirement, so that I could combine the trips with excursions, almost always including Dubrovnik. Pavao was undertaking research on the coastal islands and wanted me to go there but his schedules and mine denied me the opportunity.

Zagreb was a very different city from the closed in place the family had passed through in the 'sixties and, as with many other ex-communist capitals, has now changed very much further. I toyed with a Croatian dictionary and moved around exploring with enormous interest.

The head of tourism was putting his weight behind the congress, which arranged an opera, a reception in the grounds of an old castle, and countryside visits. I walked up to the beautifully preserved old town watching young people in full ceremonial regalia getting married in the city hall and then moving over to the cathedral. One of my favourite spots was the main cemetery up on a hill overlooking the city. I jumped to the conclusion, too soon, that the Croatians were welcoming and tolerant of other cultures in the federation. This thought was based on the fact that the cemetery had, side by side, Catholic, Orthodox, Jewish and Muslim graves.

I learned to drink slivovitz all night long and come up with only a little head. The tourist director took some of us a long winding road up a northern hill, bordered by a stream on one side and old wood mansions which could have come straight out of Canada. He lived in one with a back lawn and several plum and other fruit trees. He took us to his basement and treated us to tastes of his home made slivovitz, produced from his own plums. It seemed an easier, more relaxed life that I had experienced in other communist countries.

I found an excellent little guide to all the restaurants in Zagreb, and over the years slowly worked my way through many of them. Unfortunately my notes are thin, and I must take care not to confuse restaurant names. Of course now both the number and style of such places have expanded enormously. The service was cautiously friendly and accommodating, not the deadpan reluctance of Russia. On the whole, the standard of cooking outside the main hotels, was straightforward, simple and succulently flavourful. Most restaurants I sampled specialized in a single style of presentation – fish, game, regional specialties, Hungarian or Serbian. In fact the food offered was at the time outstanding by comparison with all other European communist countries I had visited. And most accepted credit cards!!!

Except the fish, which is esteemed and proudly presented, usually grilled. The fish itself was fresh, mostly dace, but it all tasted the same, whether in Zagreb or Dubrovnik. This was a shame. I have an excellent Yugoslavian cookbook of the period which contains highly varied recipes and a wider range of fish, such as mackerel, pike and sole. There were good offerings of oysters.

The old Hotel Esplanade by the railway station was my home away from home. It had huge rooms with high ceilings in which I could feel lost. Its two restaurants were excellent. The main one, the Rubin, had first class breakfasts, though at dinner it was toned-down international. To me its pride was the Taverna Rustica with lively music and a good variety of local dishes. You could live for a week on the Šestine platter for two – veal and beef fillet and pork cutlets, served with sliced potato, fried tomato, mushrooms, cabbage, drizzled with oil and vinegar.

By contrast the Hotel Intercontinental at the time had ordinary international food in its main room the Opera. This was a surprise since I have usually admired the way Intercontinental hotels found a good place for local cuisine, wherever they are. In its Taverna Grič, though all I knew (I did not see the whole menu) was Greek, the closest cuisine being Macedonian.

Up the road toward the tourist director's home there was a place set out in the open in a lovely setting with great trees around and a running stream. I don't know how I got there (though I did take buses from time to time). It was called Olsruljak (if you can get your tongue around that!). I don't know if I had its signature rumpsteak dish or not. But I had a very satisfactory lunch giving in the open air, which always pleases me.

On Zagreb's main street there was a restaurant called Lovači Rog which I found at the end of my visits. It specialized in game, a style which is not common in the world these days except in Central Europe. Here there was boar, venison, game birds. It was quite dark inside and I was the only diner when I sampled the menu with a venison steak. However it had a high and well deserved reputation.

On one occasion the Congress took a party of us to a motel outside the city. It was more than a motel in that it ha the finest quality rotisserie called Plitvice. Lamb on the spit is a regional favourite from Greece inward and in this case was beautifully herbed.

Numerous dishes are worth seeking out. You will b e able to find smoked goose breast, local salamis, white asparagus in a spinach sauce, melon with *pršit* (prosciutto) and shrimp, *šar oplanina* (lamb hotpot) with a huge array of root vegetables, *vipapa* soup of beans, sauerkraut, onion and bacon pie, crab casserole, offal as an appetiser, leeks stuffed with pork, whit wine, onion ns tomato sauce; squid stuffed with scampi, onion, garlic and parsley, fried trout; many stewed meat dishes; venison with fruit; chicken with walnuts; turkey with sauerkraut; pheasant; pork chops with prunes and *taramasalat*; walnut pancakes: and the famous dessert crepes. The desserts can be a medley of Greek and Central European styles.

Below the old town there was a Saturday open market. The produce on display was limited, but there was a good enclosed fish market bringing up delicacies from Split and its neighbouring villages. The vegetable vendors were mostly brawny peasant women eager to pass on their sometimes tired wares.

And up above, the grey almost Baltic buildings of the town gave way to beautifully maintained public buildings and the soft pastel colours of the homes and offices of the elite. There was a gallery devoted to contemporary glass, pottery and sculpture, and a well kept local museum.

I toyed with the idea of living in Croatia – these urges strike me from time to time but in the end there are always reasons not to do so.

It came about because of Pavao's ambition. He had the grand idea of establishing an Advanced International Anthropological Institute affiliated with the International Union. His ideas were quite vague but he assured those who listened that there would be support from the Croatian government and he had quarters already in the old city of Dubrovnik. I worked out a scheme with costs to attract international staff and ways to finance without running up against currency restrictions. But it was never heard of again.

I enjoyed Dubrovnik. The old town was bordered by surrounding hills. To the north-west there is a kind of suburbia with splendid Adriatic views. To the south east there was a string of modern hotels blended into the cliffside, with pools. One evening in the bar of the one I chose their recorded music was unusually pleasant. I'm never good at following the words of songs and assumed it was Croatian. But no. Italian ruled. So much for my ear.

It was always pleasing to walk down to the old town in the evening cool and explore the few streets, surrounded by old stone houses, and take a (standard) fish meal in a tiny restaurant, or drink slivovitz in a cafe.

That was well before the Serbians bombed the place. And before the countries of old Yugoslavia opened up to the mass of invading tourists. Just twenty years ago.

36. Egypt and Morocco

Alexandria was a disappointment. In chapter 13 I mentioned that an IUAES Inter-Congress and other meetings were disrupted by American University in Cairo student demonstrations and threats against Israeli attendance. Despite the cancellation of the academic meetings and the official business of the Union carried on. Thus for the few days of that work I was almost entirely confined to the hotel on the cornice. When I did walk out for a few minutes of exploration I found that stretch of the harbour silent with only a few fish cafes. The great romantic and historic city was closed to me.

One thing I did learn however was the pleasure of the Egyptian *foule* breakfast – a mess of cooked beans, here served with a poached egg on top! It was the only Egyptian food of note that I remember.

The Alexandria meeting was several days after another meeting in France, so I put in the time between with the most exploration I could muster. I arrived early in Cairo and had the good luck to stay in the Oberoi hotel, part of an Indian chain. It was right next to the pyramids and in the early morning I was able to photograph the camel drivers and guides as the smoke rose from their cooking fires and they prepared the camels for the day's work. I walked the pyramids, climbing a little, through the desert sands right on the edge of the city.

Exploring Cairo, except for the national museum, would have to wait for another day, since I planned to use my time elsewhere. From Canada I had booked with a firm which opened up tourism to Egypt and then throughout the world – Thomas Cook. The taxi took me to a street with dark buildings, and there was the tiny office upstairs on a corner. I was taken aback. Instead of large premises filled with tourists, there was a little upstairs room with but one small clerk-like man in charge and no one else in sight. But he pulled an itinerary and my tickets out of a drawer, and I was on my way for the first of two major excursions.

The flight to the Sinai desert was in a small plane from a small airport. I was the only Sinai bound passenger, the others leaving at a town on the western shore of the Red Sea. Most of the lands we flew over were classic desert.

The little airport was about an hour's drive from Mount Sinai with no other buildings suggesting a settlement. The terrain was already magnificently superb and I felt quite out of place. On either side of the road, which was on a high plain, scores of primeval jagged peaks poked up. They were dry, without snow, showing off their mostly black stone. They were close together, peak after peak, divided by what I learned later were deep chasms – not valleys, not gorges, but deep slits which dropped seemingly miles into the depths. Used to Alps in Europe and Canada I had seen nothing like it. Not only did it take my breath away but it sent shivers down my spine.

The "motel" was across the road from the monastery and peak of Mount Sinai. All the buildings of the motel were made of blocks of stone. The office seemed efficient and elaborate, there was a separate rotunda for meals, and the rooms were in blocks of three or four, each with its desert doorway. Up the road on a hill there was distant camp for back packers who had arrived by road in trucks on what must have been an extraordinary journey.

That night was the coldest I had ever experienced. I was wrapped in layers of thick blankets and there was a small electric heater in the room but I shivered all night and did not sleep. In the morning there was frost outside. I was alone for meals, served off-hand and unmemorable. They did give me foule when I asked for it but with no egg....

The walled monastery was a few minutes across the road, with no path to it. As I walked toward it my eye was struck by the well preserved detritus or the armies which had encamped here over the decades – cigarette packages, chewing gum and the like from British, Israeli and Egyptian soldiers. I took photos of their scattered accumulations, well preserved in the dry desert conditions.

The monastery is in honour of Saint Catherine of Alexandria who transported herself by holy magic from that city to the top of Mount Sinai. But its even greater claim to fame is as the custodian of Moses' burning bush. The little shrub outside the main monastery door is they claim the very same, despite the dispute of scholars who debate whether this is indeed Moses' mount.

The monastery is walled around its buildings and an orchard and vegetable garden, well tended. It is an outdoor place of peace, although I saw very few monks outside and none at work. It has a major and famous library.

You can see the top of the mountain from the plain, with a great cross on top. There is a path, winding along the side of the cliff. Well, I was here and better make the most of it. So off I set.

I said the path was on the side of the mountain cliff. You had better be warned. I mean what I said. Mostly it was wide enough for one set of footsteps. To your *immediate* left was the chasm. Not a valley, not a gorge, a chasm with seemingly no bottom. The view was of black peak after black peak as far as the eye could see. But better to close your eyes.

As a boy I was afraid of heights. One of my most vivid memories was freezing with terror as I descended a scoria pit which was part of a modest hill-mountain in Auckland. But after all I had skied steep descents and I thought I had got over it. And now this.

I persisted step by step leaning toward the mountain side, which is quite the wrong thing to do since it predisposes the body to slide outward. Every now and then, not often enough, the path widened, and at these points others descending from the top were just able to sidle past.

The point arrived where the path was even narrower, one foot before the other. I could not take it. That was it. I turned around perhaps two thirds of the way up, and forced myself not to slip slide as I reached the bottom.

It was Christmas day. A group of Greek nuns had arrived. They chatted amiably in the dining area but I saw them no more. And it was very difficult to persuade the only waiter to get me even one small bite of something to eat. After all it was hardly Café Centrale.

After Alexandria the tickets took me to Luxor. I was quartered in the Mövenpick hotel unfortunately a cab ride away from the city and docks, which was clearly a mistake, based upon my respect for the chain's restaurant in Geneva. I didn't really get to wander the town itself.

Once in the town it was easy enough to cross from the fertile side to the desert side of the Nile. Everywhere one looked there were photographic enticements. I was taken by the brightly painted vendor's huts against the pure brown of the sands. I did my duty by the kings and queens and the great ceremonial buildings and colonnades.

When I came home I started to read, and realized how truly ignorant I was. In later years immersed myself in novels and histories and still have much more to understand. For the first time in my life I began to realise what an enormous debt the western world, and Greek and Roman cultures, owed to Egypt. I have acquired an enormous respect, perhaps exaggerated, for the ancient Egyptian ways of life, and frustration that it is not accorded the same treatment as Greece and Rome in our educational and cultural systems.

The eastern banks of the Nile constitute a different and fascinating world. That is where the desert stops and agriculture and greenery make their marks. I didn't have time. But I wanted to get in there, to move amongst the villagers. I need several more visits which I cannot accomplish. I want to go to the high Nile; I want to experience the life of people as the Nile enters the Mediterranean, I want to see what village life is like beside the Upper Nile. Another lifetime of inspiration.

My last night was banality itself. It was New Year's Eve. The hotel put on a communal dinner where we all sat at long tables. There was music for dancing.

The crowd consisted of, literally, bored continentals. We didn't know each other and at my table there was no conversation, but several couples who seemed totally bored with each other. Very few danced. I tried but could not force conversation. I went to bed before the midnight hour.

At the other enc of the Mediterranean, at a different time, on the Spanish shore we bought a ticket to Tangier from Algeciras in Spain. It was close to another New Year. To embark the next morning we found ourselves in a massive line-up of Moroccans moving from various parts of Europe for the holidays. The ship itself was close to being overcrowded and we seemed to be the only non-Africans.

In Tangier itself we walked the streets near the port and explored lanes between small but neat Mediterranean style houses and eventually found ourselves on the main boulevard replete with cafes and *men* gossiping over coffee.

Near the embarkation jetty there was a large open space. As we walked through it to return to the ship a suited young man approached us and said "The boat is cancelled. But I can take you in my taxi to Ceuta" (some distance down the coast). My teen age companion immediately took him on. "Do you think we are fools….. You are lying….. You just want our money."

The driver did not rise to the bait but said quite calmly "Very well, come to the ferry office and you will see that I am right." We did so. He was right. The winds had risen and the Straights of Gibraltar were unsafe for the passage.

"No I won't take you to Ceuta" the driver said "The winds will probably be just as high there and the Ceuta ferry will be cancelled too."

So to the chagrin of my companion we found a hotel and caught the ferry next day.

That was my first taste of Morocco.

The next time I flew from Madrid to Marrakech, wishing I had time to visit the great desert towns. Although the city had been a favourite of Winston Churchill who stayed and painted in a luxury old style hotel, possibly the only one in the city at that time, Marrakech was just starting on what would become a major tourist boom. There were several European hotels within walking distance of the main square, but nowhere near the volume of visitors which exists nowadays.

The main square was a source of continuous action and attraction, with jugglers, fortune tellers, and a highly popular story teller squatting in the middle surrounded by a group of intense listeners. I took mint tea in one of the nearby cafes, and fell in love with the drink, made in a way that I can never duplicate.

Just off the square is the vast *souk*. I wandered among the shaded stalls as the vendors hawked their wares and bought a large thin Bedouin carpet simply decorated in black and white, which I folded up and carried with me for the rest of this trip to other parts of Africa and Asia. It was full of sand, and though I used it at home it took years of use and a couple of dry cleanings (fortunately safe) before the reminder of desert encampments was erased.

The one and only *Current Anthropology* associate had an address I could not make out. But the taxi driver could. We went to the far end of the traditional city and entered a lane through an old entrance. The lane was full of pedestrians and children and was wide enough for one vehicle only – without one way signs. The driver manoeuvred skilfully and we did not meet another vehicle, except donkey carts, before he deposited me at my colleague's home. Inside we sat on a carpet and drank tea while we talked.

Afterwards I was able to find my way out without need of a driver and walked the streets with richer and more modern houses set in tropical gardens. The streets were wide and on the footpaths there was a scattering of young men and women, in the high teens, walking slowly, heads down over open books. They were students cramming for exams, scanning the texts to drum the words into their brains, presumably because the technique of education involved rote learning.

I also found a meet market, roofed but otherwise in open air. Carcases hung from hooks, flies abounded, and bourgeois women chose their cuts. I saw no sign of refrigeration. What happened to unsold meat? Was it *halal?* I do not know.

By the time I reached home I was ready for a swim in the hotel pool.

37. Quintana Roo

Quintana Roo, as a phrase, probably doesn't mean much to you. The Yucatan Peninsula probably means just a little more. Cancun is that place in the sun that is touted as Mexico's greatest shopping spree, the centre of the best scuba diving in the world, the resort you are planning to go to some day. They are all linked together.

The Yucatan Peninsula of Mexico has a line drawn through it, more or less NE to SW. On the north western side is the State of Yucatan, it s capital being the old Spanish-colonial city of Merida, its most famous archaeological site Chichen Itza, where the Toltec observatory and pyramid do fabulous tricks at the equinoxes and solstices, attracting visitors such as circus performances.

The indigenous people, and majority population, of Yucatan are Mayan (the Toltecs conquered them and were rulers for a time until the Spaniards put them in their place.)

On the south eastern side of the line is the State of Quintana Roo, which contains the magnificent Mexican Caribbean coastline, with its resorts, beaches, endangered reefs, environmental parks and non-Toltec ruins, each in competition, mostly destructive. Quintana Roo has only been a state since 1974. The people of Q.R. are Mayan too, but Mayan with a difference. They have been, and in some respects still are, separatists. Like the Indians of British Columbia, Canada, they do not consider themselves to have been legitimately conquered; but they lack the means to make an independence stick.

To understand this, you must know a few things. Most of them do not even have Quintana Roo in the index. Books on the history of Mexico give chapters to the wars and the twentieth century revolution; and the works of Presidents constitute the organizing themes, like the works of Renaissance princes (who did a lot better). But the Mayans of Q.R.? Usually zilch. Mexico would rather forget, it seems.

Yet.

The Spaniards made their influence felt, I won't say dominant, from the very earliest years, from the sea. The first Spanish explorers were scared stiff at what they saw, sailing past the coastal fortress and religious city of Tulum, afraid of its extensive population. For years after some of the coastal islands became playgrounds of Caribbean pirates. Eventually, by persistent efforts, the Spaniards prevailed, on the surface. From time to time they were faced with Mayan armed protest, sometimes small, sometimes massive, not only in Quintana Roo, but in Chiapas and Yucatan also.

In the middle of the nineteenth century, from 1847 to 1901, when their leader Santa Cruz de Bravo was captured and executed in the mystically famous town of the Talking Crosses, Chan Santa Cruz, the Mayans were in full fledged politico-religious revolt, known as the war of the castes. That was a long long time to be omitted from the history books. And long after the death of Santa Cruz there were forceful and psychological resistances in Quintana Roo. In all parts of Mayan country there are major examples of continuing religious syncretism, many with significant political overtones.

But then even by comparison with other states, to Mexico Quintana Roo and its Mayans were marginal.

There wasn't much of an economy -- a little fishing, and great copra estates on the coast. For the rest, the Mayans were, and to some extent still are, hidden in the forests of the great limestone plain.

Once the revolt was officially quashed, the Mexicans didn't quite know what to do. They named Quintana Roo, not after a geographical or ethnic entity, but after a nineteenth century leader who was on the side of joining the Mexican State. The name continues to rankle among some. They gave Chan Santa Cruz the new name of Felipe Carrillo Puerto after a Mexican Revolutionary Governor, and made sure eventually that the streets of new towns honoured national Mexican patriots and archaeological sites, rather than Mayan heroes. They recognized that the Mayans of Q.R. were less tractable than those of Yucatan, within whose boundaries the territory formally lay at that time, or at least they were less overlaid by Spanish-Mexican power -- sporadic revolts were still going on. The solution was to newly create the present boundaries and establish a political Territory, directly ruled from Mexico City.

It didn't work. The period is an embarrassment to officials and politicians. All I know, and of all things it comes from the text attached to a poorly drawn map of the area, is that in 1913 Q.R. was attached to Yucatan, in 1931 it was moved into the State of Campeche, and in 1935 after only four years it became a federal Territory again -- until 1974. That does not sound like an easy-going peaceful kind of place.

If you cull the guide books carefully you occasionally get other snippets of information. You learn that much of the resistance was centred on the archaeological sites of Tulum and Cobal, and that Mayans still hold Tulum in religious awe, using it for ritual. In Tulum there is some continuity.

Cobal is different. It was built by people with Guatemalan roots, then mysteriously abandoned, and only re-occupied by Mayans late in the nineteenth century, Mayans who had lost contact with it and who, as it were, began all over again. Although, probably because it was in an isolated inland situation, it became a resistance headquarters, its religious significance had to be re-invented. Today local people use it for Christian based worship, re-naming one of the most easily accessible pyramids "La Iglesia".

It does not take an anthropologist long to imagine and hypothesize the existence of significant messianic elements in the resistance, and quite possibly in some Mayan thought now.

I had a couple months in Cancun in the early 'nineties, expecting little more than beaches, sun and tourists. But I came across rather more.

I will get to the food. If you are a tourist going to Cancun, what you as a consumer find by way of food will be influenced by the hidden history of the people who serve you in the hotels, drive your taxis, cook your meals, clean your rooms. Those who teach you scuba diving, comment on the tour buses, sell you condominiums, are more likely to be from Merida or Mexico. The population of Q.R. is being overlaid by national immigration. Mayan food, even that from Yucatan, is being hidden too. I wondered why?

Mexico, like France, despite talk of regional autonomy in both places, and despite the overt importance of Indian culture in that of the country, is a highly centralized state. As such it is in a continuous dialectic with a troublesome multiculturalism to which the political system has not fully accommodated. There is no university as yet in Q.R., no institution of higher learning, and the policies of research institutions such as those that deal with archaeology or museums are dictated from head offices in Mexico.

For most of its life the economy of Q.R. could be left in peace to muddle along in happy Caribbean fashion, supported by smuggling and tax free privileges in the capital of Chetumal, far to the south, on the Belize border. But the time arrived, in the '70s, when that could go on no longer. The copra industry was totally destroyed by the fall in world prices, world over-supply, and food-oil and soap-oil substitutes. Apart from fishing, there was nothing else. The people knew of greater wealth elsewhere. The place, despite minimal social services, was a drain on the central government. Something had to be done.

As in so many poverty stricken resource poor countries there was one answer. Tourism. Only the Club Med had discovered Quintana Roo, its unspoiled beaches and reefs. France was showing the way -- those magnificent built from scratch resorts along the Mediterranean coast. The Mexicans tried something similar.

Aided by computer analysis, the Mexican Government decreed the establishment of a world class resort at Cancun, centred on an island to be linked by small bridges to the mainland and to have a major airport. It cannot be a coincidence that the establishment of the State and the opening of the first resort hotel both took place in 1974. By that time the essential decisions had been taken and the infrastructure put in place. *After* statehood, the people would have a *fait accompli*. Since the huge development, with over two hundred hotels established in Cancun itself in sixteen years, would act as an enormous pole of attraction, it would pull in thousands of workers from the neighbouring districts, and *managers from Mexico*, not so subtly altering the political as well as the economic balance. New hotels are still being constructed, and the beaches all down the coast, as well as on the islands of Isla

Mujeres and Cozumel, are being occupied. It is very difficult, until you get quite a long way south, to find a piece of beach that is not claimed by some development; and then, even in the south, it is one end to end line of garbage. Only in the hotel areas is litter, partially, under control.

So what do you, my dear consumer of sun and sand, do with all this? If you are adventurous, knowledgeable, and lucky, and probably independent minded, you can explore what is left of nature before it goes. You can go off shore to scuba dive in and out of the boats that take you there. You can go south and inland into the reserved forests and take your time to explore the flora and the fauna. There is magnificent bird life, if you know where to look for it. You may be lucky, as I was, even without that knowledge, and see a troop of thirty ant-eaters scuttle in ones and twos across an isolated road. You will have difficulty camping on your own resources because of the high lime content and rarity of water supplies that characterize this huge once-underwater reef that constitutes Quintana Roo. If you are well-heeled you might try deep sea fishing.

The chances are you are not like that. If you come off the huge jets that land many times a day, you are here for a week, maybe two, of living it up. The hotels will help indeed. With a very few exceptions, their buildings and pools are Americanized blah, one hotel much like another, and almost all American owned. (A few Spanish and Mexican.)

But they compete to provide good restaurants with "international" food, and around and about you will find Mexican food designed for the overseas palate, even a little Mexican *nouvelle cuisine*, a bit of maybe Brasilian or Thai, quite a bit of Spanish. You will find McDonald's, Denny's (Mexican zed somewhat and with a bar, for gosh sakes'), Soft Rock Cafe, lots of Tex-Mex places catering to the world of the U.S. young, Pizza Hut, Señor Frog's. And outside there are taxis with drivers panting for your custom -- and line-ups to get into the chain restaurants.

You might say, why come to Mexico for that? From this point of view there is not a thing here that you cannot get as well in Miami, Honolulu, or, better, in its French versions like La Grande Motte. So, soak up the sun, visit the magnificent walled site of Tulum if you can push past the other fifty tour buses (yes, I counted them) to enter the crowded cattle pen, and go home.

You might of course rent an apartment and a car to be a little more independent. You have heard about the cheapness of Mexico, so why not? You could in my time find beautiful apartments at $200 a night, and Volkswagen Beetles and the like for $1200 a month. Yes. That is if you booked from abroad. To do otherwise takes the time of searching around and bargaining like crazy. And if you are stuck on American food you find it alright and pay enormous prices in specialty supermarkets.

Pay in advance can be the key. After all they then have the use of your money. When I went to an international car company to bargain I used a local advertisement which said $19.50 a day -- instead of $40 -- for a Beetle. Sorry, they said, that is only a promotion if you are staying in such and such a hotel (the ad didn't say that) -- and you must pay 17 cents a kilometre as well. A bit more persistence, some pro forma discussion with head office at the airport. O.K., tell you what. We give you a nice Beetle. It's waiting for you. Two months. 10,000 kilometres a month free. Good deal? $20 a day. But you pay one month cash now. Second month you can pay credit card. OK? OK.

Later I found deals could have been struck without the monthly ploy. And all around the hotel zone there were the little car hire firms that had touts offering cars for $15 a day, unlimited mileage. Indeed the touts accosted you on the streets, much like sex offering touts in Bangkok.

Outside the hotel zone, on the mainland, is the large attractive city of Cancun itself, population 650,000 according to brochures, known as Cancun town in the local *patois*. It has large boulevards, parks, many fine hotels that have much more character than most of those in the tourist hotel zone, often in quiet suburban streets. It has a main drag called Avenida Tulum, with six lanes of traffic neatly separated by great bird-filled trees, even pedestrian crosswalks that really work -- and a couple of other main streets, that are full of what the tourist imagines as Mexican restaurants -- and boutiques. Many of the restaurants are open to the air, full of action, touts calling you in, menus full of lobster and steak, huge breakfasts, mariachis, everything for a holiday. There are side streets off Tulum Boulevard where you find even more restaurants, with names like El Pirata or La Bucañero. Sometimes you can get really fresh fish. There's an Italian restaurant where you can get *tiramisu* made with rum, and some very fancy hacienda type places with beautiful sculpture and fountains, and international food (Mexican, Spanish, French, Japanese, Italian). The ambience is often smart and romantic, and in the hotel zone the vistas of sea and light can be romantically reflective.

But I was, alas, not looking for romance. I wanted unusual food. I did not spend my time trying to determine whether the Italian was as good as in Rome or the Spanish as in Madrid. Why come to Cancun for international food? You are in Mexico, and not just Mexico, you are in the midst of Yucatecan Maya culture. Don't they have food?

So I searched for it, and found it. It is not your North American Mexican, or even national Mexican, food. You will find some reference to some Yucatecan dishes in Mexican cook books, but, for example, one very good one that I have, written and published in Mexico, gives only three in the whole book. Ortiz identifies some dishes as Yucatecan or Mayan in her cookbooks on Latin America and on Mexico; the otherwise excellent book by Diana Kennedy hardly at all (although both books refer to dishes such as *muc-pil* chicken, *ixni-pec* sauce, fish in *mac-cum*, which I was unable to find anywhere in Quintana Roo, though they are probably available in Merida).

As with politics, Cancun offers a food conspiracy of near silence. The tour guides didn't feature it, and there was only one Yucatecan restaurant, Los Almendros, in the whole complex that was somewhat known in the tourist advertising world. Yet, if I may say so, it is damn good cooking, with often beautifully subtle sauces, different herbs, and lots of fun.

I cannot pretend to know what there is to know about this extraordinarily rich kind of food. In the first place I don't know Spanish, and many of my conversations had to be in pidgin Spanish or sign language. Still, it is remarkable what can be communicated sometimes. Further, many of the words used are peculiar to Mexico, and still more, limited to the Yucatan. They do not appear in Spanish dictionaries. (Another complaint: Spanish dictionaries are often poor on Mexicanismos, and all dictionaries are poor on food terms.)

Hence if you come to Cancun and look for Yucatecan food, treat this as an opening chapter, a place from which to depart (especially since there will have been many changes in the subsequent years), the beginning of a world of exploration, to mix the metaphors. You will go further than I did, and be quite content as a result. Ignore all that stuff in the hotels, except perhaps for the odd dinner -- or, better, to find ways in which the hotel chefs incorporate Mexicanisms into *nouvelle cuisine*. A very few do it, and there is an annual gastronomic festival in which they show what they can do -- rarely, though, incorporated into standard menus.

You notice I said Yucatecan food. It would be too subtle to distinguish Quintana Roo from the totality of Yucatan. What we mean here is Mayan food, as presented to the mostly Mayan public in restaurants and taco stalls. It does not necessarily correspond to what you would get in a Mayan home, but it is closely linked. (For example, you might find venison in Mayan homes, but you can't find it in Cancun eating places.) And the best restaurants for this kind of cooking -- and for many other Mexican kinds -- are to be found, so I am told, in Merida, not here. And what is very special to Quintana Roo is the seafood, of which more later. And I must of course try out some Mexican restaurants along the way, to notice the differences, and see what *nouvelle cuisine* can do with it.

But I am a consumer's representative, so off I go consuming, to see what I can find. Let it come as it may.

How to start? In the tourist brochures there are passing references to Yucatecan food, and sometimes you notice the word *Yucateca*, or something like it, attached to a menu item. But, with the possible exception of Los Almendros, one of a Merida based chain, none of the restaurants I eventually found figure in the listings. Nowhere in any of the tourist literature did I find "a visitor's guide to Yucatecan, or Mayan food". Like the Mayans in politics, it was hidden from foreign sight, except when it was transformed, as I shall show, into tourist food. Yet it is there. It has to be. The bulk of the population is Mayan.

So you ask.

One natural bias of many informants is to confuse ambience with good food. They want you to have a good time, an interesting one. So several people put me onto La Prosperidad de Cancun.

Thus I drove out along the Avenida Jose Lopez Portillo, a resounding political name of a street that would, if you let it, take you hundreds of kilometres to Chichen Itza and Merida, almost in a straight flat line. I reached the darkness at the end of the city and turned back on myself. Not far there was a brightly lit modern inn, crowded with parked cars, lively music flooding onto the street. I screwed up my social courage and went in.

The ambience reminded me of a Mexican version of a North American beer parlour, except that at the checkered covered tables there were a few families with children. In the centre of the double room a band was revving up. A mature happy looking woman put me down at a table where the stage was inescapable. An older waiter with no English took an order for tequila. On the table was a form menu with a few items price listed. Very few struck me as having anything specially to do with Yucatan -- perhaps the *cochinita* (suckling pig) were *pibil* (roasted with a marinade in the ground or its equivalent), but that was not indicated, and at $30 who was going to find out? There was *poc-chuc*, a kind of mixed grill, and *longaniza,* a spicy sausage, but no prices, so not available. The rest, though probably good, were entirely Mexican -- *flautas de mole*, *cabrito Norteña, res de carne tampiquena.*

The band got to work with a handsome lead singer, and a chorus of young skimpy ladies cavorting in limited salsa movements, occasionally taking over the microphone with not bad voices, sometimes calling up a man to strut around licentiously, but all in all very innocent. The families had left, and most of the audience were men.

A young waiter helpfully practised his English on me. Sorry but the food service stopped half an hour ago -- at 6 pm. He saw my discomfiture, brought me another tequila. All of a sudden three plates were put in front of me with a huge basket of tortillas. Hard boiled eggs (three) with *mole* sauce; something that seemed like spiced ground beef with a few carrots; something that seemed like ground pork with garbanzo beans. It was cold but tastily edible, and it was very thoughtful of them. I like those surprises, which tell me that people are thoughtful and kind -- I was very hungry. And it's one way of getting interesting food, though it may not be what you came for.

And, though I didn't stay any more for the tinselled dancers, they charged me only for the tequila.

Another, less pleasant, way of getting misled, is through the touts who are the curse of the area. They do not push their wares in front of your nose with pressing "bargains" as in the *souks* of the Muslim world. They stand outside their offices asking you to come in to look over the specs of a condominium for sale, or to hear about a special tour, to get a car at a cut price. Or they flash menus from the restaurants and offer discounts and all the booze you can drink in a night for free. They don't bother you if you just walk past. What amazed me was the high proportion of tourists who allowed themselves to be drawn into fruitless conversation -- fruitless because what the touts had to offer was not in the priority zone of their hoped-for clients.

One day I was outside the Federal Express office waiting for it to open so that I could collect mail. When it was being regular it opened about half an hour after the posted morning and afternoon times. Sometimes as in this case it was irregular and you either give up or waited patiently for an hour or so. Today was one of the latter occasions, which gave a tout from the next door tourist office a chance to talk to me, and tell me about Federal Express - and restaurants.

He heard I was interested in Yucatecan food. Well, he said, it so happens........ The upshot was that he gave me a voucher for a free lunch at a hotel where he said the buffet featured Yucatecan specialties. My part of the bargain would be to meet him there and he would show me the hotel and get a commission. Fair enough, because quite often (but not it seems in Cancun) hotels in exotic places do a great deal to show-case indigenous food, and prepare them in ways that retain their qualities but make them appeal to visitors -- witness the marvellous activities of the InterContinental's in francophone West Africa, and hotels in Mauritius and Fiji and Kenya. Furthermore my new found friend, for I was beginning to think of him as that, rattled off in a most impressive way the ingredients and herbs in several Yucatecan dishes. He knew the subject, and I fantasized I would invite him here and there to assist my explorations.

So off I went to the rendezvous. The lobby was crowded with U.S. jocks and their girl friends, eyes glued to basketball game on a huge TV monitor. The steps were filled with baggage, and young people disconsolately waiting for tour buses to take them to the airport and home. This was U.S. Spring Break, the beginning of weeks of beer drinking, hoopla, beach parties, and, if you are in the wrong place, rape.

No sign of Andre. Twenty minutes later still no sign. I went to the restaurant, showed my voucher, checked the buffet -- standard blah, wilted salads, heavy desserts, cold cuts. I said to the manager I would like your Yucatecan specials, because I hear they are very good. Yucatecan specials? Sometimes we have Mexican but never Yucatecan....

Next day I sought out my friend. Where were you? he said as he rushed to meet me. In the lobby. I couldn't find you. Did you have your lunch? No, there's never been any Yucatecan food there. Oh, did you hand in your voucher? Of course not. Are you sure, didn't the manager take it? Certainly not. His face fell. End of commission. He was not at all interested in whether my need for Yucatecan food was fulfilled -- his only concern being that I turned up, handed in the voucher, and made him eligible for his payoff.

By that time I had started on other leads, and was making progress, adding a few observations of my own as I drove the streets. Here is a list, without which you can do no wrong, believe me, if they are still in operation. I am not a tout. I have no vested interest. Even with this list you will have to explore on your own because times have changed.

The one that will be mentioned to you by almost anyone you ask (though I did hear one lady criticize it), is called Los Almendros (Almonds) on the peripheral street called Avenida Bonompak -- right opposite the stadium that serves as the bull fighting arena. It even gets into the tourist brochures occasionally.

I'll It is a big place in two brightly clothed rooms, adopting the style of Mexican restaurants that show the process of cooking with the kitchen before your eyes. Except that here much of what goes on is behind glass and invisible, the visible part consisting of hot trays with finished results being kept warm. Los Almendros is part of a formula chain based in Merida, and though it is streets away from such places as Denny's, the formula influence prevails. So the food in the trays does tend to dry out, and many of the dishes suffer as a result.

The sauces were, however, a taste bud opener. Soft, spicy where required, complex in their tastes, but their tastes always available to the palate, truly worthy of great international cooking.

Another interesting place was also tucked away a bit, on the corner of the great Avenida Uxmal, where it narrows into a small street, and joins Avenida Jose Lopez Portillo. The first time I went to Los Venados (venados = deer) I was out of luck. Like many of the "people's" restaurants, it shut down firmly at 6.30 (opening toward mid-day). This taught me to watch it, reminding me that Cancun is full of the oddest eating hours to the city Westerner[29]. Some of the fancy restaurants in the hotels have two "sittings", one for the North American early birds around 5 or 6, the other around 9 for the Spaniards, bourgeois Mexicans, and other assorted Europeans. Restaurants in the old town can have lineups from mid afternoon into the late evening; tacos bars, unless dealing with things like late movie goers, go for the lunch time jugular, and can shut as darkness comes. And some of the American style or little tacos places are open twenty-four hours (with varying degrees of alertness.....)

The second time the visit was better. Self-conscious for arriving around five, I was confronted with a small smiling woman who rattled off a list of dishes in the fastest impossible to follow Spanish with a Mayan accent (even Mexicans find Mayan Spanish hard to follow). I grabbed hold of one word I heard and had it -- succulent, large spicy meatballs. No booze. No credit cards.

The room was "typical", that is compromised not one whit to tourism. The ladies were in their normal dress, which means beautifully embroidered garments as you would see in a village, kerchiefs, and smiles. They could not be bothered helping you if you were having language difficulty -- except for the large ebullient manageress who spent most of her time watching TV. In one corner was an old bent lady busily making tortillas by hand, the guarantee for which was her finger marks on what you received. And excellent they were.

---

[29] The hours are reminiscent of asy eighteenth century Britain, with a midday or early main meal followed latter by a supper, controlled by the needs of a rural life.

The third time I came I made the waitress give me her words one by one, and wrote them down. That time I made a more careful selection. And then I noticed as I went to photograph the tortilla maker that there was actually a chalk written menu board. But by 5 p.m. most of the items were no longer available.

Then, more or less by accident, I came across an empty looking quite modern simple cafe style place at the magnificently strategic corner of Avenida Tulum and Avenida Cobal. I'd passed it many a time but did not think it had much to offer. But by then I'd started to get into Yucatecan snacks, and I noticed its name, Antojitos Yucatecos, i.e., guess what, Yucatecan Snacks.

So I went in. And was very glad. Simple indeed, with a little lady and a couple of helpers doing the work, not too many people, tourists going by but passing because there was no tout and no mariachi band and no Mexican stuff like *fajitas*. It may not be the greatest cooking in the world, but if you want to know what Yucatecan cooking is like, for next to nothing by way of cash, and with friendly people who may not be able to talk to you much, but who are totally willing to give you what you convey to them you want, this was it. Tops in my book. Without any fussing, they broke up the dishes as described on the menu, and allowed me to taste, say, three delectable mouth watering yummies I'd never had before, instead of being held to one plate of three of the same.

Three seafood places figure on my list.

I would never have found La Calamar had it not been for a lady behind one of the desks at Cancun Tips. It was away from every boulevard and side restaurant street, not far from Avenida Uxmal. Like any really local place, it too closes down the kitchen at 6.45. My first time I arrived at 6.30 but they served me with grace anyway.

It looked simple inside, neat but unpretentious. The proprietor was a fisherman who began here fifteen years before my visit. On the walls were photographs of every celebrity in Mexico, all in the company of the owner. It is nationally famous, and unknown to the tourist. The food was exquisitely prepared and of the most evident, refreshing freshness you could imagine. You know how cold raw fish can tell your palate straight away that there's been no monkeying around; and you know that that quality can survive cooking and marinating if the skills are there. It may be the owner is sitting with his back to you with a group of friends; it may be that only one of the waiters can communicate, but graciously; it may be this is not the place for gringos really; it may be that vegetables can be banal; but it is the place for beautiful fish and its sauces.

Another place also recommended in the same way, but which I did have on my list, was Los Flamingos, almost at the end of the eight kilometre or so drive, between the Isla Mujeres ferries at Puerto Juarez and Punta Sam. (There were several promising fish restaurants along this stretch of road, some of them very simple, but reputedly worth the drive).

Los Flamingos was big and bouncy, well patronized by Mexicans and tourists alike, some chic, mostly just there for the food. There was a great maritimely decorated banquet hall, an open style dining room and a verandah that jutted onto the beach facing Isla Mujeres. The waiters were busy and ignored me as I chose a table. After a suitable period of suspense, one brought me a menu.

Total disappointment. Nothing but your ordinary "fish as you like it", lobster, garlic or *meuniére*. I showed my disappointment and again was rescued by a young junior waiter wanting to play with a little English. "There's another menu," he said, "It's got more on it." Marginally, it did have, and at least gave me a chance to go further with

Yucatecan styles. It was a fashionable place for Cancun family and group Sunday outings.

The third place I found accidentally, named after the island of Contoy at the northern tip of the Peninsula, a name that was hidden from me by various awnings and decorations. It is in a part of town tucked between the junction of two Avenidas, Uxmal and Chichen Itza, only a few yards from each, yet an island of local activity where the tourist is as rare as jaguars in Mexico City. The area is known as Mercado 23, and consists mostly of small covered shops selling everything from shoes and clothes and hardware to vegetables, spices, poultry, meats, fish, shellfish.

I had come there in search of a Mexican popular (in the sense of "people's") restaurant called La Flor de Hidalgo, of which more later. It was shut, so I was walking disconsolately around, and noticed Contoy at the end of a street. It advertised *mariscos* (shellfish) from the island, and a notice board listed some unusual lunchtime tacos that I did not get a chance to explore. It was a simple place, decorated with fishnets and models of tuna and swordfish, people dropping in for real meals, discussing and enjoying their food. The payoff, as I enjoyed my meal, was a waiter who, though having no English and me little Spanish, took great pains to tell me what was what, what the chillies were, and the herbs, with no reticence and much care.

One of the first and best, for food, I found driving back into Cancun from the south along Avenida Kukulkan before it becomes the hotel zone. A sign on the seaward side said Restaurant Rio Nizuc - *Cooperativa -- Pescados y Mariscos*. So I drove off the road down a pot-holed track and found a small group of parked cars. A few yards further was the bank of a river or estuary joining the inside lagoon to the sea, with a highway bridge over it. A boardwalk led me along the side of the estuary toward the sea, with flamingos and pelicans and frigate birds. It was a Sunday. Local families were coming back carrying picnic gear, and some food wrapped in tin foil. I wondered if, at five o'clock, I was already too late, or even that I'd missed the restaurant entirely.

In the end, there it was, a small kitchen building with a large thatch out-jutting roof, a few iron chairs and tables roughly set out underneath, families outside and on the tiny isolated beach. You would not have known that the next habitation along the coast was the famous Club Med...... Rough direct service, beer from the bottle with a paper napkin around the top to indicate hygiene, no menu. With some difficulty, a waiter was found with a few words of English, "Good grilled fish...." It was the best *ceviche* of shellfish and fish I had anywhere, and as for the *tikin zic*, wait until I describe it. I had to come again with my friend Jaime Rubio to sample it, the small sward covered with eating and picnicking families, Mexican, Mayan, and some tourists off the beaten track.

There are of course innumerable seafood restaurants around town, serving excellently fresh produce, well cooked, and worth your visit if seafood is what you like. But very few indeed made any attempt to present Mexican, let alone Yucatecan, versions. An extremely popular place, which could have line-ups from four in the afternoon, was Il Pescador, off Avenida Tulum. It was unpretentious with a highly charged crowded atmosphere, with nothing Yucatecan. Less excusable was the Hyatt Hotel's Seafood Market, a pleasant open air casual place with a chef who was a member of the *Chaine de Rôtisseurs* and made a show of presenting his "regional adviser". All the fish was on display, fresh and sparkling from the sea. Just about the only sauce you could get was *meuniére*, and there wasn't a trace of such things as chilli, *achiote*, or Mayan *rellenos* (stuffing's). You'd think an ambitious chef could do better than that. Perhaps he was not ambitious. The attitude was perfectly summed up by the words of the *Maître d'*, totally taken aback by my observation -- "But, sir, we don't have Mayans here....." On the other hand, to be fair, the Bucañero has one dish called Yucatecan, cooked with *achiote*. I didn't try it, but in view of my experience with the Stelae restaurant in a similar matter, I have my grave doubts (see below).

From this I think you may gather, correctly, that top flight genuine Yucatecan food was not to be found in the fancy highly be-sculptured tourist restaurants. There were some Yucatecan dishes in such places, and in the tourist places of less pretention, such as Garibaldi or Mexicana or even Bellini, and several seafood restaurants offered the passing dish with a Yucatecan base. Nearly all such places did what Americans do with it -- they destroy the unique and special qualities, beginning of course with the chillies. They try to link it with something you know, or know about, turning Veracruzana sauce into a variety of *ratatouille* or spaghetti sauce, totally losing its character. What an enormous pity.

Even the Mexican restaurants will do that, if you don't watch out. They aim to please, not to educate. After all, that is where the money seems to be. Alas.

It is time to move away from the locations, to see what emerges when the product appears. What can a tourist like myself find for Yucatecan food?

First some *mea culpae*. In two months I cannot be an authority, and don't intend to become one. I can tell you what I found. The boundaries between Mexican and Yucatecan are not firm, and I am not setting up artificial ones. What I discovered was in and around Cancun; not in Merida, where it would be possible to find foods totally missing here. I am not always sure that what I tell you about is Yucatecan in the indigenous sense, or Yucatecan in the sense that the country is now part of Mexico, writ large. It is not *comida casera*, home cooking, except perhaps for one or two *antojitos* and perhaps for Los Venados. But I am sure that is it what you will find, and that if you persist you will find many other fascinating things as well.

As everywhere in Mexico the basis of eating lies with the tortillas, served as part of the dish itself, or on the side like our bread. Sometimes, because of the deep influence of bakeries of French origin (going back into history) you will find *bollitos*, hard rolls, or even French bread.

Here as elsewhere, corn tortillas are the thing, and handmade at that. Except at Los Venados, do you think that's what I was eating? Wrong. And in fact I did not once have corn incorporated into my main food, except when I had a light pork soup with salad floating on it at the home of Jaime Rubio. No wonder, especially with free trade and cheap imported corn on the horizon, the Mexican government, with an eye to voting patterns, is afraid for its peasant corn farmers.

Not once did I see corn tortillas on sale in any supermarket, as is possible in New Mexico or Vancouver. They were all factory made wheat tortillas (*de tinga*). In one or two places you could also get pita bread, *calle pan arabe*. (There is a long standing Lebanese influence in this part of the world). Residents tell me that if they want corn tortillas they either make them themselves, or buy them fresh in the outdoor markets early each morning and put them in the refrigerator.

The variety of things that can emerge from tortillas is legion, and totally confusing, since the same word can mean different things in different parts of Hispanic America, or even within Mexico; and nowadays tortilla based snacks are competing with various kinds of bread sandwiches. Given the nature of competition and public presentation, words are also deliberately made ambiguous so that customers may be seduced, and there is a certain amount of slippage because of the nature of a transliteration. Thus *bollitos* are hard crusted French rolls, but *bollitos* are also sandwiches, like anywhere in the world, with any kind of filling, made of French style wheat round buns. These are sometimes called *tortas* on the road sign of the snack bar, but *tortas* is also a word reserved for sandwiches made from lengths of French baguettes, very popular indeed.

We are sliding into the world of *antojitos*, loosely translatable as snacks or *hors d'oeuvres*, one of the most marvellous and rewarding elements in Mexican, and Mayan, cooking. The French influence has, for centuries and even before the French imposed the Mexican Empire on the people for a few short years, dominated baking, apart from tortillas. Since the Spanish influence has been even greater, and was responsible for the introduction of a range of food products that was at least the equal to the indigenous, it is extraordinary that one of the most typical Spanish institutions is totally unknown -- *tapas* and the *tapas* bar. Whenever I raised the subject I got blank looks, even among many sophisticated Mexicans -- what are *tapas*? Until I learned that *cantinas* in Mexico City are full of such things, under the name of *botas*, where you go to eat inventive nibbles as much as you do to drink. But not in Yucatan.... (I did see some places mentioning *botas* on their signs, but they were simply *tacos* and *enchiladas* and so on and had none of the required inventive delicacy.)

But the Mayans have something that almost takes its place, the *antojitos*. As with pita bread or a pizza you can load anything you like onto a tortilla. The tortilla can be small or large, thick or thin, crepe like or doughy, flat or rolled, sandwiched, toasted, lightly fried in oil or fat, deep-fried to become crisp. The only version I didn't find here were the puff-balled *sopapillas* of Santa Fe. Nor did I come across any of them served with honey, though that must surely happen, since bee-keeping and honey are so important locally.

The simplest forms, loaded with food like an open-faced sandwich, are the *tacos*, with their derivatives that give rise to a host of names, sometimes based on the shape and material of the taco, sometimes based on the filling. The vocabulary has some similarity to that of pasta.

An anthropologist, José N. Iturriaga, has written a marvellous little book which is both an ethnography and cook's guide "*De Tacos, Tamales y Tortas*" as presented in roadside stands and cafes throughout the country, with literally scores of descriptions. There are a few special sections on Yucatan, but not specially Quintana Roo. Needless to say, some of the fillings he mentions I didn't come across -- such as those made with turkey and black sauce, or with venison sausage -- others I mention he didn't catch up on, since the possibilities are infinite.

The first local *taco* I had was at a simple stand by the ferry terminal at Punta Sam. The *tacos* were loaded with *chicharrones*, dried pork rinds, broken onto thin tortillas, with chopped onion, cilantro leaves, red bell pepper dices, slice of avocado. Since there are no implements bar a paper napkin, you fold the tortilla over by yourself and eat hamburger style. The stand's salsa on the side was excellently strong and pungent with roasted habaneras chilies that made all the difference, onion and cilantro. You can usually depend on simple cafe and road stand salsas much more certainly than restaurant ones, which are toned down for the tourist and often have less flavourful chilies. And often the food depends entirely on the fact that you will be using a salsa, so if one is not evident, don't hesitate to ask. It will always come, even at a place like Bellini in a shopping mall, designed for tourist relaxation -- it takes the cook just seconds to put it together.

Usually *tacos* at a stand will consist of something like those called *salbutes,* fried on a hot plate, loaded with chicken strips, salad, tomato, maybe a slice of avocado, cilantro or mint. At Antojitos Yucatecos the tortilla was made from *masa de mais,* literally a lump of corn dough, and raw onion was more prominent, without the avocado. Ortiz' Latin American book has recipes under the name *sambutes*.

Antojitos Yucatecos was in fact a marvellous place to get a run through of many of the different ideas. One of my most total favourites consisted of *papadzules*. These are typically Yucatecan. At Antojitos Yucatecos they consisted of soft rolled tortillas containing chopped hard-boiled egg, covered with pumpkin seeds and a *salsa ranchera* and scattered with egg again. At Los Venados they were very much larger, with invisible pepper inside as well as the egg. They were covered this time with cream and a little tomato salsa, unchili'd. At Los Almendros the pumpkin seed was turned into a green salsa which underlies the egg, with the tomato salsa and additional scattered egg on top.

Huaraches are oval shaped tortillas with a similar range of fillings. There was a self-service restaurant on Uxmal -- pay before you eat -- which has a wide variety of such things. Mine came loaded with Yucatecan chorizo style sausage, probably from Valladolid, a city famed for such products. A kind of spicy hamburger -- and indeed chorizo is in Mexico can be very spicy indeed from several ingredients, and somewhat dry to the taste.

Sometimes you will see a sign that indicates the food will consist of Mexican *antojitos* and especially *flautas*. Unlike flautas you often find in Tex-Mex or North America, these are crisp from deep frying and really are flute-shaped tight rolls. They vary a great deal in width and length. You can even buy them in packages in the supermarkets ready for your own frying. Mostly the interior meats have been dried out by the process so that there isn't all that much gastronomic interest. But in a little wayside cafe I ordered one each of three kinds -- chicken, pork and potato. Without losing any of the crispness of the *flauta* itself, the filling was jam packed with salad ingredients and overlaid with crême *fraiche* -- just called *crema* in Mexican.

The equivalent Yucatecan products are called *codzitos* and are more lightly fried, rolled and more openly filled, preferably containing aromatic leaves. The meat is still dry, moistened perhaps with a tomato based salsa.

Iturriaga mentions that Yucatan is famed for its *tacos de ceviche*, which I imagine would be very good indeed. The nearest I got to that was at El Calamar, which served me a plate of three, one containing shark (*cazón*), another the most tender octopus, and the third conch. The marinade was minimal, just a touch of lime and cilantro, so that nothing whatsoever interfered with the paradisiacal sense of freshness and cool firmly-soft texture.

At El Parilla, a place where loud noisy music deafens tourists and makes conversation impossible, where muggy heat is intended to remind you are in Mexico (fair enough), in and out of the clichéd grills, you could find items of interest, and perhaps survive long enough to enjoy them. Examples were the *tacos de nopalitos*.

Nopale are the leaves of a prickly cactus, the idea of which puts some people off. They are delectable and should enter the repertoire of all cuisines, especially since they are available internationally in many bottled and canned forms. One writer has most accurately described them as being between okra and bean in taste, and their tenderness leaves nothing to be desired. Here they were served with slices of onion, the whole *tacos* fried.

Panuchos are another Yucatecan favourite. At Antojitos Yucatecos they came as tortillas covered with fried beans, slivered chicken, chopped raw onion, and a tomato salsa. There was a tigerishly innocent looking side salsa with chopped onion and chilies *habañeros*. The Almendros version was more complex still, with turkey.

Enchiladas and *empinadas* are Mexico-wide. In North America and elsewhere the word *taco* has been taken over by the fast food companies which market "taco shells", crispish pre-folded tortillas, into which you can force stuffing's much in the manner of open pita bread. In North American Mexican restaurants *enchiladas* are thought of as rolled. Here in the Yucatan *flautas* are rolled, but more crisply and tightly, and *enchiladas* are folded as with North American tacos but softer.

Thus it was with the *enchilada de mole* at Antojitos Yucatecos, a rolled tortilla.

But what about the filling, and that infuriatingly difficult word *mole*? One thing it most certainly does not have to be, that is a chocolate flavoured sauce, as in the classic dish *mole poblano*. By derivation from the Spanish it could imply something mixed or pressed together; by derivation from Pre-Hispanic languages, a Chile-hot sauce -- or stew!. The Mexican recipe books I have to hand make it clear that almost anything can go into a *mole*, which can be vegetarian, contain meats, aim at different colours like red or green or black. The one common denominator that I can find is stewing to the point of heavy reduction, the result being either a stew in itself as in *mole poblano* where the main ingredient of the stew is not even mentioned in the name, or a thick sauce for use over something. Ortiz, however, states that *mole* is any sauce made from any pepper, which seems a bit broad as a definition. It definitely does NOT have to contain chocolate.

In the case of this *enchilada* all I could infer was that the shredded chicken had been stewed in a dark bean and Chile sauce which was used to cover the folded tortilla. But who cares? It was delectable.

Empanadas are simply little pies or turnovers, with a thicker crust than is implied by a tortilla. I didn't seek them out very much, because mostly, unless you are in Alsace, pies are pies, and the one I remember, stuffed with spiced ground pork and covered with a tomato salsa, was, well, a pie.

At the Contoy fish restaurant there were several other kinds of *tacos*, listed as "*de tinga, de morcilla, de raja*s". I didn't get around to checking them out. *Tinga* is a complicated dish with boiled pork accompanied by fried sausage and other ingredients, which hardly seem likely here, *rajas* are strips or slices, as with *rajas de chili*, but perhaps used in other contexts, *morcilla* is a blood sausage. These were available only at lunch.

Of course I came across other *tacos* which are more Mexican or national, and have enjoyed their delicious characters. The Garibaldi restaurant, near Avenida Tulum, not always with success, and with a bit too much toutism, nevertheless tried to showcase regional Mexican food. It presents *sopes* in the form of thick homemade pork flavoured tortillas with cold shredded chicken, lettuce, and *crême fraiche*.

Molotes at the Flor de Hidalgo were like tortilla fingers, closed at both ends, with chicken and tomato filling, sprinkled with powdered cheese. *Gorditas* at the same very special restaurant were like a fried tortilla sausage roll. Mine was served with a chili hot orange coloured sauce that looked like jam but was not sweet. It was sprinkled with powdered cheese.

I didn't go in for *tamales* because I didn't find them very often. Classically they consist of ingredients wrapped in corn leaves and steamed. Any I have had I have found coarse and unappetizing. But in the Yucatan -- and I believe in some other countries such as Costa Rica -- *tamales* are made not with corn leaves but banana leaves. This gives an entirely different flavour and quality.

My one and only try was totally delicious. I was walking from the Cobal corner along Avenida Tulum and came across this little somewhat grubby stall selling beer and hamburgers to harassed Mexican shop-wives and drunken beachcombers. But I noticed they listed *tamales de chaya* and I hadn't been able to taste *chaya* leaves as yet. So in I go and order one. Chaya are the leaves of the tallish shrub, much prized for their nutritional value and for their somewhat soft spinach-like taste.

It came with the banana wrapping opened, a pleasant looking lump of whitish green. The mild but palatably tasty *chaya* had been mixed into a soft *mas de ma‹s* with mashed boiled egg. I loved it - just the sort of tasty mush I adore. And nowhere, nowhere in any restaurant (though some modern ones do try to incorporate *chaya* leaves) was its delectable dish on a menu.

The day I wanted to try an equivalent at Antojitos Yucatecos they weren't available. But the menu talked of *vaporcitos,* described as *tamales* containing chicken stewed in banana leaves.

Apart from *chaya* the two herbs most special to Yucatecan cooking are *achiote* (*exited*) and *epazote*, together with generous usage of cilantro, and such other ingredients as parsley, mint, chamomile, and garlic.

Achiote is a reddish powder made from grinding the seeds of the annatto tree, *bixa orellana*. It is available in bottled commercial form almost throughout the world, the bottling including, in one form I know, oregano and cumin and vinegar, allowing it to be mixed into a sauce or spread over a meat or fish. This gives a yellowish red colour that is somewhat similar to what you get by roasting with a paprika or even turmeric baste.

Epazote is a flavouring that is special to Yucatan, although it grows wild in many parts of Mexico and the United States. It is the leaves (NOT the seeds) of *chenopodium ambrosioides L.*, which has the common English name of, alas, wormseed. My books say that it is not used this way, even in Mexican cooking, in the United States. If so, pity. [But I have found little plants in herb garden stores in Vancouver]

Lime, orange, bitter orange, are used with considerable effect and delicacy. I did not come across other use of fruit in main courses -- unless you count raisins, olives and almonds. And of course sometimes, but not often, and usually on the side, cooking bananas or plantains.

Mexico -- and Yucatan is no exception -- has to be the land where the cult of the Chile is rarified, nurtured to be the *sine qua non* of the educated person. Never was any waiter at the slightest moment's loss to identify precisely what Chile was being used where. And you do NOT get them mixed up. Any old red Chile, any old medium hot Chile, any old very hot Chile, will simply not do. Every Chile has its flavour, and all chilies may, if you wish, be eaten raw, or marinated, or cooked, or baked, or whole, or chopped. But the decision is precise.

The prime Chile of Yucatan is small, greenish to white with touches of red, squat, and called, with reverence habañero. [The orange Scotch bonnets of the Caribbean are similar] The more you roast it, marinate it, treat it, the more a pungent full flavour emerges that few other chilies can match. It has its own character that will not be submerged. Many is the time that I have had a salsa or some other dish and searched for the identification of the flavour. Could it be cilantro perhaps? No. No other flavour was needed. It was habañero.

Other chilies are of course used. In most supermarkets there are perhaps half a dozen varieties, some dried. But in the real vegetable stores there will be a minimum of thirty to for kinds, as there will be in the marvellously localized supermarket on the outskirts of town on Avenida Cobal.

Some Yucatecan dishes have entered the national repertoire -- cochinita or pollo pibil, pavo de relleno negro, jaiva relleno, huevos motuleños, tikin zic.

Let us start with breakfast, since this is something you can get in one form or another almost anywhere, from hotels to Americanized places like Super-Deli and 100% Natural to Antojitos Yucatecos. You are likely to get a choice of three offerings: *huevos rancheros, huevos Mexicanos*, and *huevos Motuleños*. It is the last that is Yucatecan.

The first can be found almost throughout Latin America in one form or another, but in Mexico has a specific meaning that is different from, for example, the way I was served it in Lima, Peru, where it was rather like a North American Spanish omelette, spiced. Here it is fried eggs on slightly fried tortillas, with a reduced sauce on top made from tomato, garlic, onion. chilies (probably *serrano*), herbs, with refried beans on the side. Mexican eggs, by contrast, are scrambled in oil with finely chopped tomato, onion, green Chile and coriander, again with refried beans on the side. Restaurant cooks will play with additional ingredients and side elements.

Ideally, *huevos Motuleños* are more complex. The eggs are fried, and the tortillas soft fried and covered with refried beans. The egg is on top, and then a sauce, usually consisting of mixed tomato, Chile and garlic, to which are added separately cooked peas and fried chorizo sausage pieces with herbs. On top of that again is a garnish of onion rings, avocado slices and sprinkled soft cheese.

Antojitos Yucatecos serves another breakfast which I've seen here and there called *Desayuno* (breakfast) -- as distinct from *huevos Mexicano*. Apart from juice, fruit and coffee, you get a steak with fried egg, refried beans, tortilla and choice of salsa. It is quite clear that in Mexico breakfast is a serious business -- especially since it may be eaten late in the morning.

Cochinita (sucking pig) -- or its cousin *pollo* (chicken) -- *pibil* is without doubt the most recognized contribution of Yucatan cooking to the national cuisine. Pit cooking seems to have occurred in most parts of Mexico, since it is a natural form of creating an oven that can be found from Polynesia to Croatia. That is the meaning of the word *pibil* in Mayan, a word rendered in most parts of Mexico by *barbacoa*, said to be the ancestor of the North American word "barbecue". But in *pibil* cooking you don't just leave the food on the top of a grill, as in barbecuing. You dig a pit and line it with stones that will preserve the heat, create a fierce fire within, let charcoal form, remove the flames, wrap the food in moist leaves, and bury it on the heat. And you have to judge exactly when it is going to be properly done -- three hours, they say, for a skinned pig -- or you might just get a charred mess. (In parts of Polynesia, the red hot stones are doused in water to create steam, and the "roof" of the oven can consist of thick layers of leaves.)

That is not all there is to it. The meat is marinated in flavours, of which *achiote* and sour orange are the most important, and it is wrapped in banana leaves for flavour as well as protection.

Since no one these days has an open pit or *pib*, other devices have to be used. Restaurants wrap the food in the required leaves, then in aluminium foil, and cook in an oven or stove-top container with bottom high steady heat. Great traditional Mexican restaurants like Le Flor de Hidalgo, use enormous cauldrons with bottom fire to pre-prepare the food and keep it warm.

Pavo de relleno negro, is turkey with a black "stuffing". But let's stop a moment to check out this word *relleno* which you will often come across in menus, as for example in crab or *Chile relleno*. Like good cooks anywhere, Mexicans take considerable liberties with the literal Spanish meaning of words. Something or other that is described as *relleno* in all probability is not, literally, stuffed. Although sometimes the food really is stuffed, as often as not the "stuffing" mixture is served as a sauce or even side garnish.

This can be so even with peppers. At El Parilla the *chilies rellenos* consisted of bell peppers cut open and laid flat, with ground meat, bacon, mushroom, cheese, green salsa spread over, each ingredient somewhat separated from the others.

So far as I know, there is no such thing as a Yucatecan cookbook, and although I can say for sure that *pavo de relleno negro* is nationally known as something Mayans do well, it does not feature in the informative Mexican cookbooks I was able to find in Cancun. So I cannot be sure whether, literally, some part of the bird was supposed to be wrapped around the *relleno* stuffing. It would be very difficult to do, since the *relleno* is quite liquid, and much more in the nature of a beautifully contrived sauce or gravy.

I had the dish twice, at Los Venados and at Los Almendros, and once something similar under another name, a version of *nouvelle cuisine*, at Du Mexique. In neither did the turkey matter much, being stringy and tough at Los Almendros, and chunky tough at Los Venados. It was the juice, the sauce, the gravy, call it what you will, that was superb, and showed me without the slightest doubt that, as *sauciers* the Mayans can be the equal of any in the world.

At Los Almendros the ingredients included pork and hardboiled egg so finely ground they had no impact on texture whatsoever, together with almonds, *epazote*, olives, mild *quemado* Chile, and I found a couple of raisins. At Los Venados the juice was a little thinner, and had bitter orange or lime, no raisins. But it came with rice to mop it up, and a roll of ground pork, like a two inch diameter sausage without the skin. The resulting colour of the gravy was such a dark green, from the Chile, that at first I thought it was black, and the total concoction was redolent with flavours.

Jaivas in this part of the world are prized smallish crabs, about three inches. I had *jaiva (jaiba)* dishes twice, and was not thrilled. Indeed at El Calamar, an excellent restaurant, the stuffed crab shells, though powerful with minced crab, seemed to have no other flavouring, and I had to mix them with a supplied side *ceviche salsa* to make them palatable. Similarly at Los Flamingos a *salpicon* (mince) of stewed *jaiva* was just as tasteless. Yet Booth gives a Vera Cruz recipe for stuffing which contains almonds, olives, tomato, onion, egg, mustard and Tabasco sauce.....

And, truth to tell, I'm the kind of person who finds lobster, which also figures highly on all the menus of all the seafood restaurants in Cancun, totally uninteresting unless it is beautifully sauced. I did not find any special Yucatecan lobster sauce at all anywhere, but my French friend Murielle had an extraordinarily delicate Nantua-like preparation in the gourmet restaurant at the Melia Cancun hotel.

The most satisfying nationally known fish dish, which alas you will also not find in the kind of Mexican cookbook I consulted, is *tikin zic*. I had noticed it on several menus, including Los Flamingos and even places like

Bellini in the Caracol shopping mall, and I chose it for the first time at the Contoy. As time went on more and more locals said the very best was at Rio Nizuc. So one day Jaime Rubio, the manager of Federal Express which had been looking after my mails to Canada, and I set off there for a kind of farewell lunch.

The fish was butterflied and grilled with oil, brushed with a sauce of *achiote*, pimiento, garlic and orange, giving a soft red-brown colour, and crisping the skin, served with a side salsa containing the Yucatecan *habañero*. The fish was a huge *mero* (grouper), served for two, the head garnished with marinated *jalapeño* pepper, and a raw salad mostly of onion. The fish must be butterflied, or the cook cannot brush the dryish paste onto the flesh, as well as on the crispy tasty skin. At Contoy, there was also a side serving of rice. Rice, by the way, seemed always to be garnished with a variety of possibilities, most often slightly reddish in colour, perhaps with tomato, minimal Chile, beans, peas, and often fried, presented as a mound.

Other dishes are perhaps not so nationally known, at least as Yucatecan specialties. I enjoyed many, from which I select just a few.

At Los Venados, *albóndigas* meat balls, about an inch and a half in diameter, held together with corn meal, came in a light tomato and lime broth, preceded by a chicken soup with peas and garbanzo beans. On the side there was a large soup plate full of black bean purée, handmade tortillas, and a somewhat runny but flavourful salsa.

Interestingly enough, that most internationally known of all Latin American dishes, *ceviche*, is not important enough, not Mexican enough, or too easy to manufacture, to figure in the home-grown Mexican recipe books. Naturally in coastal Yucatan, *ceviche* are magnificent, always featuring cilantro, and a minimum of extraneous material like raw onion and/or tomato, lime, with side wedges, side spicy salsa for those who want Chile in it -- as was the case at Rio Nizuc. There I had a mixture of white fish and octopus.

Ceviche of conch was almost universal, with an octopus like texture -- but made me wonder where all the conch comes from, and how long it can last, just as I did with crab and lobster, since, I was told, it was not farmed. At the Contoy restaurant the *ceviche* included *mañero* Chile.

At Los Flamingos, the *chilies rellenos de mariscos* were utterly superb. Great green bell peppers stuffed to the hilt with all kinds of shellfish, wrapped in corn tortillas, and covered with a red-brown sauce containing orange, tomato, puréed mild Chile.

Snapper (*huachinango, guachinango*) is the most internationally famous of Mexican fish, primarily because of the way it is almost universally served with a Veracruzana sauce in Mexican restaurants outside the country. In Yucatan it is sometimes replaced with a similar fish called *boquinete* for which I have been unable to trace an English name. In any event, you don't have to have it with Veracruzana sauce, which, moreover, can be disappointing unless done by the best.

At El Calamar it was offered in four styles, and, exploring as I was, I chose the three that were unfamiliar to me, all on the same plate..... Believe it or not, it worked.

I left out the one with *mantequilla* (butter) sauce, and instead chose *ajo* (garlic, out of curiosity), *chipotle* and *xcatic*, the last two being varieties of Chile. Seldom have I had as pleasing a fish, and, where fish is concerned, I'm very hard to please. The fillets of snapper were grilled in butter, firm, quite thin. On top of one was the *chipotle*, a red Chile, sauce. On the other, the *xcatic*, a green chili'd sauce with tomatillo. On top of both fillets were tiny chips of roasted garlic, scattered. Nothing else. Alas, garnished on the side with a useless helping of raw cabbage and some cooked carrots.

Once again it's time for a linguistic diversion. The Mexicans, who more or less invented tomatoes, don't use the word the way it is used in English. Our kind of intended-to-be-red tomato is *jitomate*. Somewhere along the historical line the word *tomatillo* came into North American English to describe a green fruit, like a tomato, of the genus Physalis. Nobody who writes cook books seems to know how.

Just to confuse us poor foreigners, the Mexican word *tomate*, sometimes *tomate verde*, means tomatillo, which, botanically -- and don't let some of the cook books deceive you because they sometimes get it wrong -- is not a tomato at all.

There are other interesting foods. *Longaniza*, a long thin dryish spiced sausage, served as an *antojito* with three different salsas at Los Almendros, *jicama*, a tasteless hard "fruit", which, however, is capable of absorbing flavours when properly handled, *pepino* or cucumber marinated with vinegar, lemon and cilantro as an appetizer and salsa (Contoy), *sopa Azteca* or *sopa Maya*, chicken based broth containing *tostadas* (triangular toasted tortilla chips like North American nachos), not very tasty, until you squeeze in juice from the supplied lemon wedges and add some side salsa, when it starts to bear a resemblance to the Greek *avgolemono*.

But if you are here for any length of time you will want to go beyond Mayan only, and try out the way Mexican food is presented in the resort. Rather different. The restaurants divided into three -- traditional and family, tourist and bourgeois, and *nouvelle cuisine*.

The most exciting and genuine of the whole lot can be hard to find. I would not have known of it but for a chance remark of a lady on the staff of the little hurricane-destroyed Cancun Museum. First of all, it is normally open only on Sundays from early morning until three in the afternoon, though in some seasons you can have a meal on Saturdays. It is there for Mexican family Sunday treats, adjacent to Mercado 23 away from the tourist routes, upstairs over a large vegetable and Chile store. Flor de Hidalgo, as it is called, was run by a charming lady who will do her best for you even if you have no Spanish and she no English, and seems proud of her enterprise. The main room is huge and packed, and there is another, verandah style, overlooking a square.

Clients come and go, busy, talkative, enthusiastically examining their food, most of the men of huge girth. Tables come together for parties of six, eight, ten, babies, children on laps, balloons in the air. People get up to look at where the food is cooking, others come in and take dishes out wrapped in the universal foil. Flor de Hidalgo is clearly an institution for Mexicans expatriated to Mayaand.

I wandered over to the open cooking area. Girls patting tortillas into shape, frying the *antojitos* in great pans, huge hot cauldrons of the *moles* and stews, the back wall hung with equipment and pans of all descriptions, men and women sweating and joking as I photographed, huge pottery bowls of salsas of a dozen kinds.

I had a wonderful *ensalada de nopales*, prickly pear salad, marinated like a *ceviche* with onion, tomato and cilantro, *molotes* as I have described above, and for main dish the wondrous *mixiotes*. Take very tender lamb, marinade it in the outer membrane of the leaves of *agave (maguey)*, a family of spiky leaved plants some of which produce Mexico's indigenous drinks. In the marinade include *ancho* chili, garlic, oregano and avocado leaves. The classic recipe calls for the lamb then to be wrapped in pouches of the *mixiote* leaves and steamed. Here the lamb was in large chunks, dripping off the bone, wrapped in aluminium foil, and presumably baked in the marinade, the reddish sauce having been brushed over it. Whatever, it was totally seductive. Other items on the menu were just as mouth-watering and away from the tourist clichés.

Flor de Hidalgo, with its nice black skirted white bloused waitresses, if you can pull yourself away from the beach one Sunday, is a must to experience in Cancun.

Among the more bourgeois, atmospheric Mexican restaurants, not quite into *nouvelle cuisine*, but presenting their food in style were Rosa Mexicana off Tulum and La Habichuela boulevards tucked beside a residential park. For me, the trouble with such places can be that, even when catering to the Mexican elite, they modify their recipes and presentation so as to please, if not to not offend, foreign palates. It is touch and go as to whether you are going to be satisfied, though the style is usually careful and gentle.

Rosa Mexicana was more like the tourist's expectation of a Mexican restaurant -- bright table cloths, candlelight, attractive hostess and graceful waiters, lively music, a patio surrounded by tropical plants, and a menu with most of the expected dishes, plus a few others. I tried my first *ensalada de jicama* and found it almost inedible, with large slices of wooden tasteless *jicama* and ordinary salad trimmings. (*Jicama* is the root of a plant which Ortiz identifies as *exogonium bracteatum* and Kennedy as *pachyrrizus erosus*). The supposed marinade of lime and mild Chile could not be tasted. Off-putting, but exploration is not always successful. A dessert of *dulce de papaya* more than made up for it, the papaya baked in cinnamon and honey, tasting for all the world like pear poached in wine.

The main dish, *puerco en naranja* consisted of slightly dry pork loin slices baked in a banana leaf, in a smooth soft delicious sauce of orange and lime, said also to have *ancho* Chile and garlic which I could not find in my tastebuds at all. Western style baked potato and sour cream, boiled carrot and onion on the side.

La Habichuela ("the bean") could possibly have won the prize for the most romantic (alas I was alone) and expressive restaurant in Cancun. Both exterior and interior were a blend of superb modern-Mayan sculpture, falling water, and tropical plantings. The main dining room, softly darkened, had panelled woods, metal and wood separated alcoves giving privacy, decorated with well chosen artefacts, and the outside patio (reserve for it) was a dream Mexican garden out of a novel by Grahame Greene, D.H.Lawrence or Malcolm Lowry, occupied by the chic and also alas the soul-less. It was the place for you, for you to make your own mark for your inner self. Although many come in casual Cancun wear, it is a place worth dressing for, where you can please your partner's eyes.

But the food. The Cantina shrimp soup was described as "a favourite of Mexico City cantinas". Fair enough, but I wondered, in this form. It was a smooth bisque with cosmetic touches of potato and carrot, but no life. On the side were lime and Tabasco sauce; the lime at least made a difference.

Chicken Tenango, named for its origin in Tenango City had beautifully tender chicken -- in the commoner restaurants one does not expect tenderness -- in a totally mild tomatillo sauce. At the side on the plate were the most tender sautéed beans imaginable, guacamole with a minimum of tomato chopped in, cheese, and a purée of dark refried beans. I had no way of knowing the degree to which the character of the original recipe had been removed, but to me it felt like high class Tex Mex.

I wanted to try other classical Mexican dishes that one finds abroad -- *posole*, the corn and meat stew, *mole poblano*, a really decent snapper *Veracruzana* -- to let me establish standards. Alas, time, and weight, ran out on me.

Twice I did have something called *Veracruzana*. The first time it was just spaghetti sauce. The second time it did have olives, but the tomato and onion were presented like a thickish *ratatouille*. Nowhere did I find the *jalapeño* Chile, marinated Chile, Chile powder, cinnamon, garlic or lemon juice, or the required density of the olives. There should be a law.

And in Jaime Rubio's home I called one day to find a wonderful pot of *mole* stewing away slowly and contentedly. In its dark black juice were pieces of meat, whole *chayote* (small christophene squash, *sechium edule*), and on a table nearby sprigs of *epazote*, tomato and onion to be introduced later.

Before I conclude with Mexican *nouvelle cuisine*, a few words about drinks. Here I can mostly only give you hints for you to explore, since I quickly found my favourites and stuck with them, and because many I was not lucky enough to find.

If you buy fruit juice for the frig in your room, and if you don't like the addition of sugar, you are in for a disappointment. If packaged presentation is any guide, Mexicans must be crazy about sugar. All the supermarket juices have at least 5% and sometimes more. There is one, however, called Delli, which makes the most scrumptiously thick unsugared orange juice I have ever had the luck to find. And Super-Deli carried, expensively, Dutch packaged unsugared juices of various kinds.

Throughout town, though, there are ice cream and fruit juice bars, and even the Americanized cafes, that offer you the most exotic huge glasses of readymade, freshly pulped, whatever you want, including many from fruits like *mamey* you have never heard of before. They are delicious, as good as anything in any tropical country including

Kenya, inexpensive, and come in the hugest glasses -- so that on demand you can mix them, as I did, like a combination of papaya and banana.

Atoles are more difficult to find. They are non-alcoholic drinks, designed as refreshment, based on semi-dissolved corn meal, with a variety of flavours, including especially cinnamon and vanilla. The only one I managed to try was a hot chocolate *atole* that tasted just exactly like hot chocolate......

Jaime Rubio, when he took me home, decided to experiment for his first time with Mayan *posole*, which is NOT a corn based stew as in most of Mexico, but a corn-based *drink*. He bought the makings in the market, bringing home two big round balls of a kind of *mas de ma‹s*, corn meal. With our fingers we made it dissolve in water; to that you could then add vanilla or chocolate or anything you like.

The national alcoholic drink of the Mexican centre derives from Aztec times, *pulque*. It is brewed like beer from an *agave* similar to, but different from, that from which mescal and tequila are distilled. (Some books, quite erroneously, infer that tequila and mescal are made from *pulque* -- not so, and the plants are different.) Archaeology tells us that *pulque* had sacred properties, its use limited to ritual. History tells us that the Spaniards recognized a good thing when they saw it, worked hard to turn it into a common popular drink, established *agave* plantations and breweries, making their fortunes in the process, and, until the government started to get restless, by which time it was too late, inventing *pulquerias*, or drinking pubs patronized by regular clients, or brotherhoods. They still exist.

But *pulque's* fermentation only gives it a short shelf life, so that it cannot be successfully bottled for national distribution as with beer. It does not survive the journey to Cancun very well. Cancun therefore lacks *pulquerias* and it is almost impossible to find as a drink. When it is a little past its truly fresh prime, it can be mixed with fruit like a sangria, or otherwise jollied up, but it is not the same. I was given addresses, but didn't get to taste. Nevertheless, you may be luckier or more determined. Here they are.

There is a cafe on a side street near the main post office -- I do not have its name -- which has fruit added *pulque* if you get there at seven in the morning as people go to work...... Le Flor de Hidalgo has two types of *pulque* on its typewritten menu. The day I was there they were not available. It was firmly promised for the following Sunday, but I was leaving town. My guess is that you would have to be there early.

Tequila, distilled, is a form of mescal made from a special *agave* in the area around Tequila township, a town of distilleries. There are numerous mescals with their own characters made in different parts of the country, from different varieties of agave. The naming is now controlled, the distillations differing in colour and age[30].

I confess I like the stuff, but not when I follow the mystiques sometimes attached to it. Contrary to Mexican mythology it is not stronger in alcohol content as most distillations in other countries, and it may be drunk with fewer side effects. It is, in fact, an uncomplicated drink with full flavours that is worth sipping.

Because of the mystique of its power, it has become something of a macho drink, which it definitely is not. It is frequently served with slices of lime or dollops of salt on the side. The erroneous but persistent theory is that knocking back a shot of tequila requires counter action, so, before or after taking the poison you add a counter irritant --

---

[30] In later years there has been an ezpansion of high priced "premium" tequilas

salt and/or lime. This is the Mexican way. I have seen Mexicans put either the salt or the lemon into the tequila, which, to me, destroys it. What a waste of a good drink...

Because of that mystique, foreigners developed the Margarita cocktail, with its salt-rimmed glass and its lime. And you have other tequila based cocktails, mostly to be found in foreign hotels and restaurants and bars. To me they are the pits. To me, tequila does not mix. Its flavour is special, to be enjoyed directly, slowly, savoured. Mixing creates ugly tastes. Leave it alone.

There is, however, one custom that deserves encouragement, and is not often available overseas. One way of savouring tequila is to have it in its own shot, with a parallel shot of what is known as *sangrita*. (No relation of sangria). *Sangrita* can be found in a commercial bottle, which I think of as thin and weak. Better, barmen make it fresh and the better bars don't charge extra for it. It is tomato juice or pulp, flavoured with orange, *serrano* and *piquin* Chile, very slightly sweetened. When properly made it is itself yummy. As something to sip in and out of tequila -- but never mixed -- it is superbly refreshing. Trouble is, of course, that not all barmen do it right, and sometimes you get a concoction that is probably spiced Clamato out of a bottle.

For centuries wine making in Mexico was illegal. But it happened. And now Mexico has some good table wines, and an enormous variety of brandies and liqueurs, that go way beyond the over-rated Kahlua. They are not expensive, they are often available in shot sized bottles, and they are well worth experimenting with.

And Yucatan makes some excellent beer. The two I know are from Merida, Montejo and Léon. The latter is especially worth exploring, a dark beer that is refreshingly light in taste.

Cancun, naturally enough, has some pretentious and possibly excellent restaurants catering to the international set. I know for sure that those in the Melia hotels will do you proud, that many of those in other hotels are unimaginative, and that the Italian restaurants, though Mexicans enjoy them, have sadly ordinary menus.

There is in fact a festival of Mexican *nouvelle cuisine* that had its first competition in early 1991. The photographs look great, but then I have learned that in competitions of this kind, even the great international ones, it is the looks and lists of ingredients that count, and the tastes often don't matter. Here in Cancun you get the good and the terrible.

The terrible I experienced at Stelae, a pleasant looking luxury place in the Flamingo Plaza. The menu seemed to have at least some challenging dishes, so in I went.

For the adventurous, it said, try our Mayan plate of selected delicacies. I nearly fell for it. Surely this must be tapas-like *antojitos* or *botas*? Fortunately, I asked. No, no, said the waiter, it is one plate only of breaded chicken stuffed with shrimp. Chile? No way.

I nearly walked out, and should have. But there was a filet of fish in *chaya* leaves. Give it a try. Start with a truly beautifully presented plate of *ceviche*, then on into the future.... The future came, and it was like a shudder from the past. Pleasantly textured white fish, probably *boquinete*, with a few distressed *chaya* leaves trying to say "here we are" through a sickening plaster of floured white sauce, the kind that all fish used to be served with in England. Push it off and try to eat the fish without it. At least the vegetables were not steamed to death.

What a missed opportunity! I can imagine *chaya* being turned into its own sauce, as a French chef would deal with sorrel.......

From there to the sublime. Well, nearly sublime. A French chef by the name of Alain Grimond operated a chic restaurant in the chic restaurant area of Avenida Cobal, called Du Mexique. It has curved white walls, sea-green-blue decorative plates (for initial viewing, not for eating from), an art gallery of derivative sculptures and paintings, unpretentious service, undemanding musack.

The menu was as imaginative and inventive as anyone could want, based almost entirely on Mexican ideas and ingredients, with fancy and unintelligible Mayan or Aztec names -- but the carte does explain. I went wild. I chose the *naiysnallo,* crepe of *cuitlachoche* -- the fungus delicacy that attaches itself to corn -- and *tochtlyimmoli, mole* of rabbit. Sorry, said the waiter, they are not available......When will they be? Please ask the kitchen, and I'll come back. Later. Sorry, the kitchen doesn't know.

Try again, why not. *Xocotizin,* stuffed apple with *jicama.* Maybe it will be as bad as at Rosa Mexicana. Now, was that something? I discovered for the first time the real possibilities of *jicama.* It was slivered, mixed with raisins and a slightly sweet dressing, loaded into a crisp cool fresh apple, with some additional apple on the side on a lettuce leaf. It was totally delicious, perfect for the palate on a warm muggy day.

Then on to the *Iluhicatl Yayanco,* modestly described as stuffed chicken Yucatan style. They could have made much more of the description, because this was no less than a modernly wonderful *relleno negro.* Not only was the chicken breast fork tender, but the black-green sauce, judiciously ladled over it, had been inventively modified. In addition to the puréed boiled egg and chili *quesada,* which gave a sharp peppery taste, Grimond has substituted puréed veal for the traditional pork. If it were necessary, he proved beyond the shadow of a doubt that *relleno negro* deserves, under its own name, to be in the forefront of the *repertoire de la cuisine internationale*. The classically light dessert, a tiny tortilla filled and surrounded by a white chocolate sauce, was the final touch of a master.

Enjoy the beaches. Enjoy the reefs. Go to Señor Frog, Mama de Tarzan or the Pizza Hut if you must. But there are other adventures in store -- if you reach out.

After Cancun I decided to take a look at Costa Rica. I had only a week in San Jose which is not enough to get a true taste of the country. But I was impressed enough to toy with the idea of making it my retirement location and to that end attended one of the numerous seminars which tempt North Americans to invest in mahogany plantations and thus earn the right of residence, with all its advantages – generous immigration and relocation procedures and health services in one of the best regarded medical systems. I checked out the central market which I found disappointing and did not have time to find good food. Expatriate homes around the capital were of neat bungalow style but otherwise taking little advantage of the upland climate. I took a tour to the volcano crater puffing its smoky puffs and on the way admired the Swiss like mountain side with groves of trees, smooth meadows and grazing cows. The showpiece orchid farm seemed limited although there are renowned tropical ecosystems at sea level.

I decided not to pursue the idea.

38. A Brother in New Mexico

My brother Michael was seven years younger than I. In his youth my parents sent him to boarding school. I myself was finishing university at home and then inducted into the New Zealand forces. Michael naturally resented this and had a difficult relationship with the rest of the Belshaw family as a result.

My parents took him with them to the United States when my father worked for the Institute of Pacific Relations in New York and took up academic appointments in California. There Michael studied music and architecture. Then he moved to Columbia University where he took his doctorate in economics and anthropology and married a charming Chinese American, Clara, who worked for the United Nations. Michael wrote a good book on a Mexican community.

Michael developed a passion for the land and did not have an interest in creating an urban home and family. This led to a parting of the ways with Clara who later left the U.N. and established an antique enterprise in New England. I had visited them in New York and Betty and I took in Clara's enterprise during a tour in the East when Diana and Adrian were at university themselves.

Michael by then had moved to Arizona where he had a post in Prescott College. He was able to purchase a large tract of land with the determination to protect it from developers. H led the rural life. On one occasion he fell down a canyon and was saved by his dog who summoned help as Michael was dehydrating.

Michael visited us in Vancouver and we kept up a superficial contact at Christmas and birthdays.

Despite his feelings Michael attended the funeral on behalf of the family when my father died on a mission for the F A O in Rome, while I looked after my mother who was unwell in Vancouver and could not attend herself.

Prescott College closed and Michael was on his own, his only asset being his land. He publicly fought the developers but eventually sold the property and moved to New Mexico. In the meantime he specialised in the construction of adobe houses, had a small plane which he gave up on his move, and some earthmoving equipment which he held on to until the end.

In New Mexico he acquired a unique piece of land north of Santa Fe in the midst of a national forest. It had one access road which he himself constructed and could not be built around because of the forest reserve. There he constructed a simple but comfortable home, entirely self sufficient. His source of power was solar panels; he had a radio phone as his contact with the outside world. He collected rainwater off his roof in the time tested New Zealand fashion. He had a friendship with the nearby Hispanic settlers and a number of friends but his life was largely as a hermit.

And then his passion became his wolves. He bred them (with a small proportion of Alsatian within them.) He sold some to aficionados, carefully selected for the understanding of the breed, and became their fierce defender.

The wolves were quite superb animals. After my trial I was able to visit him on several occasions, including one Christmas. As Michael resented his family, so I too had resented Michael's lack of interest in the care of our mother. But in New Mexico with Michael and the wolves I could not be more contented.

Michael had them in specially constructed pens. Wolves have a deep fear of humans (stories of the aggression on humans are much exaggerated – wolf packs were more interested in the food humans had than in their bodies). So when a wolf gave birth, Michael would softly enter the pen, squat down with the nervous mother for hours at end and allow the cub to smell him and get used to the human scent.

Inside his cabin his old and loyal favourites were allowed to enter. One in particular was his constant companion and would walk the land with him.

During my visits I would sit inside with Michael. We listened to his great collection of CDs – he kept up his solid interest in classical and world music. He had a curious habit as he relaxed, blinking his eyes as he talked and using his head to emphasize his points. His politics were "conservative" and truly American by now, but his opinions owed nothing to the main U.S. parties. They were dominated by land and wolves and sustainability.

As we sat his main wolf friend Chamako would sit there too. Then the huge animal would approach me. His head would come to my shoe. He would sniff at my leg, gently. The head would rise to my lap. Then slowly it would work its way up my body until head and paws would surround my neck and the animal would relax there, almost asleep. As intimate a relationship as I have ever had with a canine, although my earlier Samoyed loved close contact. Michael provided two wolves for my young grand daughter and her mother in their rural settings northwest of Vancouver.

When I visited Michael I either rented a car locally or drove my own down through Washington and Colorado. Gastronomically the route was a desert, but it all changed the moment I crossed the New Mexico border. I stayed in Santa Fe, one of the most charming towns in the United States although it is encircled by the typical disaster of strip malls, and one of the very few to which I am attracted. During my last visit especially I sought to demystify the tangled web of food, searching not terribly successfully, for the "indigenous" Hispanic food and life, traced back to the original Spanish occupation.

Spanish expeditions reached New Mexico, after months of travel, in 1540. The territory was "conquered", from 1607 to 1692, in the search for lost golden cities and a passage linking the Atlantic to the Pacific. It was definitively lost to the United States by treaty in 1848 after a disastrous war and years of military skirmishes, along with Texas (already de facto occupied by the Americans) and New California.

Santa Fe itself is not the oldest Spanish settlement in New Mexico, but its founding as an administrative capital in 1610 makes it the oldest capital city in the United States, and it has been continuously such ever since. Despite a rambunctious history, though not nearly as macho as that of Texas, and waves of immigrants of several varieties, it has managed to retain styles of life and an aesthetic flavour that makes it, to me, the only city in the whole of the U.S. of A. to which I could think of devoting some years. Taos. nearby, has its undoubted charm, but seems dilapidated and uncared-for by contrast. Bustling Albuquerque has no character for me, even though it does have the airport.

The town is 7,000 feet above sea level on the rise of a plateau, in the lee of a hill where skiing is possible in winter. The quite small central core of the town maintains the layout and many of the buildings of the original Spanish occupiers, churches, mansions, haciendas, old government buildings, the plaza.

The Spaniards of course were not the original occupiers of New Mexico. Their settlements were surrounded and in competition with those of the Indian pueblos, corn growing communities sheltered by soft coloured clay-adobe houses, some terraced upward to several stories, that to this day draw thousands of tourists, and have captured the senses of artists and writers, including D.H.Lawrence.

Spanish officials did not understand much of their Indian neighbours. They had known such people in Mexico itself, especially in the north and west; but they had also crossed arms with Toltecs and Mayas who had worked their great stone pyramids and temples, their astronomical observatories, and expressed themselves in writing. The New Mexican pueblos did not command the same respect. From time to time they revolted, fought back, often with a background of U.S. intrigue.

Even New Mexico has its regions. Santa Fe is regarded as the beginning of Northern New Mexico, as distinct from the hotter, closer to Mexico, south. I have to bear this in mind, because the food I write about begins with Northern New Mexico, and resists being blended into something wider, like that of the U.S. Southwest. Thank goodness for that. Tex Mex, with stuff like Chile con carne, and Californian Mexican, in which everything is mushed together, has not yet quite taken over. You can find it in Santa Fe, alas, but there is other food too.

The climate of Northern New Mexico is mostly dry and clear and for most of the year hot in the day, cool at night. The clarity of the skies are characteristic of desert lands, but with a difference. The lights, particularly in the early morning and at sunset, are full of radiant colour, aquamarine, turquoise, pale beige, rich russet-brown, peach colours, colours that are present in the land itself. For in the land there are sands and stones of almost every hue imaginable, which, ground down, are used in the magically-healing sand paintings of the pueblos.

The adobe structures are as much a part of the landscape as anything made by nature. In remote villages you will find centuries old churches of adobe, their flowing forms matching the hills around them, some sanctuaries and places of pilgrimage and healing, as holy and magnetic as anything in Europe. They are still places of faith.

The Spaniards adapted the style for their palatial and domestic buildings. They added more out-jutting beams, and built their rooms around garden or utilitarian courtyards, with cool fountains and shady terraces and balconies. As Americans came down, they added wooden cottages in the middle of lots, very different. But in the centre of town the two styles live pleasantly side by side, the adobe dominating as nostalgia governs city planning.

The city spread up canyons and ridges, and as it did so the newly rich and the newcomers, even commercial firms and hotels, mostly adopted adobe styles, adapting them to modern living. My brother built some for a while. They can be totally phoney, that is ordinary structures with a bit of sand coloured cement thrown on. But in their architectural expression, their soft colours and gently moving lines, minimizing sharp angles, their ability to blend with the landscape and yet create oases of courtyards, shady spots, gardens and vistas, they are without compare. Many world renowned architects found their inspiration in this countryside.

So too have artists of every description, painters, sculptors, workers in beads, cloth, silver, jewellery, potters, traditional Indian geniuses, immigrants who gained inspiration from Indian motifs and techniques and the soft colours of the countryside. Indian art itself grew and adapted without losing its truth. It is mostly soft art. But it also mostly speaks to the soul.

So that, whether you look at pottery, textiles, jewellery, painting, sculpture, Santa Fe is, downtown and along some of the canyon roads, one great artistic show-case. It is much more than those little European towns like Les Baux de Provence or even Carcassonne, because it is not just a front for history, transformed to make a living. Santa Fe is itself living artistic history. It has its own momentum, dynamic and looking to the future. The visual arts spread to music and, in modest ways, to drama.

I had been to Santa Fe several times, but always just for a few short days. At the time of my last visit I had not thought of going, but I was suddenly confronted with a December season for which I had not made plans. Every place I thought of going was cold and\or wet, cloud covered, or else the sort of place that was crowded with European holiday makers already booked solid, or else demanded impossible amounts of planning and money to get to, and fierce hotel bills when you got there.

One night I woke out of a dream and said Santa Fe. Not your jet set Cooks Tour sort of place at all. Yes indeed it can be cold at 7,000 feet, but sunny sunny cold. The food I want to check out. And since I didn't have time, either in advance or for length of stay, to book an inexpensive villa, there was the next best thing, the Residence Inn, with its well equipped kitchens including microwave, its "We'll buy your groceries for you" service, its King size beds and roomy suites with sun catching balconies, its reduced, but still uppity, prices for longer stays. So, a month ahead, I was on the phone. To my surprise the crucial days of Christmas were fully booked -- I had discounted the attraction of the small ski area -- but eventually there was a cancellation.

You cannot fly into Santa Fe unless you have a plane of your own. The commercial airport is at Albuquerque, an hour away by car. The winter flight from Europe was a mess -- late into Chicago, missing the last United flights to Albuquerque, transferring to another airline, catching it by the skin of my teeth, tired and cross with 184 kilos of baggage, mostly books and computer stuff. But it worked out.

The road, especially when one is tired at night, is dull. And the outskirts of Santa Fe are as off-putting as they are in any other U.S. or French city, the charm almost totally stripped by the free-for-all endless unregulated stretches of shopping malls, *grandes surfaces* and supermarkets, auto salesmen, junk food drive-ins, drive-in banks, all that mess. In the daylight, it is true, some of the structures around Santa Fe pretend to some adobe, which takes only just a little of the bite off.

Michael lived about an hour's drive from Santa Fe, renting for the moment a small ranch house on the outskirts of the old Mexican village of El Rito. You may have difficulty finding it on the map. And once you got there Michael's directions were not always of the clearest. Just ask, though, for the "wolf man" and you' would arrive -- if you don't hear the wolves singing well before. He had open house on Sundays, a day when the curious and the children from all around come and talk to the magnificent animals. Otherwise it was by appointment, and you should show you're serious, maybe thinking of buying one of the chirpy young cubs, fluffily tumbling over each other in their runs.

The wolves were demanding of time and attention, and the drive from Santa Fe, though easy, itself takes time. But we thought we might spend a few moments talking, exploring Santa Fe food, chatting up the wolves.

The Arctic Express, roaring down from Alaska and Canada and the North Pole, had other ideas. It dumped heavy snow on the whole region, with record breaking low temperatures. When the clouds lifted the sun was gorgeously rich -- I could even sunbathe in my room -- but the roads were icy or slushy or both and the drivers unprepared. We did visit alright, but in a reduced way. And once I fell asleep at the wheel and woke to find myself bumping over sage brush...... There were days when it was not even wise to go into town.

But I did find food, and what a joy and challenge that was. On previous occasions I had checked mostly at the well-reported tourist places, some of which are of pleasantly high standard, often using New Mexican ideas in their modern menus, some of which I shall mention. This time I wanted to go for the Spanish roots, and try and distinguish northern New Mexican, Santa Fean, from the "national". In particular I wanted to educate myself about the real food, as distinct from the fast-food influence that pervades "Mexican" outlets in North America, with its mushy conglomeration of everything into one great slush. Maybe that's what I would find. It was and it wasn't.

Modern Santa Fe has several layers of population, who live in somewhat suspicious harmony with a measure of repressed hostility. There are the Indians of the pueblos, who will welcome you into their villages as a tourist, even to observe ceremony, provided you pay the shot and observe strict rules. They are in town, portraying themselves as indigenous artisans, sitting on the pavement of the plaza to sell their colourful carefully executed wares. Some of the gifted among them sell their creations to art galleries under their own names, as do any good artists world wide, and are known locally and nationally for their outstanding work.

It was Indians, here and in Mexico, who provided the baseline for the kind of cooking I was to find, even though much of their food nowadays is known by the introduced Spanish names. The starting point was corn, corn of a score of colours, eaten directly, turned into flour, then into tortillas, wrapped around fillings, incorporated into poultry and venison stews, made into drinks. There were tomatoes and chillies, pumpkin, the flesh of the prickly pear (soft and delicate) several beans, piñon nuts, potatoes, riverine and lake fish, herbs like sage. Did they use the wild epazote? The books don't say so, which seems strange. But then nor do North American gringos.

Because of the climate, what they did not have were things like avocados and papayas, coffee and chocolate, oranges. Later immigrants had the networks and techniques to import such things, but they are not indigenous to northern New Mexico styles, and much of the local cooking mostly ignores them.

Before coming to New Mexico the Spanish colonists had overcome their snobbism to the extent that they learned that this food was good food, and necessary to their survival. The Mexicans adopted it as their own, with a much richer variety of available ingredients, which had to be filtered out in the north. But everything in the pueblo repertoire became New Mexican.

In addition there was the introduction of new elements - cilantro, saffron (both the expensive imported stuff and a local plant of a different family) and other spices, pork and beef, the former becoming the readily available staple, with chicken, wheat flour in parallel to corn flour, rice. The ingredients are ready, the mix is about to begin.

(But first, an aside. The third wave of immigration was Anglo-American, dominant now, though by no means unchallenged, in business and administration, in tourism, and in the national style restaurants, from old established family to newcomer. And the final group, discounting American immigrants of other cultures, is the present wave of Mexican, socially, culturally and economically marginal, snubbed by the older Mexican families whose roots and lands, after all, have centuries of precedence. Each group makes its mark on food, but I did not explore those results systematically.)

The historical threads, the variability of that thing loosely called "Mexican" cooking, and individual ideas, inevitably bring about considerable indetermination when it comes to food terms and words. *Posole* means something different in an Indian pueblo, in a New Mexican cafe, or a food outlet in the Yucatan. I will try to sort out what I can, and stick to the usage as I found it, where I found it, with whatever inconsistencies may emerge. They will be the inconsistencies of life, and perhaps reflect the rich dynamic of the world.

To find out, I asked questions, of Michael and of some people in the food business. Where is the best northern New Mexican food? In almost every instance the answers indicated small casual cafes. Sometimes there was the inevitable overlap with Mexican- Mexican, U.S. style, or with nationally recognized "Southwestern" and sometimes with the good innovative modern cooking that uses the traditional as a base. I include these as comparative commentary.

The cooking of Santa Fe is extremely fortunate in that it is methodically and accurately described, in recipe form, in one of the great books of the cooking repertoire, Huntley Dent's *The Feast of Santa Fe*, which I have used extensively to check my data and observations. My purpose, though, is different from his: it is to describe the food as you, a stranger, will find it if you look.

Another feature that was welcome, I must say, is that because the food is in casual places and outside the tourist down-town area, it is often, indeed usually, inexpensive. Seldom did I pay as much as ten dollars for a very satisfying meal with beer.

The three characteristic ingredients, which demand a lot of attention, are tortillas, corn and Chile.

In Spain, the tortilla is an omelette. History does not tell us how this changed in the Americas. Here it is a corn or wheat crêpe, a variant of the almost universal phenomenon that is naan in India, pita in the Middle East, pizza in Italy (though that is more crusty), injera in Ethiopia (though that is softer). The original tortilla, as developed independently of all that by American Indians, was of corn, and it is not found in Indian areas where corn was not grown.

Tortillas come unleavened and leavened, and nowadays of various styles of wheat as well as corn. In U.S. supermarkets the cases are full of both corn and what products. Yeast and baking powder can be used for leavening, but traditionally a "pumice-like substance" called *texquite* (which you can buy) was the stuff to use. I doubt though if I have ever tasted tortillas made that way.

In New Mexico there is a bit of difficulty in deciding what to call what happens with them, because of the mixed up influence from other brands of Mexican cooking. On the whole one can say that enchiladas here are rolled tortillas, tacos are deep fried and stuffed and can come crisp (as in supermarkets) or soft, burritos are rolled and stuffed with sauce on top. Fried tortillas made from flour are much tougher than those made with corn, often far too tough for my taste.

Tostados are hot fried crisp tortillas cut in quarters, the basis of the modern nachos (In Mexico they are sold whole, with a deliciously nutty taste result). Nachos are triangular nibbles nowadays served with a salsa in Western-oriented restaurants as a kind of earnest of genuine Mexican, but not normally provided in those restaurants that are in fact genuine, except perhaps for a couple popped into a sauce or into refried beans to serve as garnish and scrapers. In supermarkets nachos compete all over North America with potato and other dip chips.

Empanadas are filled pies, not to be confused with the adjective empanizado = breaded, as with breaded fish, though of the same derivation.

Then we have to watch for quesadillas (small corn tortillas filled with anything, then fried), sopapillas, chalupas, and Mexican chimichangas, as we will when we proceed.

The preferred medium for frying in this part of the world is lard rather than oil although most restaurants use oil.

Corn is only one of the many staples of the world that Central America has contributed. It comes in an enormous range of styles which are really only just being discovered in Western cuisines, and could take off to become the newest fad in yuppie culture. The variant that is now making the grade throughout North America, but which you don't see in Mexico itself, and not much of in traditional New Mexican cooking, is the blue pueblo variety, available universally as blue nachos (to me it tastes just the same, the appeal being purely cosmetic.) If it makes money for the pueblos, fine, but I don't think they're getting much of that.

Spanish dictionaries will tell you that *masa* means a lump or a mass. That is not its connotation in Hispanic America. *Masa*, or *masa de mais*, is your basic humid cornmeal reserve used as a mix in a thousand recipes.

If you steam green corn and dry it on the cob, then shell it, you get the famed southern hominy, here called *chicos*, providing a base for a whole range of dishes confusingly all called *posole*. Some are drinks, some are gruel, some are stews. Dent points out that strictly speaking that *nixtamal* is the base of whole-kernel corn, often used in stews, by inference treated with lime. If not treated with lime, says Dent, they are called *chicos*.

I had a cup of the first kind of *posole*, half way between a drink and gruel at La Choza in Santa Fe, and a bowl of the stew kind at Josie's Casa de Comida. At Josie's the *chicos* were mixed with white beans and stewed pork. If the menu does not describe what kind of *posole* is intended, it is wise to ask.

Now chillies are a different story indeed. In my Philistine Canadian way I knew that chillies come in differing degrees of heat, that *chillies asados*, toasted, which you can make yourself or buy prepared, have a special role in cooking, that dried chillies come powdered or chipped, and that there were different names for chillies. Thai cooks had told me that the chillies used in Thailand, of Central American botanical origin, had different qualities because of the way they were grown. I knew that Hungarian and Spanish pimiento differed in taste from each other, though from the same mildish plant. And I knew that sweet or bell peppers were from the same kind of plant. Indeed in the summer I grew some of these things in a northern Vancouver garden.

What I did not do in Santa Fe was to ask about cultivation and the effects of climate. The range of chillies available directly to the northern New Mexican cook, especially off the land, is infinitesimal by comparison with the range available in Mexico itself despite their high reputation.

I do not know for sure what varieties can be successfully grown. The huge wonderful red and red-brown bunches of dried chillies, the *ristras*, hanging beside every traditional house, and many other buildings, even as Christmas decoration, so characteristic of the New Mexican scene, are but the most common variety.

And the situation has been made more complex by the emergence of highly localized varieties grown in particular places with particular soils, rather like the way varietal grapes differ. And of course by international trade, since now a number of chillies not locally grown are readily available to cooks from supermarkets through importation from other parts of the southwest and from Mexico.

Furthermore, what is important about chillies, to an experienced cook, is the taste, the flavour, not just the size and shape and hotness. This I had discovered more seriously in Mexico. It is difficult to convey in writing, so does not often appear in text-book descriptions, yet it is so important that cooks who cannot get the right variety, grown in the right place, can be driven to despair -- not because of the "heat", which can easily be matched up, but because of the taste blends they aim at.

Just as starters, here is a blend of two lists of chillies reported by the owners of the Pink Adobe Cafe and the Coyote Cafe. I must stress that neither of these are in the class of traditional restaurants, both being highly up-scale and innovative, so that many of these chillies will definitely not be used in the purist northern New Mexico cuisine. Dent also has his list of chillies, and a long extremely informative account of ways of dealing with them in the kitchen. It is interesting to note that both he and other non-Mexican writers place great emphasis on such matters as handling with gloves, which no Mexican-in-Mexico bothers with. But there is very useful information on drying, roasting, skins and seeds. If you explore cook books about Mexico, you will find that some of the names can be used slightly differently.

Anaheim ex California. long, one pointed end, mild

Ancho, mulato, pasillo from Mexico,. oblong, wide, dark green, mild with distinctive flavour.

Cascabel, round, red, mild.

Cayenne, bright red thin pointed very hot 4-6" long.

Cubanelle, light green yellow, mild, sweet.

Española, milder, from the local Española valley, looks like Hatch, to which it is related.

Fresno. 2" red Chile, tapers, 1« wide, very hot, similar to red jalapeño but broader in shoulder.

Gero, generic term for yellow, usually for banana or wax chilies of Santa Fe Grande, which are mildly hot, slightly sweet.

Habeñero, green, yellow or orange shaped like a small bell pepper 2x2" 15 - 20 times stronger than serrano, caustic.

Hatch, hottest native from town of Hatch, S. New Mex., thick, 5 - 7 ", green to red.

Jalapeño, very hot, small, dark green or yellow. When dried and smoked called chipotles.

New Mexico Green 4 - 6" x 2" med to very hot.

New Mexico Red ripened version of green.

Pepperoncini, pale green to yellow, thin, pointed, curved, 2x1" mild.

Pequin, usually home grown, small bush, extremely hot.

Pimento Red, heart shaped 4x3-4" sweet, slightly hot, used in Spain and Hungary for paprika.

Poblano, green form of ancho 4-5x3-4 medium to hot usually cooked or roasted.

Serrano bright green or red, cylindrical with round or pointed end, 2x¬", hottest common Chile in North America. Good for North American salsas.

Thai bright red or dark green, long, thin, pointed, 4x3/4". one Thai = three serrano.

All this having been said, in New Mexico as distinct from Mexico itself, it is only the special restaurants and refined cooks who seek out the rarer varieties. Many of the popular, as distinct from the gourmet, cook books simply refer to "green" or "red" chilies, mostly meaning by that colours and degrees of power that depend on the stage of ripening. Where a restaurant specifies the kind of Chile that they use, I will mention it; otherwise it is up to the discretion of the cook, and his or her sense of taste. This is not the case in Mexico itself, where, as we shall see, the flavour of the Chile creates much more discrimination. I imagine that the New Mexico situation is the result of the limited range grown locally over the centuries, with importation from the south being expensive and not frequent until recently.

Perhaps I should have included beans among the staples, especially since the version known as *refritos* or refried beans is such an important part of the garnish to many dishes, and others like garbanzo and pinto and chick peas figure in some forms of *posole* and stews.

Refried beans is a bit of a misnomer. There are several ways of preparing them, usually aiming at *claro* or light forms, or *nero* or dark forms. The methods of preparation remind me so much of the ways of doing potatoes in Alsace, except in this case *refritos* are always mashed to a smooth puree. The similarity is that you change the taste of the bean minimally by using pork lard to fry the beans as you puree them, and you may add bacon or ham and\or onions to give additional oomph, always however pulverized in such a way that the additions cannot be seen. Some beans will be soaked or have water added to begin with. You can't do this with any old beans but must choose your type.

I assume the idea of *refrito* came about because after this preparation, and maybe storage of the product, you warm them up in a frying pan to serve them, that is refry them. In other words, refried beans are not twice fried, but prepared in order to be fried.

In the small restaurants I checked out and in the localized Indian and New Mexican cookbooks, there are some notable omissions in the repertoire of the cuisine. Duck and goose one might expect to be limited by the dry environment. But venison, game birds, rabbit, mutton and turkey, which are locally available, though they must appear in home cooking, do not figure in the non-gourmet restaurants or in the simple recipe books, except for Indian ones. (Dent has some turkey and lamb recipes.) Nor does epazote, a herb that grows wild in North America and is used in Mexico, or the more difficult achiote, although it is available in commercial sauces. Coriander does not figure much in home cooking, and there is next to no reference to mint, though both must surely be used (Dent has minimal reference to cilantro, and does include mint in a couple of recipes). But cinnamon and cumin figure, obviously imported. I was in fact struck by the relative lack of reference to specific herbs, both in restaurant menus and in the simpler cookbooks.

To me, much cooking in the United States reflects the powerful force in that country toward standardization through the application of a cultural lowest common denominator. There is a tendency in the culture for the majority to push aside anything that is different or makes a strong ethnic statement. Hence "Mexican" cooking, amongst many others, has arrived at a style that in being totally inoffensive to the majority, which still treats it with suspicion, lacks authenticity and difference.[31] Not so in New Mexico, unless you go out of your way to look for that sort of thing.

I will never forget my first introduction to authentic old New Mexican food.

In the very first cafe in the very first village of Raton after I had driven down from Canada I ordered real fajitas, taken for granted on the ordinary menu for ordinary people. Strips of grilled loin on a hot hot hot dish, with the standard, but still real, garnish of salsa, guacamole, refried beans, tomato. I knew I was in a different country, where ordinary working people had different ideas of what food was all about.

There is a cafe in the little village of El Rito called El Farolito. If you are not familiar with this part of the world, you will pass it by, since it is located in a simple house, not terribly well repaired, like many another. But if you are hungry, you may stop, since there is only one other cafe in the village, and the village is many miles from other resources. And if you do, you will be in for a treat[32].

---

[31] Cuisines of other cultures are now much more widely appreciated than they were during my visit.
[32] If it is still there.

El Farolito (there was a different place of the same name, a bed and breakfast, in Santa Fe itself) was named after one of the ceremonial observances that even the new Santa Feans hold onto as a mark of their special individuality. At Christmas they deck out their homes and streets with festive candles set in sand, sheltered with paper bags, a sight reminiscent of the liberation day candles that light the windows of Amsterdam once a year.

El Farolito (does the word have some etymological link with faro = lighthouse?) is neat and tidy, with only half a dozen tables, and a pay phone that brings in friendly people who greet each other and stop for a chat.

It was here I had red stuffed *sopapilla* (Dent calls them *sopapillas*). *Sopapillas* are tortillas made of flour mixed with lard and a leavening agent, deep fried until golden brown, used either for savoury fillings, or, more frequently in restaurants, as dessert or sweet side dishes. They are not generally known in Mexico - a New Mexico invention. The *sopapillas* of El Farolito were fried in a heat that did not puff them up, then rolled and stuffed generously with ground meat and herbs, placed on a deliciously smooth hot red pepper coulis, accompanied by pinto beans.

In many restaurants you get very deep fried *sopapillas* which are served on the side instead of tortillas or bread. The extreme heat of the oil – 400^0 - and a small hole made in the mix to let the air out and puffs them up like huge pop corns. Sometimes egg is included in the mix. I do not know whether there is any technical difference between these and what is known as Indian fry bread. You serve them with very sweet local honey, without which a New Mexican meal would hardly be one, or with a sugar and cinnamon mix.

Guadelupe is a perimeter street near the old railway station, yet fortunately well within the newer strip perimeters so that, despite development, it has retained much of its historical character. There you will find old buildings turned into malls, and many little houses that are now bookstores, specialty food places, office copying enterprises, boutiques, all that jazz. It abuts simple residential areas, in which there are restaurants and other attractive places.

La Choza was one of these, across the railway tracks from the Guadelupe traffic, but well patronized for all that. You had the same plates at lunch and dinner with of course different prices. There were, as is typical, several large rooms, a roaring fireplace in winter, and your typical Hispanic semi-artistic decoration. The waitresses were energetic and fast serving, including a tall blonde southern Amazon in baton twirling boots and a luscious smile.

Not all places in Santa Fe do the North American trick of serving nacho chips and salsa, but they do here. What is also usual is to provide wedges of lime with your beer, a garnish I enjoy with the lighter ales, of which Santa Fe makes a reasonable brew, more interesting than the mass produced U.S. liquid. (Incidentally, France has now taken up the idea with its panaché beers, bottled with lime or peach flavours added, refreshing on a hot day.)

Here I sampled *Chili verde con papas*, which came as pork and potato soup with strong green chilies, a salad served first, and a tough flour tortilla with butter. I found most side tortillas chewy to eat, and was amused by the cafe idea of providing them with butter, a half way house to a dinner roll -- sometimes with jam too at breakfast. You will note that the type of green chili was not specified, taken for granted, and probably New Mexican.

There was more careful cooking, with a little more innovation, yet retention of old values at the Maria Ysabel Restaurante, a pleasant adobe building not far away, with courtyard, small and modest in presentation.

As usual, I was there for lunch, sampling the carnitas, strips of beef marinated in wine. They were served mixed with sautéed mushrooms and onions, delicately. I liked the way the *refritos*, refried beans, were placed on the side of the plate so that you could either mush in the American manner, or, better still, taste them in and out of the beef, Mexican style. The green chili salsa was in a side cup.

Among the more interesting items I did not have a chance to try were nacho pie with *refritos*, red chili, *chicharrones* (deep fried pieces of pork skin, often eaten as chip-like snacks), cheese and lettuce; *bistec a la Santa Fe*, a rib eye steak smothered with green dhal, cheese and mushrooms; shrimp enchiladas with white mushroom sauce.

This was one of the few places I tried a local desert, warm capirotadá. It reminded me of the old English bread pudding we used to get as boys - bread lumps soaked in a honey sauce with raisins and cheese (in New Zealand cheese was not included!).

Tomasita's, in the same district, has more the air of a Western beer parlour that forgot its mission and decided to serve food, busy simple rooms and tables, but with line-ups by mid-day. (The best time to be sure of a lunch table in all these restaurants, if you haven't reserved -- and many places don't take lunch reservations -- is not later than 11.15.) Here you could get meat and bean stuffed *sopapillas*, *tamales* with green chili, rice and refried beans, and tortilla burgers, which, since they are not sandwiches, would probably be called super-tacos in Mexico.

I tried the *chalapas*, Santa Fe style. These are large broad-rimmed cup-shaped crisp tortillas, in this case topped with layers of chicken (at the bottom), cheese and lettuce, some nearly invisible guacamole, an overpowering mixture of red chili salsa and sour cream on top, overpowering in the sense that it smothered the rest most uncharacteristically. When I say sour cream, I mean a soured cream used in New Mexican cooking that is a bit like crème fraiche. The whole was accompanied on the side by a surprisingly leathery *sopapilla* that we complained about with a sweetened sour cream.

We're in the United States of A., with its 50's nostalgia, so what would be more natural than a diner, and diner it is at Zia's, though they couldn't stop there, and had a large restaurant style room and a summer terrace as well. But it had your bar stools, booths, and floor tables and a lively young staff, entirely non-Mexican (though I did not see the kitchen).

As people turned up for Sunday lunch I found myself a table away from a threesome including a large lady with a loud voice, a tall dark handsome man dressed with the kind of jewelry that announced "I am an artist" and a softly chic woman whose style bespoke aesthetics. As so often in Santa Fe, it seems, the artistic community has to talk business -- this was a learnedly practical discussion of how to make sure your creations received appropriate show attention in a commercial gallery..... not just hung around an obscure corner.

Searching from something New Mexican in its diner-oriented menu I hit upon meat loaf with pine nuts and green chili. It was juicily moist, with specks of green that were presumably the mild chili, but it wasn't easy to taste the pine nuts or the chili. It was there, though, since I had chili indigestion after. The modern diner atmosphere was reinforced by undercooked carrot and broccoli and diner style mashed potato and gravy.

I must have been tired of keeping my weight under control that day, and totally seduced by the notion of blackberry banana crumble pie. Though I couldn't taste a hint of the banana that had enticed me, it was still a pie of the kind Americans can do so well when they make up their minds to it -- marvellous   blackberries and wonderfully thick crunchy crust. Not Mexican, but still....

In the Mexican part of the menu you can find green chili and cheese pie, black bean flautas, tostadas, West Coast Snapper Vera Cruz. And there are the diner-yuppie favourites, establishing modern cooking credentials, such as corn and asiago cheese pie, baked brie in phyllo,   humus and pita. You get what I call the international conglomerate message....

By way of contrast to New Mexican, Michael took me to a Mexican cafe in a shopping mall, the Old Mexico Grill, neatly set out in a simple tiled manner. Here there was more emphasis on fish. I had a tortilla with chicken, bell pepper, onion with beans, Mexican rice and garnish. Michael was pleased with excellent looking fajitas, which come in chicken, grilled beef, vegetarian, shrimp formats. There was the inescapable *huachinango* (snapper) *en la salsa di dia*, with beans, Mexican rice, but it wasn't available our day. Or *camarones en salsa verde*, sautéed small shrimp smothered in *salsa verde*, mild green chili and tomatillo sauce, with cheese, black bean and rice, the beans served in a side bowl. Definitely of more care and interest than many other U.S. Mexican outlets.

In the centre of the town, which is after all only a few blocks' walk from the Guadelupe area, there are a number of places that consist mostly of converted houses, some ancient, some colonial. They are extremely popular and some are open only for lunch. Mostly they consist of small rooms interlinked, and sometimes there is a rear entrance as well as a front one, and you are never quite sure where the lineup is or who is in charge of finding a place for you.

One of these was The Den. The guests I found there were typical of the "in" restaurants of the downtown area --

young people getting married talking to parents from Illinois, women in Confederate style chic hats, shoppers, feminists, grey-haired, grey-bearded anxious-eyed men who are so busy with their mothers within that they have not yet found their fathers. The Den was in an old colonial building inside a courtyard near the Plaza. Hand painted beams, fretwork over the windows, a generous supply of paintings. No credit cards.

The tacos were not folded as in El Paso brand supermarket supplies, but open as they should mostly be. The ones I sampled had a mixture of beef, chili, onion, tomato and cheese on a layer of hot lettuce, with two blue corn tortillas on top, accompanied by pinto beans and a small serving of *posole* without the stew part. On the side French garlic bread. It had clearly been designed to fit contemporary healthy food tastes, hamburger style.

Another such lunching hole was Josie's Casa di Comida, also near the Plaza. It had an extensive menu with lots of sandwiches and famous pies, and emphasizes its fashionably casual style by a crudely written nearly unreadable board which listed extensive specials of the day, as well as New Mexican specialties. It had no licence and didn't take credit cards.

I had thick juicy well chilied tomato salsa and excellently crunchy corn chips. Then chicken enchilladas, chicken slivers on blue tortillas overwhelmed with red bean and cheese in an uncharacteristic Americanized thick mush, with rice and more refried beans on the side but somehow included in the mush, garnished with lettuce accompanied by a tough floury tortilla with butter. When you get such mushy servings, especially with cheese, the cheese strings stretch from plate to mouth and, like spaghetti, need something to break the flow, or you'll be all day sucking it in. Pieces of tortilla are excellent for this.

The deep pear pie with ice cream -- now that might have been worth it, good American cooking, not pretend Mexican.

One place downtown I liked for its frank kind of made-over counter-culture atmosphere with yuppie prices was Cafe Pasqual's[33] a highly popular corner-store sort of cafe with mammoth breakfasts lunches and dinners. Dead centre there was a large oval table for singles. The food was not terribly spicy, but showed variety, ingenuity and respect for ingredients in its preparation.

This time I had the quesadilla, large crisp tacos of good quality, with a weak side salsa, jack cheese, avocado, scrambled eggs and minimal chorizo (last two an extra charge). In the United States, American jack cheese, vividly yellow, but mild, tends to be used where in Mexico there would be the thinner, runnier white crême fraiche kind. It was tasty and easy to eat with the fingers. I could also have had, for example, local trout grilled in cornmeal with chili and toasted piñon nuts.

You may have noticed quite a transition taking place as we go through the restaurants, from those which try to stick close to traditional New Mexican styles, through those which muddle along offering some token dishes within an essentially casual American menu, to those which use New Mexican, Mexican, and Southwest styles generally as a basis of innovation.

It would be possible, indeed delightful, to take a different tack from the one I did in the short time available to me, and look for the most innovative styles of cooking, building upon Mexican ideas more generally. There is plenty of that in Santa Fe, some of it highly successful; indeed it is a trademark of the upper-scale chefs and

---

[33] Saint Pasqual is the here the patron saint of cooking.

restaurants. Within American innovative cooking, the chefs of Santa Fe are undoubtedly deserving of their national reputation, and sufficiently proud of their accomplishments to publicize what they can do in an unusually wide range of recipe and menu books[34].

Here, though, you have to be very careful, because there is a characteristic among such chefs sometimes to go wild, to combine ingredients in ways that sound exciting and beautiful, but which simply don't work once the product is inside your mouth. In the attempt to create the unusual, there can be a clash not only of cultures but of taste-buds.

The most famous of all Santa Fe restaurateurs is Mark Miller of the Coyote Cafe, a man I am intrigued to think of as a colleague, but whom I have never met in my three visits -- partly because I didn't know I could claim him as a colleague until late in my last trip. He should be writing this book instead of me -- perhaps he will write his gastronomic autobiography one day, since he was young at this time and has many productive years ahead. He has the kind of personal history of which I approve -- as if my approval matters.

Mark Miller is a product of the Berkeley 'sixties, with an advanced degree in cultural anthropology, turning it to the advantage of the world of cooking. Apprenticed in California restaurants of the highest calibre, he struck out on his own, and eventually settled down in New Mexico, determined to build a cuisine in the new style based on a thorough knowledge of ingredients and their uses in their cultures of origin. He has widely travelled in Asia and Latin America and has studied the foods with an anthropologist's eye.

---

[34] I obtained several and posted them to Canada, but they disappeared in the post.

His lavish and accurately informed book *Coyote Cafe: Foods from the Great Southwest*,[35] is I believe destined to be the bible of southwestern cooking. The section introductions are full of lore and information, the recipes outstanding for their innovative styles, respect for traditions, and care for the selection of ingredients, all presented with the passion and verve characteristics of classical chefs.

Yet.

Yet, despite Craig Claiborne's accolades ("perhaps the greatest Southwest cooking in the whole region") and the poetry of the recipes, in the three meals I have had there I have been disappointed. The first time I was presented with one of the toughest most uninteresting dishes of grilled venison that has ever let me down. At others I found the combinations affronting the taste buds with their clashes.

Mind you, even then the cafe is an experience. The tables are set out split level, full of fashionable Santa Fe, crowded and alive. And it is fun just to be at the grill bar, watching the grill chefs at their task. When I did that the dining room chief kept a minute and detailed check on the passage of food from order to cook to table. I was sitting almost next to where the maitre d' stationed himself with his copies of the order slips. Depending on the appetizers, he checked the timing of the grill mains as if he had a stopwatch in his head. "Fire 10" would come his call, "Fire 25" and so on and on, the cooks responding, getting the product to the table with industrialized split second timing.

That alone was not enough. As each plate was complete it came to him. His nose, his fingers, his eye, checked it all out. A little pushing here, a little poking there,

---

[35] Berkeley, Ten Speed Press, 1989

and it was ready for service. Not a plate escaped his attention, for the whole, packed dining room.

Bearing in mind my cautions, some of the poetry from the book needs quoting. Hear this.

"Poblano pesto, with poblano chilies, lime, sweet pepper, garlic, pine nuts, used with oysters; chili mignonette, with shallots, cilantro, chopped assorted chilies, wine, vinegar; tamarind chipotle sauce; green chili and oyster chowder; squash blossoms, stuffed with cheese, sour cream, marjoram, eggs, cumin, coriander, chili powder, cinnamon mixture then deep fried in peanut oil; goat cheese and mint tamale; currant and cinnamon tamale; curried oysters with banana salsa; scallop hash, with chili; tuna tartare with cilantro mayonnaise and avocado *crema*; pan-fried quail in red chili cider sauce; braised duck with posole; pheasant with chorizo and blue corn bread stuffing; smoked rabbit enchiladas; rack of lamb with rosemary-serrano aïoli; pork tacos with wild mushrooms and tamarind chipotle sauce; pecan and wild boar bacon waffles with bourbon syrup."

I don't guarantee that these will be on the menu of the Coyote Cafe the night you call. And it might be an idea to find the book to see how it is supposed to be done, experiment yourself, and get the taste balances right.

The Pink Adobe is one of the earliest up-scale innovative restaurants in the town. You might be attracted by, for example, brie with green chili soup; rolled stuffed breast of veal New Mexican with piñon nuts, coriander, jalapeño jelly, roasted green chilies, and chorizo); sautéed shrimp in chili coconut milk sauce; Southwestern stuffed artichokes -- stuffed with mayonnaise, sour cream, chili, artichoke hearts, Parmesan, Worcestershire sauce, Tabasco; swordfish *borracho* with *salsa fresca* -- in herbs, lemon, lime, dried chili, marinated in tequila, with salsa. If some of it seems a bit overdone, maybe you could be right.

Such is the nature of the world's merry-go-round.

That visit was also the last time I saw Michael. Some years later he had written a small book called *A Kiwi in Cowboy Land*. He had always talked of travelling – back to New Zealand, and with an earnest interest in Patagonia, but he never did.

He was finding the harsh winters of the hills of New Mexico too much for him and spent years trying to sell his land and exchange it for a tract he had his eye on close to the Mexican border in a warmer climate. At long last it happened. He had long given up breeding wolves and had minimal income. He bought a trailer in which he was to live until he had constructed a new adobe home. He had made new friends locally but his letters to me were lonesome and penurious.

Melanoma made its appearance. I did not really know how dangerous was his situation until the end, not even when I phoned him. He travelled frequently to Albuquerque for treatment. The chemotherapy, as so often happens, upset him and invaded him with depression. He could not stand it. He stopped taking the medication.

A neighbour passed by. Within a couple of days, Michael had died, sitting in his chair.

He deeded his land to an environmental charity. I do not trust them. The land will miss my brother.

And I ask myself, why Michael, not me? When I was a boy I frequently had serious sunburns which created enormous pain – sunscreen was not known in those days and coconut oil made the burning worse. And I have spent many an unprotected time on beaches and in deserts. Why Michael?

39. Hi jinks in Stockholm and Lively Leiden

Over a decade ago I decided to put down my thoughts about the state and future of the global society, no less. The draft I then wrote was amateurish.

Later, in the new century, I decided to undertake it seriously. I had written a printable draft when in 2004 an e-mail informed me that there was a competition sponsored by a group in Stockholm with the acronym SOC which would crown the World Utopian Champion. There had been one earlier competition.

So why not? The total book draft would be too much for the judges, so I selected one of the first chapters, on reforming education, and the last two chapters, one on reforming world government and one on how to get there in the 21st century. There were two interlocking themes. One was a holistic approach to world society, and the other a theory of innovation (whichwould make change possible) which I had already published in an earlier form.

Much to my surprise and delight I won, and received an accolade from Tom Moylan[36] one of the judges.[37]

---

[36] Glucksnan Professor of Contemporary Writing and Director of the Railihin Centre for Utopian Studies in the University of Limerick

The award was to be presented at a gala of supporting artists in 2005. But how to get to Stockholm? I am not one to miss that sort of party. I was broke, and SOC had so little revenue (by way of Swedish grants) that they had to wind up after the event. The main movers and shakers were Jon Brumberg and his colleague Annika Drougge two Swedish artists. I tried for funding from Canadian sources, but was either out of synch with funding calendars or considered to be too old. But the Canadian government did have a programme of support for such travel. So the Swedish colleagues got to work and approached the Canadian consul in Stockholm. At the very last minute the grant came through.

It was generous but not sufficient to cover costs in the normal way. The Swedes decided that they had to economise on the air travel so that more nights could be covered. A Stockholm travel agent, with great initiative, managed to find a KLM flight which enabled modest but good accommodation to be covered for three nights.

I had major scruples about travelling through the United |states because of the Patriot Act and the way fellow Canadians of colour had been hassled at airports while being honoured at literary events. I squished my principles. The cheap flight took me from Vancouver to San Francisco by Alaska Airlines. Then KLM took the polar route back across Canada to Amsterdam, and thence to Stockholm. Paradoxically, many more kilometers were covered on this route than on the direct

---

[37] See http://www.soc.nu/utopian for details of the competition, the judgement and the concluding gala

KLM flight from Vancouver, such is the logic of present day air travel.

Although I had been to Stockholm once before I had not noticed the millions of lakes and islands, still covered with ice in the early spring. Two things almost immediately struck me as they had not done before – the fact that Stockholm is a city of islands and waterways; and that there is a substantial German population in the south of Sweden, which no doubt contributed to the Swedish neutrality in the second world war.

Most of the members of SOC were Swedish artists, and thus I was immersed in an artist community and the gala itself took on the atmosphere of that community. The organizers had obtained a large gallery area for the event, with a well stocked bar below.

The place was packed. I sat next to the runner up, Per Norböck, a Swede from a small Swedish town who had made use of the internet to galvanise young people to take an interest in civic affairs and had created a virtual network which gained seats on the local council and pressed through with reforms. My contribution was theoretical; his was practical and received high marks from the Australian judge.

There were enhanced videos about the needs of the world and Soc's role. It was of course in Swedish, and not until afterwards did I realize that a part of the story was that SOC was at least temporarily winding up. It too was broke.

When my win was announced I was called up onto the stage and asked how I came to be interested in Utopia. I was worked up and launched into an impassioned statement of my mantra. It was people like those in SOC who would make the essential difference in the state of the world. The differences we all wanted would come about through determined changes in the way of life of every individual, from family through to politics.

When I stopped, Swedes revealed themselves. This was no quiet, polite, clapping Canadian crowd. The Swedish artists erupted. They clapped, they stamped on the floor, they shouted, they whistled. One man afterwards told me he had tears in his eyes. I have to believe him. These people wanted, almost desperately, to change the world.

Then there was a party. The hall was emptied of seats for dancing. Most of the audience, however, descended to the bar. Jon and Annika danced on the bar itself, and pulled me up to join them, a not unusual occurrence in Sweden. Somewhat tipsy I climbed up and made what movements I could muster without falling off.

Jon and Annika were wondrous hosts, enthusiastic and accommodating, and with them I explored food as you will now see. I wanted to find traditional Swedish family food.

The answer to my query was Yes, it is there but you have to look for it. Stockholm food, like that of all other major cities, is international and global. But a long weekend showed me what to look for.

I asked Annika and Jon – pronounced June with a softer J. They thought and said it might be possible, but frankly if they wanted good Swedish food they visited their mothers. I forbade to ask what happens when this generation of mothers pass away? My advice: find the food and support the good restaurants which do in fact serve it.

The discussion happened on the way from the airport to the little bed and breakfast hotel, the Art Hotel, they had found for me. The Art Hotel, furnished by volunteer artists, is central and simple on a one way street. As I was freshening Annika did her research at the front desk and with delight produced not only an address around the corner for the Pelikan restaurant, but a full menu of true Swedish cooking. We had a most satisfying comfort meal.

At one of the big bookshops next morning, which carry shelves of works in English, I searched unsuccessfully for the translation of a new novel which bears the title "Hash", with a story built around Sweden's most elemental comfort dish. I said to the cashier, "Where can I go around here to sample a true Swedish lunch?." With furrowed brow she said, well it's not totally Swedish, but if you go to the terrace at the Eden hotel across the street you will find something".

And something it was. In and out of the international menu there was a smooth mouth-watering smoked salmon and an eye catching plate of frikadelle meatballs– so different from the stuff served nowadays at Ikea. Never have I tasked such a fresh lingonberry sauce, not the sweetly sickening jam that comes bottled. At a buffet dinner preceding the Gala I asked the same question, and I said, correctly, that the guide books were less than helpful. Wherever you go in the world, if you ask such a question, immediately there will be a standards committee struck on the spot. For an hour the opinions flowed thick and fast, with the result that I obtained a list which you won't find in any Swedish guidebooks. Here it is. You are privileged to read it. Keep it safe.

Good places to eat traditional Swedish food (my spelling may be a bit off since I am not sure I interpret the writing correctly).

Pelikan – "Great place and great food in an old beer hall."

Operabaren – "classic"

Bakfickan – "Classic"

Gondalen – "Great view of Stockholm"

KB – An old artist hangout"

Eriksdals Värdshus – "Half an hour from the centre"

Prinsen – "Also a hangout for artists"

Ulla Winblach

Grodan

Folkhemnet

Tranan

Clearly good old Swedish food is alive and well, if not in the guide books.

Unfortunately the long weekend was too preoccupied (with pleasing activities) for me to sample widely. But on my last night we visited Fem Smö Haus, a long standing favourite where Annika and Jon – pronounced June with a softer J – used to hang out as art students. It is in one of those once working neighbourhoods now becoming gentrified, but retains its older character and clientele. The entry is through a large bar into a dark wooded room with white tablecloths that only Old Europe can produce.

There was the famous hash on the menu, so I chose it. Not exactly your gourmet choice. It was indeed a huge plate, of chopped meat, with an egg on top. Highly filling, not possible for one like me to complete. I found it totally tasteless, so full was it with gruel. Jon – pronounced June with a softer J – let himself go with a venison stew. The friendly, helpful, homely waitress brought us a round of good *Swedish* aquavit served with shot glasses in a bowl of ice – to be drunk in one gulp, but I prefer to savour the herbs in my poison.

Stockholm is a charming city for both food and ambience. The clear sun warmed the city, and the waters of the myriad bays and inlets and boat passages – for the town is built on scores of islands – sparkled as front drop for the gently coloured Baltic architecture. Friends gathered on street corners and in squares to greet each other after the long winter. Sunday morning congregations stepped forth from churches as the bells tolled for the next service. Despite activity streets were so quiet after Vancouver. In the three plus days I heard not a single emergency vehicle and, although there is crime and unhappiness, saw not a single policeman or homeless person.

....

At the end of Chapter 26 I described a conference in Leiden sponsored by the university's Afrika Institut. Had it not been for their financial efforts I would never have managed to get to the meeting. Leiden is above all a university town and has the verve and cheek to go with its younger inhabitants. The university itself is spread over a huge area. To make it more confusing there are *two* Afrika Institut locations. One of these is in a combined student and classroom building in the centre. When I lost my way, as I often did, and asked directions it was here I was always directed. But the main research Institut was in a separate building quite some distance away. While the African participants seemed to have no trouble finding it, I, the anthropologist, could never discover it on my own.

I arrived by the beautifully smooth train from Schipol a day early and was able to do a little preliminary exploration.

At the station there were huge bicycle parks, including a major automated one on several levels. And by one of the entrances a bicycle repair shop doing enormous business with students continuously bringing and taking their bikes. As throughout Holland there are special bike lanes. At first I found it too easy to wander into them, only to be brought up sharply when a descending torrent of English bikers descended on me without mercy yelling "Get out of the Way". I soon learned but not before my very life was in jeopardy.

This was in the early days of Skype, the extraordinarily useful internet phone service. My first hotel was on a residential street opposite the medical school with good rooms and the ability to surf the net so that I was able to phone Vancouver and Toronto for next to nothing. We later moved as a group to a motel outside the main city and I spent two extra nights in the well known Hotel Minerva. In neither place could I use my laptop independently of their own terminal so I used the JWire search engine on my own machine to find the location of a wireless connection. The only one was in the public library, but that didn't work either. When I went to the library I found numerous studious people working on the library's machines but I could not find an independent connection. The librarian was concerned and guided me into various corners of the building. Only in one place did I get a weak and useless signal and then I had to turn the laptop 90 degrees. In a university town!!! I am sure that in the subsequent years matters must have changed considerably.

The city was full of life as you might expect. As I was walking in the centre there was a weekend festival. A band led a military parade over bridges and down the streets. With the Netherlands flag there on an equal footing were the Stars and Stripes and the Maple Leaf of Canada. The Dutch do not forget.

I drooled over the Saturday market, colourful and crowded and discovered where I could by my favourite Alsace eau-d-vie for a pittance – in Vancouver when you can buy it at all the price is prohibitive, though fortunately there is now a local product which is nearly as good. And on a bridge beside the market, with barges and rowboats floating with happy parties there was a most wonderful orchestra enthralling packed listeners. For me this was a time of sunny happiness, for photography and audio recording.

I had my eye and taste buds open for good food but since the main clientele in the city centre is students good food is very hard to come by. Close by the station there are fast food places and in the station square there was a small caravan grilling up mouth watering seafood. I was often hot and tired so I would hop into one of the numerous cafes where they would serve me coffee with cream, the cream sometimes being on the side. I learned more about drinking *yonge jenever*. One of the more amusing dishes which was common was called *bruschetta*. It could not have been more different from the Italian original. It was a large piece of toasted bread with something on it – in one case, for example, *kip*, i.e. fish, in another egg and mayonnaise.

On one occasion the Afrika Institute hosted the group to dinner at the major Chinese restaurant in a main square. It was a most ornate place, sparing nothing in the way of oriental ambience in décor, resplendent in reds and golds. We were close together and enjoying ourselves. But I had to say to myself that the food itself was not well executed.

I looked for the better restaurants and they too were a disappointment, though most of those praised in the guides were well away from the central city. I found Jill's to be a popular place, well recommended. The atmosphere was comfortable and friendly. I can't now read my poorly printed bill but remember the execution of the dishes left much to be desired.

I had passed by an elegant looking place with open rooms and white tablecloths and thought I should go in one evening. At first I was put off because a waiter was stationed outside in the manner of a polite an elegant tout, but a tout nevertheless. They were not keen to accommodate a single diner. After a while I was admitted and reassured as the place filled with well dressed patrons on their night out.

The whole setting was pretentious beyond belief with astronomical prices and a banal international menu. When I asked for a glass of tap water I was refused. "We have to make our money on bottled water" was the wry explanation.

I thought that at the very least great fish would be available, and there is a well thought of specialty fish restaurant on a side street in the town centre. When I first tried for admission I found that it was only open three nights a week and this was not one of them. I did manage to get there on an open night and was turned away. "We are totally full". No apology. That was that.

Clearly I was not going to do a Stockholm and find traditional Dutch food. When I inquired from Institut staff they were discouraging. "It would be pretty heavy stuff" was their verdict. I learned that there was one Leiden participant who was an expert in the matter. He promised to bring me a list, even if I could not visit them, on the next and last day.

This was the day I well and truly lost my way on the campus, missing the short final session. I missed my contact too and was not able to track him down, by email or any other way. I did learn, though, that traditional restaurants were well away from the city centre.

TWO SPECIAL MEN

40. Raymond Firth: Mentor

As you may have read in Volume I Raymond Firth was my academic mentor mentor and in many ways controlled my early career. I owed him the benefits of guidance and understanding. When my student finances were in jeopardy he always came through with solutions which not only saved us from penury but gave me valuable experience. His wife Rosemary was hospitable and became close friends with Betty.

To many colleagues do I owe wisdom support and critical advice during my hurly burly life, in its quiet times and noisy ones. Two in particular were there from the beginning when I tried to be an anthropologist, but one with a view outside the discipline itself. They were Raymond Firth and Harry Hawthorn. Sometimes they were disappointed in me. Once again I write from memory without benefit of what is in my archive boxes. It reflects my own sense of our interactions, rather than the kind of issues that were really preoccupying them at the various times.

One cannot think adequately about Raymond as human being without thinking of Rosemary his wife. Rosemary was a good hearted woman who had partnered in Raymond's study of Malay fishermen. She was moving into social psychology and social work, which deeply affected her thoughts about individual people. I don't recall how it was that my wife, Betty, and I met her, but it must have been early on for she invited we students to spend one Christmas in their home. It was Betty who was the catch, not me. It was kind and generous and somewhat disastrous.

Raymond was ill with a dreadful cold or fever. Bravely he descended to the living room in his pyjamas and dressing gown sniffling and snuffling, his eyes and nose streaming.

And I, still naïve about the ways of the world, had bought a bottle of wine. Some cheap Cypriot plonk. Raymond looked at the bottle in the kitchen and sniffed as only he could, with or without a cold – "if he doesn't know anything about wine he shouldn't bring it………"

Indeed in the 'fifties and 'sixties Raymond was often unwell and I had cause to worry for him.

During one of their visits to Vancouver we were dining in the downtown University Club. At the arrival of the main dish Raymond, without the slightest warning, keeled over and fell to the floor. Panic all round. The staff were all for calling a doctor immediately. But Raymond quickly awoke and brushed it off and he and Rosemary both averred that it happened quite often.

Whatever the problem, Raymond not only survived his ills, whatever they were, but continued in a heavy programme of travel, charming students all over the world with his kindly wrinkled eyes and deft seminar skills.

They managed to come through Vancouver together, or Rosemary separately, from time to time, but in the course of my own ever-widening travels, I did not revisit L S E.

Rosemary formed an attachment to Betty and took a personal interest in my growing daughter, Diana. Sometimes to Betty's irritation, she would use her perspectives to lecture us on how to bring up children. As Diana continued her life she maintained a correspondence both with Rosemary and the Firth son, Hugh, whom I have never met.

Raymond's personal influence was not limited to U.K. or commonwealth universities. He personally advised the Wenner-Gren Foundation for Anthropological Research. I was fortunate enough to be included in one of his first conferences in the romantic castle of Burg Wartenstein, in the early sixties. The Foundation operated the castle as a seminar centre. This one was on credit and capita in peasant societies. There was the usual classical music in the open courtyard and oom-pa-pa dancing to the sounds of the nearby village band. But work was done in the conference room, followed by Austrian wine. Raymond was in his element as co-host, enjoying both the debates and the relaxation.

He was also close to the academic side of UNESCO as distinct from its policy side. Again he called me up for a session in Kyrenia on Cyprus organised by Peter Lengyel, an Australian UNESCO staffer who took a great deal of the responsibility for liaising with social science activities. Eyebrows are sometimes raised by the exotic locations for some of the UNESCO activities. What critics do not realize is that they were a necessity. Cyprus, for example, paid its dues in its own currency which had limited exchange value. Placing seminars in that country was one way of making use of the fund.

I remember the lively way in which Peter organized expeditions into the towns and villages, sampling Greek table dancing, food, wines and brandy. Raymond excused himself from such boyish antics but was with us on the cultural tours to all parts of the island. Here he exhibited his wide knowledge of Orthodox church architecture and the historical mysteries of its symbolism.

I also remember a nattily dressed gentleman who arrived late in the middle of discussions, was not introduced, and immediately participated confidently in the debates with a thick Bronx accent and impeccable English. He was a Soviet economist, a rare creature in those days of the cold war, who had acquired his language skills during his boyhood as the son of the Soviet trade representative in New York. On the way home through Athens I determined to beat the tourist crowd and get to the Parthenon in the very earliest of the morning. Lo and behold I met this colleague already walking *down* from the top, his inspections completed ! I wish I had met him again.

In the 'seventies I had little direct contact with Raymond except to receive recommendations for appointments to the department at U.B.C. I'm afraid after several experiences I learned to read them with a jaded eye. Raymond's generous side included a principle that he would never criticize anyone, at least in print. Let's leave it at that. He also probably had a hand in my appointment to edit *Current Anthropology*. He would certainly have been consulted.

In the fateful year before Betty's death we had agreed to live in the Firth's London home, and visit their Devon cottage while they were on a trip to New Zealand. I checked in ahead of time and over dinner they were both very appreciative. In Rosemary's presence, Raymond tended to let her manage the conversation. As I have recounted earlier Rosemary was ebullient and flattering and very pleased we were to stay in their home.

Poor Firths! My troubles were soon to begin, very publicly, and caused immense confusion, particularly in Rosemary, with which Raymond had to deal. For in a very public investigation (despite its supposed secrecy), in which Rosemary was interviewed by the police, it became known that I had been having an affair at the time of Betty's death. The Swiss police were highly manipulative and took advantage of Rosemary's shock, using that shock to attack me. My lawyer in turn met with Rosemary in London and was himself shocked at her state of mind. Raymond himself kept out of it, at least on the surface, and did not give testimony.

When I returned to some sort of life I was myself in a not very stable emotional state and protested to the Firth's about some of the things Rosemary was reported to have said. Raymond himself replied saying "let's leave it at that".

While incarcerated I was persuaded not to resign the Presidency of the International Union of Anthropological and Ethnological Sciences. I did not want to resume such responsibilities, wanted to opt for the simple life. The English delegation was wondering what to do about me – as no doubt were many others. It seems that Raymond advised the Royal Anthropological Institute – his services were later acknowledged. I am not privy to what went on, but I rather think that he advised calm and sticking to proper procedure.

Which is what the British delegation did. As I have mentioned earlier at a Council meeting in Amsterdam the British delegation properly moved that my position be examined during my absence from the room.

So Raymond and I, he in his last years, lived as it were apart, Rosemary's perspectives between us. Long after Rosemary's death I wrote to congratulate Raymond on his birthday. He replied with a warm and generous letter. I am relieved communication ended on a good note even though I did not see him personally after 1978.

41. Harry Hawthorn[38]: Pioneer

This is by no means a biography of Harry Hawthorn. There are many parts of Harry's life that have always been closed to me. It is a sketch of my memories and feelings. I owe as much to Harry, possibly more, as I do to Raymond.

Harry was a private man and only occasionally did he reveal to me, and then *sotto voce* that the inner man was other than the public man, the man most readily recognised.

His name has come up many times in previous chapters – the man, for example, who, with his wife Audrey, welcomed me into their home and fold from the first days of my arrival in Vancouver until we had a home of our own.

I have only superficial knowledge of Harry's life before he came to Vancouver. Like Raymond, he was a New Zealander, an immigrant who had to make his way. Like Raymond he retained, underneath his new culture, a strong attachment to the country of his birth. Unlike

---

[38] This is the correct spelling of Harry's name. Even in the Encyclopaedia of British Columbia is was erroneously spelled with a final e. I don't know what Harry thought about this but such an error would have annoyed me.

Raymond he was originally a shy man and I am told took Dale Carnegie courses to remedy his lack of confidence. He succeeded extraordinarily well.

For some reason I never discussed with him the steps which led him to come to the University of British Columbia. He must have been well received by the president of the time (both ardent fishermen). Whether it was a condition of his appointment or not I do not know. But from day one of the re-energised post-war university he was the beneficiary of a major long term grant from the Foundation which enabled him to create a presence of anthropology on a scale and with a reputation unique in the country. It was well established at the end of the grant, when the university took over its financing.

More than anyone else, Harry was personally behind the recognition of anthropology as an academic subject in Canadian universities, as his students gradually and then quickly began to staff other departments.

Although Professor Mcilwraith of the University of Toronto had preceded him, representing what even then was an old fashioned approach. It was not until later years that that department reached its zenith. Thus Harry can truly be judged as the pioneer of modern anthropology in Canada.

It was also in the orientation of the discipline that he pioneered. He had been brought up in the stream of U.S. comprehensive anthropology, including prehistory, physical anthropology and linguistics as branches of the discipline, as well as social and cultural anthropology.

But he had instruction from Bronislaw Malinowski, the pioneer of the new British social anthropology, when the latter visited the United States. It must have made a marked impression on him

He did not make British social anthropology the mandate of the nascent department. When I arrived in 1953 the half dozen teaching staff were all versed in the American tradition, though some like Helen Codere were thoughtful about other approaches. Others were intense ethnographers, more interested in oral statements than in day to day behaviour. And they were students of North American indigenous peoples, with little comparative interest. Harry himself wanted to revolutionise those studies from the social anthropology perspective. He saw me as the thin edge of that wedge.

I could not overcome my despair at the conditions of the Indians of British Columbia, a perspective reinforced by my contrasting south seas experience, and though I gave speeches to meetings south of the border, I must have disappointed Harry in that regard.

The role of both Harry and Audrey in understanding the significance of Northwest Indian art as a central theme for the retention of culture has been documented. Yet no words can fully recognise the warmth and empathy that characterised their understandings. The relationship they created with a handful of Indian artists was one of direct respect and equality of homes. They were welcome in the Hawthorn's living room, a rare event in those days when Vancouver was notorious for its racial prejudice.

The Hawthorn home was a beautiful place, and to visitors like myself a haven of tranquility and a hospitality that to me spoke deeply of the best of New England.

It was through the Hawthorns that I met Bill Reid. At the time I had no idea what lay ahead for Bill and I cannot claim I knew him well. I do not know how the Hawthorns discovered the genius of his artistry and sculpture. Bill Reid would have reached the pinnacles of his talent without the Hawthorns, but their help in the early days and their percipient recognition of him says much about their ability to put their finger on talent. Bill and another First Nations artist, Mungo Martin, were part of a totem pole rescue mission that Harry established on the U.B.C. campus when classic poles were in a sad state of deterioration throughout the Province. I frequently visited the poles newly erected on the campus with my children but at that time they did not speak to me. I was blind to West Coast art.

Now of course the renaissance of Northwest Coast art is in full swing and has been for decades. To me it is miraculous that such a high proportion of First Nations people are individually producing so much extraordinary and innovative art which now does indeed speak to me. Bill Reid's majestic sculpture (on display at the Vancouver International Airport) with its wealth of mythical and humorous figures is to me a work of sculpture at least as impressive as The Burgers of Calais or the works of Rodin, and it is not nearly the only one of such dramatic skill.

The meetings were in the Hawthorn's living room, especially when we did not have our own house. When we did so our style of living was much less the day to day openness than that of the Hawthorns and we ourselves as a family did not have the same skill at reciprocating or spreading our wings.

Harry had impressions of my beliefs which were often quite wrong. One persistent theme of his was that I must be opposed to museums on principle, as a graduate of the early British school of anthropology, which indeed often sneered at museology and even at archaeology as it then was. But I did not have t hose opinions about modern trends. I was excited by the Hawthorn's powerful and imaginative, even pioneering, creation of the campus Museum of Anthropology which has gone on to greater heights and a pioneering international reputation over the subsequent years.

The museum began with a gift of South Seas material from a collector, housed modestly in the basement of the library, to which the Hawthorns added Northwest Coast material. As far as the South Seas were concerned Audrey, the curator, had little knowledge and some of the labelling mistakes continued for a while into the ultimate building.

In the creation of the modern museum the Hawthorns made the best use of their connections. Harry's previous work on Indian affairs together with the help of the politically minded President of the university and Geoffrey Andrew, his number two, ensured the attention of the federal Liberal government, which was prepared to designate the project as a British Columbia centennial event. Harry was able to enlist the imaginative support of the architect, the already famous Arthur Erickson, who had Simon Fraser University among his credentials. The partnership worked like a dream, although Arthur's well known capacity for going over budget became evident. The Hawthorns had also cultivated a friendship with the Koerner family, refugee lumber barons, whose philanthropy was central to the university's growth, and who had outstanding collections of Northwest Coast art and Central European materials which they deeded to the Museum and which became central to its early collections.

And Harry made an excellent though at the time controversial choice in appointing Michael Ames, one of our former students, to the post of Director.

I was for part of the construction time Head of Anthropology and Sociology and involved, on the margins, in some of the policy. Harry made it abundantly clear, though, that he agreed to make the dream come true *only* if he had *complete* control and the ability to overrule any committees, such as a user's committee. This was Harry's style, even when Head of the academic department. In this case it worked. In particular my own headstrong ideas were kept out of sight, to the benefit of the ultimate result.

I began to notice that more and more, and in subtle ways, Harry and I were becoming distant. His inaccurate feelings about my beliefs played a considerable role, and indeed as far as the museum was concerned I might well have raised some troubling issues. For example, the site is at present magnificent, imaginative and powerful. Will it be there in a hundred years, situated as it is on the edge of a cliff subject to sea and wind erosion? I also had a different idea about its location on academic grounds. I wanted to see anthropology and sociology moved to a central location, with the museum adjacent or even physically linked, and part of a central social science core relating to the existing locations of geography, fine arts, and Asian studies as a beginning. This was not to b e and I certainly did not press the idea. Nevertheless, both the department and the Museum are detached, almost isolated, from the rest of the campus from which they are separated, both physically and mentally, by a main road.

This had nothing to do with the nature of the museum as such. But Harry felt that my ideas, whatever they were, would be too much influenced by the prejudices of functional anthropology.

He himself had mixed feelings. On day when we were walking on the lovely campus he put his head to mine and in a low voice, almost a whisper, said "You know I could not care less about museums. I am only doing this for Audrey". As I look back I cannot believe he was truly honest at that moment. Somehow he was trying to get back into what he thought were my evaporated good graces. The work and skill he put into the completion of the project could not have been done by anyone who lacked the emotional determination to succeed – and to make a statement which would reverberate through the Canadian, even the world, community of anthropological museums.

If he did it for Audrey, what would Audrey's role be? Audrey had taken care of the nascent collections but had no ambitions, as far as I know, to be Director, which would have involved different skills and way of life. It was natural for her to become a senior curator.

Here another advantage of the Hawthorn involvement began to show – their sensitive and friendly links to First Nations communities throughout the Province. Mike Ames was completely on board and the team began to plan for unique cooperation with those communities, slowly at first and then becoming a lynch pin of the museum's character. Michael extended the concept to other ethnic communities who have become central to the museum's outreach and style of live events.

With all these activities Harry's scholarship seldom translated into writing for academe. His major works addressed the analysis of ethnicity, especially in relation to public policy. One was on Doukhobor life at a time when that way of life was under mainstream attack and two, with colleagues, on Indian affairs, one concentrating on British Columbia and the other nation wide. I had participated in the first of these two, but not the last. Harry did not approach me for the latter, I think making a decision on my behalf that I might not be interested in view of my international roles. He also had to make room for other national scholars such as Marc-Adelard Tremblay.

Before this Harry approached me one day and said "Don't you think it is time we made a contribution to Polynesian studies?" We talked and he invited me to contribute to a joint paper on Polynesian chiefdoms. We both thought that the conventional wisdom was too rigid, that there were more dynamics involved in the recognition of chiefs and their relationship with other members of society. So it was agreed that Harry would produce the data, with which he was more familiar than I, and that I would construct the text and argument. I was satisfied with it and it was published in the Journal of the Polynesian Society, since when it has been pretty well ignored and the conventional view rules.

Harry was also usually an awkward speaker, possibly a carry over from his earlier shyness which still underlay his character. And I am sure that the pleasures of his garden and of talking among friends competed successfully with the pain of writing. But he had no trouble holding forth amongst friends, whom he frequently corrected on matters of esoteric fact. In other words, he absorbed knowledge but like many others with the same capacity had difficulty using it for creative academic contributions.

His attachment to New Zealand was real and perhaps slightly romantic. He had seldom visited his country of birth before his retirement. Then he determined to live in New Zealand during the southern summer and in Vancouver for the northern one. His son Henry, an up and coming architect designed and built a house near Auckland somewhere near where my own father had lived when he had retired.

Audrey however was not well at the time and her doctor forbade her to take such a long air trip. She had he same doctor as I had at the time, and he too forbade air travel for me, but a second opinion eventually put an end to that veto in my case.

In a party at their house Audrey sat next to me and confided that she was not happy at all about the idea of living in New Zealand. She felt there was nothing there for her.

Nevertheless she accepted the plan. They changed their house in Vancouver for a smaller one and for some years were seemingly contented migratory birds.

When Betty's death was announced the department of English hosted a beautifully moving campus memorial which touched all the emotional buttons that Betty exhibited in her love of literature. The Hawthorns called on me and escorted me with Adrian to the service. "What are friends for?" Audrey said.

Upon my arrest everything changed. They said nothing at all, but when I returned home they gave me the complete cold shoulder. I could understand their emotional turmoil and their desperation not to have to deal further with the issues. I wrote asking for talk and sent them cards letting them know how much Betty and I owed to them over the years. I did not pester them but felt it important once in a while to hope that they would say what was on their minds.

It was no use. Silence prevailed. And after Audrey died Harry was in very bad and sad health and further attempts were out of the question although I did send cards. From time to time I heard of him through Mike Ames and Ken Burridge who visited him, as I would have liked to have done. I last saw him from a distance at Mike Ame's memorial service[39]. He was a sad spectre of himself with difficulty maintaining his mental hold.

---

[39] Michael Ames died of a virulent cancer at a far too early age, shortly after his retirement.

WHAT PRICE RETIREMENT?

42. Perish the Publication!

During my lifetime I have been fortunate in publishing academic books, a couple for the general public, professional articles and even some contributions to popular magazines. In editing *current Anthropology* and the on line *AnthroGlobe Journal* I have been able to compare the respective advantages of print and world wide web for academic communication. I have even experienced self-publication. The one form I have not yet tried, which now embraces hundreds of thousands of titles, is that of e-books. So what have I learned?

Large and famous publication houses, which still retain their imprint, such as Routledge, Penguin, Random House, are now absorbed into large units such as Taylor and Francis and Bertelsmann. Once upon a time I could offer a manuscript to my publisher and a contract would be on my desk by return mail. This has no longer been the case for decades. University presses would send the manuscript to referees, and they still do, but now they often reject the offering based on title and description, without reading samples of the text.

For non-academic works the stakes are even higher. Many well known publishers insist that an author first submit to an agent. The agent becomes the filter undertaking work that was once securely in the publisher's hands. Agents themselves have become swamped with submissions and set up their own pre-filters. Some even indicate that they do not deal with first time authors. Many do not acknowledge receipt of the manuscript, even with a routine postcard.

Specialised academic books, such as anthropological field studies, do not sell well and often require subsidies from scholarly agencies. None of my early books had a print run of over 1,000, though some have been re-issued in hard bound library editions. Indeed of the 1,000 the main purchasers have been libraries, and because libraries were sure-fire purchasers, they guaranteed the viability of the publication.

This, though, is an expensive form of communication and makes it difficult and sometimes impossible to ensure global distribution as many libraries in the poorer countries have to economise on their expenditures.

Thus it was little surprise to me that my last piece of writing, *Choosing our Destiny* segments of which won the World Utopian Competition in 1955, was rejected by something like fifty agents and publishers. Min you, my sub-title was off putting, using the phrase: "Utopian World". and publishers had lost sight of what I was up to since I had not published a book, except for a restaurant guide, in the past twenty years. None of them read a single page of what I had written. One might think that, given the explosion of titles, in every language, in the bookstores, the entry into publishing is easy. It is not. There is also an explosion of *rejections*. Indeed a disappointed author, looking at the bulk of what he or she sees in the stores, would be forgiven if in his or her heart there would be a whisper "But my work is better than most of that !!!!"

For the criteria have also changed. Most publishers are in a tough competitive market. Look at the success of book stores which specialise in handling "remainders", the volumes which did not sell their print run by normal means.

So some authors, including myself, determined that their work would be available, turn to self-publishing. The firms which cater to this part of the industry are now numerous and varied in what they do and what they charge the author. Some offer nothing but the printing job, leaving the author to do his own distribution and marketing. Other are big businesses with highly technical programmes for marketing, warehousing, printing on demand, return policies and listings in, for example *Books in Print*, the bible for booksellers. They sometimes even have representation at the global and national book fairs.

For these services there are substantial charges to the author. They can run into thousands of dollars and results cannot be guaranteed. But if the author limits their services and specifically targets them, say, to university libraries, the outlay can be modest, perhaps $1,500 a book.

With one well known firm, XLibris, I purchased some of the marketing support. They produced a handsome volume for sale on demand, and there were electronic and print forms of publicity.

But I found, too late, that *at that time, 1996,* there was no return policy and hence retailers did not take the risk of stocking the book. They would supply by special order - but who even knew the book existed?

Yes there was a review programme for which I paid. But review journals did not care to review books which were not automatically stocked with retailers, and since this was print on demand and retailers were not happy with the processes, the result was no reviews whatsoever. And the review papers on offer were all in the United States. I had to send the book myself to any papers overseas. There was a time when every book I published was immediately reviewed in the *Times Literary Supplement* – but not for this kind of publishing. At least the book was listed in Amazon's various branches, but again, in the absence of reviews the book was unknown.[40]

---

[40] Since then XLibris has expanded its programmes but I have invested too much in the book to invest any more. If these programmes had been on offer in 1996 I would have adopted a more effective strategy including advertising on Google through keywords.

This story may suggest that self-publishing is not much good. On the contrary, I believe that if properly targeted and if the right programmes are chosen, it can be the way to go. Self publishing was almost the norm in the nineteenth century, involving many famous figures including Dickens, Marx and Jane Austen[41]. It has been responsible for many excellent books overlooked by conventional publishers. After all publishing choices are subjective and many judgements are erroneous.

And now there is digital publishing. I cannot report accurately on the comparative success of e-books, of which there are now scores of thousands. Whole libraries are now being digitalised, making it possible for readers globally to consult vast materials on line.

But I do have experience which enables me to contrast the print publishing of *Current Anthropology* and the on line publishing of *The AnthroGlobe Journal*.

From about 2004 I was experimenting with three quite different web sites, including *Anthropologising* and *Enjoy Vancouver Electronically* (or Eve), which morphed into *Adam's Vancouver Dining Guide*. *Anthopologising* is my rough and ready personal web site on which I am very slowly placing my archives, including multi media, when I have the time.

The other site was a web magazine which have described earlier.

---

[41] I seriously doubt whether *Das Kapital* would be accepted for commercial publication if offered now as from a first time author. Initially it was of course a self-publication with the financial assistance of Engels.

The AnthroGlobe Journal in particular prompted me to think more about the advantages and disadvantages of print versus digital publication. These thoughts were additionally stimulated by attendance at the conference of African librarians, archivists and publishers which I have mentioned in earlier chapters. I went there not only to speak about my experience but even more to learn, and learn I did.

In many respects some African writers were more open to digital publication than my colleagues in the North. Books are digitally published in South Africa for continental distribution. Libraries are using digital formats for more secure and accessible storage. Medical systems are linking country doctors and aides not only to central information guidance but to relevant publications. The participants knew what they were talking about and were eager to learn from the experiences of others. [42]This is what I have learned.

Printed materials have a long shelf life, but they are static in form. Libraries, especially university ones, are becoming archived repositories, not only of books, but of all formats, including film, music, the printed word and manuscripts and web pages. As time goes on their book lending function will diminish or be converted to on line access as the internet continues to expand. Indeed much of their storage is already in digital form,

---

[42] The papers are on line at the Afrika Institut of the University of Leiden.

accessible through personal computers. Thus their physical lending function will change.

Authors need to have their work in printed and/or in digital form in at least national libraries for the safe keeping of the record. Journals keep digital copies in libraries.

The internet has vast advantages beyond this. Some of these I was trying to exploit in *The AnthroGlobe Journal*[43]. The first is immediacy. A paper can be put on line in a matter of minutes whereas journal publication may take over a year.

The second is flexibility. Length is not pre-ordained but can be anything from one or two paragraphs to book length. Authors can, over time, *modify* their materials as a result of discussion with others or new information and thought. This is a particularly valuable characteristic, although it requires keeping track of changes from the original in the interests of the history of thought.

Articles can be multi-media. Anthropology papers can for example include audio speech to illustrate concepts and language; video of events and ceremonies, agriculture, dining with hierarchical implications, indeed an infinite world limited only by ever increasing bandwidth.

Since materials can be uploaded in very short times the "journal" may be continuously published rather than appearing at fixed intervals.

---

[43] which is now managed by the Department of anthropology Centre for Anthropology and Computing in the University of Kent, U.K

The material is by definition globally distributed. Book and journal publication suffers severely from this perspective, since even libraries and universities in many countries simply cannot afford to keep up with the mass of literature created daily. And it may be expressed in numerous languages with, increasingly, the possibility of computer translation.

Some scholars are reluctant to put their materials on individual internet sites. With search engines such as Google individual sites can be noticed, though they may be pages down on search engine results. It usually pays, therefore, to put the material into a site such as the *AnthroGlobe Journal* which is more frequently visited and is indexed. This also has the advantage that visitors will come across materials which did not appear in a search engine under the heading they are interested in. An article deals not only with its main theme but has along the way information which may be of use to persons not interested in the main indexed theme itself. This is the equivalent of browsing library stacks or flipping through print material.

Now I have to admit that my colleagues are staunchly conservative. In my watch the nearest authors got to multi-media, despite continual encouragement, was still photography or illustration. But even this can be done on a scale which would be too expensive for print journals.

If we are going to change the forms of publication we may as well introduce other publication reforms.

When editor of printed *Current Anthropology* I became disenchanted with the refereeing system, though that in itself had much broader procedures than did most other journals. I found slowness of response and sometimes outright prejudice. When I started on this path of criticism other things appeared to me.

Evaluations of this kind are in terms of the immediacy of the state of knowledge. A paper will be accepted or rejected in terms of its contribution to the now accepted paradigms.

But which papers will be considered ground breaking in one hundred years? That should be the (impossible) criterion for serious publication. And of those rejected, how many would have been valuable to the future had they seen the light of day?

So the *AnthroGlobe Journal* **had no referees**, though it did have a corpus of specialty editors whose function it was to seek out appropriate material. If a paper was decently written (in whatever language – we even had material in Indonesian) and was directed clearly to its thesis, it would be published, regardless. *The **future** would be the judge of its value – not the editor's personal ideas).* All papers were open to discussion and debate, though that rarely happened.

It is easy to obtain statistics of "visitors" to internet sites. One can monitor the countries from which readers emerge. I found these figures to be not what I expected. There were many from Russia, mainly because of a frequent Russian contributor and assignments to students.

So the "journal" became in essence an archive itself. The papers would always be there, although some which did not attract readership might be shunted into a subsidiary storage area.

Publication of paper journals is a wasteful and expensively inefficient process if limited to print. In some subjects other than anthropology scholars *have to pay* often large sums to get their work published. This comes out of research grants. It is a burden on sponsors. Surely the funds could be used more effectively in direct enquiry. Where this is not the case foundations and governments often underwrite the journals. Again it is money which could be used directly in research. There is no logic to this – only the failure to face up to its reality and make the necessary changes.[44]

The trends are clear. Paper publishing in the future will have a quantitatively smaller and a more specialised role for scholarly work. The internet will take much of its place and the increasing volume may well require adaptations in the size and features of the internet itself.

There are indeed issues with regard to e-books and similar long materials. One may print them out for easier reading.. There are now handheld readers about the size of a normal book which will accept an e-book and allow you to read at your leisure away from the computer. But for someone visually impaired like myself, who has to use a magnifier to read print, this can still be physically awkward. It is much easer for me to read on the admittedly less mobile but magnified computer screen.

There is also another major problem for this scenario – the conservatism and lack of imagination in

---

[44] The *Economist* has been making this argument in numerous articles for years.

university committees which demand publication in refereed print publications as part of the process of deciding about appointments and faculty promotion and tenure.

This is archaic and, to my mind, unintelligent. When necessary it is easy to evaluate what is on line for these purposes. In fact it is easier and faster than posting wads of publications to evaluators. All the committees have to do is to point to the URL and ask an evaluator, what about this?

So why don't they do it?

Perish the publication evaluation process in its present form.

Now I must add an addendum for thoughts which came to me after this chapter was in draft. It is in two parts: what is the significance of this for ethnography? And how will this book you are looking at get published?

I have mentioned earlier that in my view much of ethnography is valuable data with only modest theoretical interest despite the attempts of the author. As we all know a great deal of this is embodied in theses and research reports. It is increasingly difficult to get ethnographies physically published in print. I know of many which have been abandoned even by their authors, though with invaluable material. Libraries are increasingly reluctant to buy them. If printed the run may be 500 or less and the distribution limited. The answer? Publish as a e-book which will increasingly become available globally at a tiny fraction of the price, and will be noticed by search engines.

And how about this book? If you are reading it at all you will have decided it sparks your interest, at least in some part. I am tired of dealing with conventional publishers with all that wastage of time and energy.

So I am doing it myself. I have discovered a system which has none of the drawbacks I described with respect to my earlier attempt. I have little money. I don't need it to get the book printed and only a little to get it distributed. It is fast, a matter of days rather than months. I can do it both in print and as an e-book almost simultaneously.

So much so that I have plans to republish some of my out of print books and use the system to republish those anthropological classics which are to be found only in expensive antiquarians.

Can I do this by the end of 2010? Perhaps. We'll see.

43. Ao-tea-roa

Sport - rugby, cricket, yachting, horse racing. They are about the only things in New Zealand which have not changed fundamentally in my life time. Boys who used to chant Waitemata, Taranaki, Ao-tea-roa in mock *haka* would likely now be rapped over the knuckles for cultural insensitivity if they did it all. City populations have expanded manifold and the ethnic mix is much more evident and complex.

On my leave from the Solomons Betty (whose place of birth was clearly located in Hamilton) and I searched for the town listed on my own birth certificate, Waddington, near Christchurch. It did no exist. It had been swallowed up in the nearby city. And I have no memories of the place since I have become, well, sentient.

What I do have are memories of Auckland, the town where I grew up. And those memories tell me that New Zealand was the almost perfect place for a youth to reach manhood.

To get outside the city was easy and one could wander the hills of the Waitakere[45] range, which we called mountains, where my father had a cabin, at will, hiking to waterfalls or down a stream to the dark surfing beach at Piha or roam the open grassy cliffs to the east of

---

[45] Near-by and in the once agricultural lowlands Waitakere is now New Zealand's fifth largest city.

the city. The forests were special with exotic ferns, brilliant tree flowers and even more brilliant birds with exotic calls. There were even a few massive *kauri* trees.

Inside the city I would lie flat on the grass reading, pretending to absorb for exams at which I was mostly dreadful, or lost in adventures in far off lands. The dormant volcanoes of Mount Hobson, where I lived, Mount Eden and One Tree Hill provided immediate climbing and close friendship, usually with Will Tuck, killed during the war. We gazed at starry skies debating about the universe and we biked the streets endlessly.

The pubs stank and the race track betting called, but not to me. I did not smoke or drink. My early try outs for rugby were a failure. I never played the game, but became known as a field hockey goalie. To many I must have seemed a prig.

I found enlightenment working beside my father, a left wing economist, as he in turn worked with the Maori people. In my teens he had me as his amanuensis taking notes as he discussed economic prospects and political future in *marae* and *pa* across the North Island. He organised an event called the Maori Young Leaders Conference which brought together men (I do not recall women) from all the tribes to discuss their ways forward. There I helped with publicity and organisation. As a boy I had sat at the feet of my uncle, Vic Fisher, who was the ethnologist at the Auckland War Memorial Museum. He conducted classes in Maori lore and even a little language. But the Maori were still a marginal people.

I visited New Zealand again during my expatriation up to the end of the 'fifties, mainly to visit parents in Wellington and Auckland and driving between them. It seemed little different. I was much the same, but no longer did I feel that it was the centre of the globe. That was the feeling during my youth. We led the way in social security and political equality for women, our voice was idealistic and liberal in the League of Nations, not liking what we saw of imperial expansion by European powers such as Italy. We could be shocked at the rise of Nazism in Germany and its idolaters in other countries. We were proud of the Commonwealth. For many years I was able to vote freely in Britain, Australia, Canada without fuss of citizenship. My New Zealand passport meant something. The last time in this period was to settle my father's estate, enjoy the simple modernity of his home outside Auckland, and breath the air of a Waitemata estuary – and confirm my ill mother's residence in Canada.

As the years developed I felt obligations to Canada which had received me openly and easily, which had overcome its early racism and union bashing to start on its road to eventual multiculturalism, and whose federal civil service seemed unusually enlightened – and willing to use such services as I had to offer.

So the next time I visited New Zealand it was as a Canadian in 1972. And all of a sudden New Zealand was different and in a way desperate. It had become almost a command economy and there were restrictions everywhere, many left over from the war. My father had been able to bring a modern American car, a Studebaker of which he was inordinately proud, when he returned from his lengthy work abroad, but almost everyone else had jalopies which were falling apart. I managed to find someone who rented me a vehicle and remember vividly driving at night behind another when suddenly sparks erupted as it lost a wheel which raced wildly ahead. The incident seemed to epitomise the state and mood of the country.

No longer. There was a huge break before my next and probably last visit in 2006. The visit was just for ten days and I kept it to Auckland. My own relatives were scattered, no longer in the city and some were in Australia. One of the latter, my maternal cousin Deidre Greig had worked up a major study of my mother's family roots. Another,. my uncle, Jim Belshaw, an economist and historian, had unearthed material about my father's ancestry. They were both fascinating stories of migration from poverty in Britain to upward mobility in the colonies. But this time I wanted to concentrate on Auckland, to revive my memories of youth, and to visit Betty's sister and her sons.

Alastair Smaill, one of the sons, and his wife Ann were frequent visitors to Vancouver where they spent time en route to major cross country skiing expeditions inland. We had formed a bond and I stayed with them.

My, how things had changed. The first obvious thing was that the energy and entrepreneurship hidden in the country's population was free to build a thriving economy. No more commercial import and export restrictions. Local industry seemed thriving and exports now contained items that were hardly recognised as being of commercial interest in my time – wine, kiwi fruit, even household appliances. The publishing industry, always vigorous, was vibrant.

Auckland had grown into a large untidy metropolis without the effective planning that needs go with it. Not only did it sprawl, as all big cities do, but it was choking with traffic as the freeways moved into the very heart of the city, in some ways smothering its soul.

331

I recognised many of the small locations – Queen Street, Karangahape Road, and especially Newmarket and the roads I used to wander along on the way to Auckland Grammar School.

Around Queen Street there was a collection of seemingly unrelated buildings, and condos were sprouting by the harbour. The trams of old were now efficient buses and I found it easy to get around, at least to my old haunts. To go further afield by public transit was not on, and I did not re-visit the Waiktakeres.

The old house my family lived in on Mount Hobson Road was still there, but without the vines which provided me with kiwis, Chinese gooseberries, passion fruit and many other succulent snacks and there was no vegetable garden on which I had slaved on my father's orders. The great pohutukawa on the hillside which I had turned into my den was gone, replaced by a younger tree still fenced for protection. The symbolic tee on One Tree Hill had been hacked down by a protester and was now bare. But the lovely hillside parks were still verdant and flourishing with populations of neighbours, tourists and sheep. They seemed smaller.

I visited a butcher who ran one of the new shops replacing the old corner ones near my home. For a long time I have been puzzling over the disappearance of mutton as a preferred food – lamb, which is often hogget, being now the steady favourite in both New Zealand and Canada. So I asked him about the situation. *Both* lamb and mutton are now less favoured on New Zealand plates he told me. You just might find some mutton if you go to the western 'burbs, the area where urban Maori and Pacific Islanders live.

That was a part of town I did not get to and represents the increasing divide between the urban wealthy and the urban poor. New Zealand literature and news record a seamy side of life, with family violence, rapine and abuse frequent that were unheard of, or perhaps suppressed, in my youth.

The tribal Maori, however, are undergoing a renaissance in art and culture and in politics, the latter often rambunctious, energetic, focussed and sometimes deliberately provocative and aggressive. I heard many stories which seemed to indicate an undercurrent, especially among the young, of poking their noses at the *pakeha* whites and seriously teasing and testing those with liberal ideas..

Ironically this comes at a time when New Zealand is adopting aspects of Maori culture into its main stream. The country has adopted Ao-Tea-Roa, the traditional Land of the Long White Cloud, as its adjunct name. In computer country lists you will usually find the words New Zealand (Ao-Tea-Roa). Official documents from the now University of Auckland spell Maori "Maöri". The Maori language is taught in schools, and *pakeha* take pride in pronouncing Maori words and names correctly. Maori culture is embodied in the country's life in a way that was not at all present in my youth.

At the same time there is an evident racism which I found disturbing. While I was there I read articles in papers advocating and calling for the enforced return of Asians back to their original countries. They are blamed for unemployment. Yet to a Canadian visitor they are not particularly evident – locals disagree – except as workers, alongside Pacific Islanders, in retail.

When I looked out from the Smaill's verandah it was to a lawn with fruit trees, mandarins falling on the ground amid the chatter and songs of birds. As I was driven from the airport I realised that the roads were bordered with trees which were now much larger than I had remembered. At another house I looked from a hillside balcony *down* onto a canopy of green leafed treetops, some festooned with blossom (it was early spring) and brightly coloured birds whose names I had forgotten. The city is verdant, not with pines, but full thick green leaves.

I missed floral gardens displayed from homes. They were there, of that I am sure, but *behind* the homes, invisible to the passer by. Did I romanticize? This was not the Auckland I seemed to remember. (My sister-in-law Joan's husband Graham was an avid gardener and their home was surrounded by floral gaiety.)

I did not have time to explore the plethora of restaurants. It is well known that New Zealanders are coffee crazed and Betty's nephews Alastair and Ann Smaill are aficionados. There are scores of coffee houses, both old fashioned and modern, with "flat white" being one of the more popular orders.

Some are operated by Lebanese – in fact I found a more than usual frequency of Lebanese humble eating places. They operate normal cafes, rather than unseated takeouts common in Canada. And I did not notice pizza delivery and takeouts, now more common than hamburger joints in Canada.

There were two magnificent home dinners. One was hosted by the family of Betty's brother Barrie Sweetman. He was visiting from his home in Fiji and his Auckland family were Fiji-oriented. With his wife Anna and their daughter in law they put on a show of wondrous spicy Island foods of a splendour of taste that I had never experienced in the days I was in Fiji. And the Smaills produced a lavish family dinner for the clan straight after Ann's return home from work. Chicken and the doings, not lamb.

And there was a memorable meal of modern delicacy at a small restaurant in a Mount Eden neighbourhood that was a perfect setting for a family reunion. This visit, though, was not about restaurant exploration, but it made promise of gastronomic adventures at some later time.

New Zealanders complain that their best foods, other than wines, are exported. I saw no great reason for the complaints. Fresh food seems amply available. One surprise was the relatively new fish market. Here I was astonished to find tray after tray of strange looking *deep sea* fish. One explanation was that overseas trawlers had diminished the upper level fish stocks. Yet deep sea fish commerce is itself illegal in many countries.

Like a silly Canadian I had brought packages of smoked salmon. The first surprise was at arrival customs. New Zealand is justifiably extremely protective of the possible migration of foreign species (having suffered extraordinary depredations by introduced plants and animals in the nineteenth century.) So there are rigorous inspections and massive fines for infractions to prevent infiltration.

I declared the salmon and was praised for doing so and also I knew that the detecting apparatus would have found it anyway and I would have suffered severely in the pocket had I not done so.

The agricultural official inspected the packages and didn't know what to do with them. I would have thought they would have been common presents from Canadian travellers. Eventually, since the fish was smoked and processed, it was let through.

Then I found that it was like carrying coals to Newcastle. New Zealand has a massive *farmed* salmon industry. The fish was common in the market and everywhere in supermarkets.

Given the controversy over fish farming in other parts of the world, I was curious. Would this not be damaging to ocean fish, and could it not lead to a stock of wild salmon from escapes? After all the famous New Zealand trout had been introduced.

Oh no, I found out. The fish farms are fresh water, inland, in association with hydro-eclectic dams. Escape would be nearly impossible.

Here, it seemed to me, was another Kiwi invention[46] which the world could notice. Why do the dangerous Canadian seashore farms not move inland???

For its size of population, New Zealand is a country of marked innovation. After all, who would have paid any attention to New Zealand wines when I was a boy??? (My rather did occasionally buy some plonk.) Now I drink them with great pride and pleasure and by choice.

Immigrants everywhere are faced to varying degrees with identity questions. Am I myself a New Zealander rather than a Canadian? After all these

---

[46] Am I right? I have learned that much Norwegian farming is up from the salt water.

decades I still have a New Zealand accent, though modified. When it comes to language I am prejudiced in favour of older New Zealand English though I have adopted many Canadianisms. I am proud of the All Blacks, sailors, and other New Zealand sporting victors even more than I am of Canadian successes, though I root for those. I tend to watch ice hockey, though I want to see it reformed. I do not think of reforming New Zealand society the way I feel committed to changed in Canada. My children are Canadian, true and blue, in every respect, although they were born in London and Canberra respectively. I am proud of being a hyphenated Canadian, though one does not hear the term New Zealander-Canadian in the way one hears Chinese-Canadian.

I would love to spend more time again in New Zealand. This urge is not an urge to return to the land of my ancestors, who themselves came from families outside of New Zealand. My roots are thoroughly now in Vancouver. I feel them that way because there is much in Canada outside of Vancouver which feels strange to me. I must recognise though that this is as much a function of age as it is of national identity. I am a New-Zealander-Canadian if anything – at least by the end of this chapter.

44. Why Vancouver?

When the family moved to Vancouver in 1953 we had a hard time (see Chapter 6). Vancouver was a hick city, a backwoods country town living on the fruits of extractive industries, land speculation and a port. And the weather! Thick fog with the strong smell of sulphur from pulp mills, frequent deep snow and ice, and in the summer cloud cover and rain rain rain.

It is a wonder we stayed during the seven years before we had a home of our own. Looking back I think we must have been overcome by some sort of inertia, felling that to move – we did not consider establishing ourselves again – would b e out of the frying pan into the fire.

It was particularly hard on Betty for I had an escape into my work.

The city grew and was home to many highly creative people, often better known abroad than in the then anti-intellectual environment. When we went away on leave in the 'fifties and 'sixties we always noticed major changes, at least in the buildings, and then in civilised facilities. Visitors praised the beauty of the location and the avenues of grand trees and the gardens with their ever-expanding rhododendrons. I began to take pride in the place and described it as the city of the future, not of the past.

And that is what it is. Some immigrants still bewail the so-called lack of history and grand monuments and stimulus in a so-called laid back life style. As each year goes by they could not be more wrong. There are a few modest statues as reminders of the pioneering past and there are institutions of global renown. There are even some buildings of great architecture (somewhat lost in the banality of others).

After all, Vancouver as a city is younger than Sydney, Melbourne, Auckland, let alone San Francisco. It was founded by pioneers moving overland from the East, not by mariners from the Pacific, and then by migrants working up the North American west coast or seeking work from Hawaii, and that took time.

The speed of change over the past two decades has been breathtaking and uneven. The present character of the city took hold only some fifteen or so years ago. Douglas Coupland has rightly called it the city of glass[47]. The transformation is by no means finished and has a momentum which is spreading from the city core to distant suburbs and local neighbourhoods, admittedly with anaesthetic urban sprawl.

City councils, despite showing many faults, have made a scattering of great decisions. One of the very first, at the beginning of the town's official life, was to set aside the promontory at the harbour's entrance, the thickly wooded Stanlley Park, which has become the city's icon and pride.

Others followed from time to time. Built with private British money the Lions Gate bridge linked the

---

[47] Although his eponymously titled book of photographs does not back up the statement.

house filled ridges of the North Shore mountains creating the opportunity for homes with extraordinary vistas of sea and a total ring of mountains, just ten minutes from their work downtown. Almost everywhere you go there is a vista often combining forest, sea, mountains and city towers.

Scenery alone does not make a great city. It is what mankind does with the location which establishes its character. The site of Geneva is enhanced by the town itself. Hong Kong is too vibrantly fussy, much of the appeal related to the continual movement of ships and small boats in the harbour and the never sleeping crowds on the streets.

Vancouver is another story. The second major decision of the city council, forced into it by an angry populace, was to nix the entry of super highways into the town core. That decision prevented the kind of masculation and overbearing traffic gridlock that has shattered the beauty of much of Seattle.

Another decision was to establish an elected Parks Board whose decisions and staff are creating, often with private contracts, beautifully planted walkways around almost the whole of the extensive shoreline, kilometre after kilometre, The Board turned ugly gravel excavations into places of colour and softness, favoured as sires for wedding photos. And throughout the city are dotted small neighbourhood parks, frequently equipped with community centres, well conceived playgrounds, tennis courts, bowling greens, natural ponds. And neighbouring cities in the metropolitan area have followed suit, Burnaby for example setting aside natural waterways which in their own way rival Stanley Park.

I met an Australian in the elevator. "Why on earth do you live in Vancouver?" I asked. "It's the parks" was the surprising answer. Not the city beaches which could not possibly rival Bondi, not the opportunity to play tennis in the morning and ski the nearby hills the afternoon. The ever expanding parks - with building developers required to make a payment in support of turning downtown blocks into greenery and brilliant flowers and well designed seating areas and meeting places for dogs.

The present character of the downtown commercial and business area where I live has come partly from a large preserved residential area, with fine old and new homes, but mainly, recently from forthright planning which was one of the first in the world to reject the decades old theory of the separation of functions, i.e. the idea that retail should be here, offices over there, industry over there and residences somewhere else.

Until recently the downtown area was dead at night, totally sterile, except for one or two streets dedicated to cinemas and nightclubs. From the mid-nineties all that started to change. Residential towers replaced single family homes or office blocks, the appeal being what is now known as eco-density. Vancouver downtown is on an isthmus with land at a premium. To go up is a solution, now starting to be applied to the main routes through the suburbs.

Almost overnight the city acquired a vibrancy which had been lacking over the years. Live where you work became a mantra. Condominium living took hold. Where I live on the 29th floor I am in easy walking distance to almost everything I need or want – the public library, a branch of the university library, the central retail core, more cafes and restaurants than I can possibly use, cinemas and theatres. Buses bring young people from the university area to the entertainment locations beginning at nine or ten at night, I must admit with sometimes crowd-stimulated alcoholic and drug created results.

This is at the centre. For the rest the homes set in gardens are typical of the New World, though with much more use of wood and stucco rather than, say, brick or stone. The streets are shaded with huge deciduous trees, or brightened with prunus and cherries, many a gift from Osaka. For a long time I lived in such an area, quiet and bird-visited, near the university. Only now do I realise that, in terms of Vancouver living, it was isolated. For the most part though the 'burbs are well served with supermarkets, little stores, even boutiques. There is a certain air of gentrification about these streets, despite one area of destitution, despair and homelessness in the town's old historic centre.

Immigrant populations are everywhere. At the same time as the planners changed the downtown there was the beginning of an immigration surge, at first from Hong Kong and Taiwan and then mainland China. The flow from India and Southeast Asia and Europe (particularly Britain Germany and Eastern Europe) increased. This had marked effects.

European immigrants had always been the force behind opera, symphony and choral creativity. Some of the new immigrants were well off, investing in expensive penthouses, almost all with panoramic views of mountain, city and sea. And many of them invested in the arts, financing theatres and galleries. Offshore money flowed in seemingly without end. As in most other Western cities these days numerous diasporas have arrived contributing to all groups in society. In my own building there are New Zealanders, Russians, Japanese, Americans, Australians, Koreans, Taiwanese, Vietnamese, Latinos, Indians, Italians, Middle Easterners, African and still others. At one time such immigrants might have been limited to residence in certain areas, but now they are spread through the community. There are however notable concentrations as well – Iranians on the North Shore, Indians of varying origins and faiths grouped in separate districts in South Vancouver, Greeks around Fourth avenue, Italians in East Vancouver and Commercial Drive, West Indians in Commercial Drive and New Westminster. All categories of Asians have revolutionised the nearby city of Richmond with its huge and modern Asian shopping malls and temples and Indians have done the same in Surrey. These are not by any means ghettoes. They visit and shop everywhere in places where, thirty years ago, you would never see a coloured face or hear another language, as you do now in all the main streets and supermarkets.

The city is enriched and knows it.

The phenomenon is reflected in the variety of cuisines which are available almost everywhere. Japanese food has taken hold with sushi bars of varying quality throughout the city on every commercial street, more common than pizza parlours and Middle Eastern kabob and shawarma stalls.

The top end of the restaurant industry was helped by an unusually wise policy of the Provincial government of British Columbia. Making use of powers granted by the Federal Government it has identified immigration priority for executive chefs. This allowed some of the most respected chefs of Honk Kong and

Taiwan to set up business in Vancouver. French Italian and German chefs are notable.

When that happened local people woke up. Young men and women attended excellent cooking schools and a belated system of apprenticeships gave them extra training with outstanding mentors. Thus many of the best restaurants have Canadian *chefs de cuisine* and executives. And behind the pots and pans you may find an Asian Canadian in charge. French chefs have come to make their name after being perpetually subjected to some major figure in France, and to bring up their children in a different atmosphere. As I write two major French New York chefs are branching into Vancouver. One of the two, brilliantly innovative, is however being criticized as not doing as well as the already established local multicultural chefs.

Not all cuisines are well represented. Only recently have Mexicans ramped up their menus to go into new dishes beyond the banal fajitas and tacos. The same comment applies to Indian and Thai. We still need good German cuisine (despite hosting notable German chefs) and Scandinavian, Spanish and Portuguese restaurants are hard to find. Yet thirty years ago there was none of this. The change too has been helped by environmental movements insisting on prime quality of eco-friendly food and the very late emergence of British Columbia wines of high quality and international note.

Given my late attachment to and love of food it is no wonder that Vancouver is my favourite city. I am not alone. Both the London *Times* and the Chicago *Tribune* have listed Vancouver as one of the tope three or four restaurant locations in the world – in the case of the *Times* only after London, New York and Tokyo. It has been reported that in 2008 a thousand new restaurants opened, and many of these were of outstanding quality. The people of Vancouver are crazy about food, so much so that Barbara-Jo's Books to Cooks has been rated by *Gourmet Magazine* as one of the top ten cook book shops in the world.

Mind you the critic in me shouts at imperfections, particularly in menu descriptions, some of which can even make overseas visitors cringe. The word *bouillabaisse* is overdone, often referring to a fish stew which has nothing in common with the real thing. All of a sudden *tapas* has become an insensitive synonym for appetiser[48]. What a pity for Vancouver would be stimulated if it had the institution of the *tapeador*.

I still keep tabs on what is happening in the city, noting in detail the reports of the newspaper critics. The remains of my dining guide are on my hard drive and I devote a certain amount of time to entering the new information. I stopped monitoring events on line in order to complete these memoirs and other writings. Might I restart the on line site as Vancouver Groumand? It would necessitate my walking all the main streets to check the locations which have disappeared and find new ones. That in fact can be fun, a way to contact interesting and often devoted people and to keep in touch with the city's life.

All this though does not come without a cost. Whereas the *Economist Intelligence Unit* and other rating firms place Vancouver as one of the three of four best places in the world to live in (after such as Vienna

---

[48] However as I write I learn that a well established restaurateur is spending several months in Spain prior to opening a new bar specialising in the real thing.

and Zurich) U.S. television shows and the BBC have concentrated on Vancouver's undoubted seamy side. The port is a major source of illicit drugs and the very old centre of town is a shooting gallery with evident destitution and poverty. The citizens are worried and ashamed and have at last created an institution known as Insight where addicts can inject under the supervision of nurses, adjacent to a therapy centre.

As in most major cities the homeless are numerous. Belatedly small hotels have been taken over to help house most of them. A large proportion are mentally ill, suffering from a short sighted Provincial policy which shut down residential facilities for the mentally ill on the flavour of the month theory that they would be "better off" in the community (though without adequate community support). There are signs of a modest reversal of this policy.

Vancouver has always had gangs who erupt in violence. Nowadays they have been getting even further out of hand, so that nightclubs use high technology to sort out potential visitors with firearms. Contrary to some opinion they are by no means all Asian – some have memberships as mixed as the city itself, and others are Latino and some of the most notorious are white Canadian.

The appeal and beauty of Vancouver cannot be guaranteed into the future. The city is not always the master of its own fate. A reactionary government in Ottawa threatens to close the Insight drug relief programme. The Provincial Government has been going through a phase of adoration for roads and bridges. These are planned to be outside of Vancouver proper in order to increase the flow of heavy traffic into the port. They are also to serve the huge number of commuters who live on the eastern side of the Fraser River. The effect, as has happened in Seattle and other cities, will be to increase the flow of personal vehicular traffic to and from the city itself, which in Vancouver's case simply cannot handle such a surge. The alternative use of rapid transit gets lip service except in the city itself and the better use of rail would require legislation to bring the railway companies into line with more effective port and metropolitan service. Of a sudden the first class though limited public transit system is faced with a financing freeze, losing its CEO to ---- New York. Such shames are from the red faces of senior governments, not the cit itself.

Vancouver's outstanding way of life is fragile indeed. Immigrants understand this, some politicians don't. Fortunately for me, if the worst comes I won't be here to see it. I hope there is a wake up call and the worst is transformed into a continuation of the best.

Meanwhile I will take full advantage of the present to warm my feelings about the good things in life in a world which has far too few of them.

Acknowledgements

My thanks to those who read parts of the manuscript in draft and made wise and pertinent comments: my cousin Deidre Greig in Australia, Elvi Whittaker who has worked in many similar contexts, Ken Burridge who is in no way responsible for what I say, grand daughter Juniper Belshaw who gave a lively and pertinent reaction to what I wrote about colonial life and not least to Clive Moore, whose knowledge of the history of the Solomons and Tulagi in particular revived many of my memories. And Jon Bromberg tried to correct my Swedish spelling.

In special measure I am grateful to those whose wisdom and skill keep me functioning - (Dr. Dan) Daniel Ezekiel, Melville Shaw, Jaime Wright, Craig Beatty, Suren Sanmugasunderam, David Maberley, and Peter Dolman. What a team!

www.ingramcontent.com/pod-product-compliance
Lightning Source LLC
Chambersburg PA
CBHW020734160426
43192CB00006B/214